Ken Hooto
3-21-83
Coquille, OR.

RESURRECTION

The Bible Study Textbook Series

NEW TESTAMENT

The Bible Study New Testament Ed. By Rhoderick Ice	**The Gospel of Matthew** In Four Volumes By Harold Fowler (Vol. IV not yet available)	**The Gospel of Mark** By B. W. Johnson and Don DeWelt
The Gospel of Luke By T. R. Applebury	**The Gospel of John** By Paul T. Butler	**Acts Made Actual** By Don DeWelt
Romans Realized By Don DeWelt	**Studies in Corinthians** By T. R. Applebury	**Guidance From Galatians** By Don Earl Boatman
The Glorious Church (Ephesians) By Wilbur Fields	**Philippians - Colossians Philemon** By Wilbur Fields	**Thinking Through Thessalonians** By Wilbur Fields
Paul's Letters To Timothy & Titus By Don DeWelt	**Helps From Hebrews** By Don Earl Boatman	**James & Jude** By Don Fream
Letters From Peter By Bruce Oberst	**Hereby We Know (I-II-III John)** By Clinton Gill	**The Seer, The Saviour, and The Saved (Revelation)** By James Strauss

OLD TESTAMENT

O.T. History By William Smith and Wilbur Fields	**Genesis** In Four Volumes By C. C. Crawford	**Exploring Exodus** By Wilbur Fields	**Leviticus** By Don DeWelt
Numbers By Brant Lee Doty	**Deuteronomy** By Bruce Oberst	**Joshua - Judges Ruth** By W. W. Winter	**I & II Samuel** By W. W. Winter
I & II Kings By James E. Smith	**I & II Chronicles** By Robert E. Black	**Ezra, Nehemiah & Esther** By Ruben Ratzlaff & Paul T. Butler	**The Shattering of Silence (Job)** By James Strauss
Psalms In Two Volumes By J. B. Rotherham		**Proverbs** By Donald Hunt	**Ecclesiastes and Song of Solomon** — By R. J. Kidwell and Don DeWelt
Isaiah In Three Volumes By Paul T. Butler		**Jeremiah and Lamentations** By James E. Smith	**Ezekiel** By James E. Smith
Daniel By Paul T. Butler		**Hosea - Joel - Amos Obadiah - Jonah** By Paul T. Butler	**Micah - Nahum - Habakkuk Zephaniah - Haggai - Zechariah Malachi** — By Clinton Gill

SPECIAL STUDIES

The Church In The Bible By Don DeWelt	**The Eternal Spirit** By C. C. Crawford	**World & Literature of the Old Testament** Ed. By John Willis	**Survey Course In Christian Doctrine** Two Bks. of Four Vols. By C. C. Crawford
New Testament History — Acts By Gareth Reese		**Learning From Jesus** By Seth Wilson	**You Can Understand The Bible** By Grayson H. Ensign

WHAT THE BIBLE SAYS SERIES

WHAT THE
BIBLE SAYS
ABOUT

RESURRECTION

By

Charles R. Gresham

College Press Publishing Company, Joplin, Missouri

Dedicated To

RUTH

Faithful Companion

and

Sharer in Resurrection

Power

Table of Contents

Preface

This book is the product of many years. For thirty-two years the author has been interacting with a large number of students in the College and Seminary classroom. From this community of faith and scholarship, under the judgment of the Word of God, have come the insights presented in this volume. The author would be remiss if he did not express his gratitude to these who have contributed to his thinking through the years.

Others, more recently, have also made major contributions to this work. Colleagues at Kentucky Christian College have given encouragement. Professor Edward Moretto has been particularly helpful both in proofreading and serving as a reactor to certain ideas. Ann Stanley and others on the College staff have provided yeoman service in typing the manuscript.

The book is set out in thirteen chapters so that it may be used as a text for an advanced course or elective course in the Church School (the thirteen chapters fit the quarterly system). It may have other uses as well. The various appendices are provided for those who wish to explore critical issues or who desire broader knowledge in certain associated areas.

The volume is sent forth with the prayer that it may strengthen faith and provide deeper understanding of the resurrection, the key issue of Biblical faith. It will serve its purpose well if it reflects the grandeur and glory of what the Risen Lord has done for us. May all come to "know Him and the power of His resurrection" (Phil. 3:10) better!!!!

Chapter One

INTRODUCTION: SETTING FORTH THE ISSUE

He had come to Athens the intellectual center of the Empire. Here Socrates, Plato, Aristotle, and other philosophers and teachers had broken new ground of speculative thought. That tradition begun four centuries before continued, although somewhat tarnished from its original luster. But speculative interest had not died, for Luke the historian wrote: "For all the Athenians and foreigners who lived in Athens spent all their time in either communicating or listening to new ideas" (Acts 17:21, Author's own free translation). While this statement may be purposefully exaggerated for emphasis, it indicates what was still true in the first century of the Christian era.

But Paul of Tarsus was also an intellectual. Though he had been born in Tarsus, "an important city" (Acts 21:39), and was a "Roman citizen by birth" (Acts 22:28), he had been "brought up" in Jerusalem, "educated under the care and guidance of Gamaliel" (Acts 22:3), that great and learned Pharisee (see Acts 5). He himself said that he had "advanced in Judaism" beyond many of his own age, so extremely zealous was he for the traditions of his fathers (Gal. 1:14).

But, his intellectual attainments and his Judaistic studies had now become subservient to an obscure prophet from Nazareth named Jesus. At first he had "persecuted this way" (Acts 22:4) zealously. In speaking of his former activity to Herod Agrippa II at an informal hearing at Caesarea he said:

> I was convinced that it was my duty to combat the influence of Jesus of Nazareth. I did so in Jerusalem, having many of God's people imprisoned under powers granted me by the

1

chief priests. When some were put to death, I voted for their execution. There was not a synagogue where I did not often punish them, forcing them to renounce their faith in this Jesus. In an excess of fanaticism and enraged fury I extended my persecution to foreign cities, one of which was Damascus (Acts 26:9-12, Author's own free translation).

But, outside Damascus he met this Jesus! He knew that he had been executed as a blasphemer; yet here in the dust of the roadway, a dazzling light blinding him, he encountered Jesus. Listen to Paul's account:

"As I fell to the ground, I heard a voice asking me, 'Saul, Saul, why are you persecuting me?' I answered, 'Who are you?' He said, 'I am Jesus of Nazareth whom you are persecuting'" (Acts 26:7, 8, Author's own free translation).

The dead Jew was the risen Lord! That encounter with the risen Jesus turned Paul's life around. Almost immediately following his conversion and baptism (Acts 22:16f.), he began to preach this same Jesus that he had been persecuting.

His zeal to preach Jesus as promised Messiah and risen Lord to both Jew and Gentile had brought him to Athens. He was "exasperated" (Acts 17:16, Goodspeed) at the sight of the many idolatrous temples and shrines which filled the city. He had discussions wherever he could gain a hearing— in the synagogue with Jews and devout proselytes, even in the market-place taking on all comers (Acts 17:17). His activity came to the attention of certain Epicurean and Stoic philosophers and they took issue with him, supposing that he was just an "amateur" (Acts 17:18, Berkeley). Perplexed by both his ability and his testimony about Jesus and the resurrection (some, apparently, supposed that he was speaking of two new gods, assuming that *anastasis*, resurrection, was the female counterpart to Jesus), they "took him by the sleeve" (Acts 17:19, Knox) and brought him to the Areopagus which was a public open-air auditorium.[1] Thus, Paul was given opportunity to make known these "new and startling ideas" to a large crowd of Athenians. Paul, the Jewish intellectual, captured by and committed to Jesus, the promised Messiah and risen Lord, faced other intellectuals. The introduction of his "speech upon Mars Hill" is a masterpiece of eloquence as he sets out the true nature of the living God and the implications of his creative power. But, the heart of Paul's message was not to be in conclusions drawn from reason; it was to center in a call to repentance which is made imperative by impending judgment, guaranteed by the resurrecton of Jesus. Listen to Paul's transition from his introduction to the intended body of his message:

> Such former ages of ignorance God has overlooked; but now he charges all peoples everywhere to repent because he has appointed a day in which he will judge the whole inhabited world with justice by that man whom He has destined to accomplish this judgment. He has given proof to all men that this will occur in that He has raised from the dead that one whom He has appointed as Judge (Acts 17:30, 31, Author's free translation).

The majority of Paul's hearers "began to laugh ironically" (Acts 17:32, Rieu).[2] After all, every Athenian knew that the

---

1. Here a court met which at one time functioned as a Senate. During Paul's day the court functioned only as an arbiter of religion and morals. Since Paul was seen as setting out "new deities" it would be natural to bring him before this court for a public hearing. One of the judges, Dionysius, apparently became a convert. See F. F. Bruce, *Paul: Apostle of the Heart Set Free* (Grand Rapids: Eerdmans, 1977), p. 238.

2. It may be that Rieu translates "mocked" in this way because the Athenian playwright Aeschylus, some five hundred years before, in describing the institution of the court of Areopagus by Athene, the city's patron deity, had made the god Apollo say: When the dust has soaked up a man's blood, Once he is dead, there is no resurrection. (Aeschylus, *Eumenides*, 647f.)

idea of a bodily resurrection from death was absurd. Immortality of the soul? Yes, but resurrection of a vile body, the prison of the soul, could never have occurred.[3]

These two attitudes seen here among the intellectuals—Paul and the Athenians—have continued to this present moment. Today, the skeptical attitude of the Athenian philosophers has been adopted not only by their philosophical descendants but by others who have been influenced by the skepticism of scientism. Under the guise of the "scientific method," many have reasoned: "Since resurrection hasn't been empirically verified in our day, it does not happen." It is but a short jump (perhaps a "leap of faith") to move from that to another position: "Therefore, the resurrection of the dead has never occurred and will never occur." This skeptical faith (for "faith" it is!), based upon the partial knowledge and limited evidence of scientific empiricism has permeated a large segment of twentieth century thinking.

But, on the other hand, Paul has many contemporaries who believe firmly that Jesus has risen from the dead and will indeed "judge the living and the dead at his coming" (II Tim. 4:1, 2). To them the resurrection is not just an isolated doctrine, nor a philosophical position. It is an essential part of the full disclosure of the Redeemer God, who has created all men and has revealed to men His purpose toward them. The ground of resurrection, therefore, is the very nature of God. Paul's question to Agrippa and that group of dignitaries assembled at Caesarea is still the relevant question: "Why should it be thought incredible that God should raise the dead?" (Acts 26:8).

The question is this: Do we believe in a God who could raise the dead, do mighty works within human history, and

---

3. See the Appendix by Oscar Cullman, p. 273.

4

manifest Himself fully in the person of Jesus of Nazareth? Resurrection, miracles of healing, miracles of nature, transformation of human life—all are consequences of a greater reality, the living, Creator-God. If we believe that this universe is the result of some kind of evolutionary process, a closed system, then the belief in a God who has created and works out His will is impossible.

But, like Paul of old, believers today are committed to a God who is not the passive being or dynamic impersonal force of the philosophers, but an active Being, creating, directing, sustaining, and revealing. Such a God acted in ancient times in the lives of Adam, Noah, Abraham, Isaac, and Jacob. Such a God called a people to Himself, leading them out of Egypt in mighty power through Moses, and continued to direct this people through judges, prophets, and kings. Such a God prepared this people to be a servant people, and through this chosen race brought forth His incarnate Son, Jesus of Nazareth. Such a God acted through His Son in a miracle ministry and an atoning death to make salvation possible for all who would respond. And such a God gave all men a guarantee that He was active in this process in raising Jesus from the dead, "declaring Him to be the Son of God with power" (Rom. 1:4), and raising Him "for our justification" (Rom. 4:25).

Those who follow Paul in the attitude of faith in the living God believe that God has revealed His will and that Holy Scripture presents that revealed will. In the Bible then, there is an account of God's activity of which resurrection from the dead is a vital element. Our concern is to survey what the Bible teaches about resurrection. To do this we shall first look at the background of this belief in immortality and/or resurrection in the ancient world separated from the revelatory activity of the living God. Then we shall move to an analysis of the Old Testament teaching, the developments in the intertestamental period within Jewish thought, and finally, what that final revelation in Jesus Christ, enshrined in the new covenant Scriptures, teaches us about resurrection.

Chapter Two

HOPE AND HOPELESSNESS IN THE ANCIENT WORLD

"If a man die shall he live again?" (Job)

Ancient men faced two realities—birth and death. The discovery of death, the awareness of one's own mortality, stirred profound emotions in the ancient's breast. "If a man die shall he live again?" is indeed the poignant question of all men. As S. G. Brandon notes: "The realization of one's own mortality and the natural dread of its occurrence are personal experiences and calculated to make the individual disturbingly aware of the fact of his essential loneliness."[1]

Within the context of these experiences of loneliness and hopelessness, ancient man frequently developed funerary customs that reflect his unwillingness to accept death as ultimate.[2] Burials with such equipment as weapons and tools, personal ornaments and food, show a definite belief in survival beyond death.

The archaeological record shows that early man was not totally engrossed in the demands of his immediate environment. He was already conscious that his mere existence and participation in human life raised profound questions which transcend his physiological needs, his instincts and his emotions. He is apparently aware of fears and hopes unknown to the animal world; these are translated into his primitive art found on the walls of caves. The best interpretation of

---

1. S.G.F. Brandon, *Man and His Destiny in the Great Religions* (Manchester: Manchester University Press, 1962), p. 7.
2. Lord Tennyson poetically comments on these ancient practices:
   Since one dying race began,
   Ever, ever, and forever was the leading light of man,
   Those that in barbarian burials killed the slave and slew the wife
   Felt within themselves the sacred passion of the second life.

7

these cave drawings of early man shows that dim gropings after personal significance are in process. Because of the human ability to produce a sense of time, the ancient is deprived of that animal faculty for immersion in the present, and he is conscious of his essential insecurity in a world of ceaseless change. Already ancient man experiences what W. B. Yeats expresses:

> Nor dread, nor hope attend
> A dying animal;
> A man awaits his end
> Dreading and hoping all.

Sir James Frazer, whose investigations of ancient thought and custom are beyond question, summarizes the results of ancient man's understanding of his destiny:

> It is impossible not to be struck by the strength, and perhaps we may say the universality, of the natural belief in immortality among the savage races of mankind. With them a life after death is not a matter of speculation and conjecture; it is a practical certainty which the individual as little dreams of doubting as he doubts the reality of his conscious existence. He assumes it without enquiry and acts upon it without hesitation, as if it were one of the best-ascertained truths within the limits of human experience.[3]

Frequently, if not generally, this belief in immortality was grounded in ancient *psychology* not *religion*. As John Baillie points out: "It was in no sense a product of ethical idealism or of religious faith and aspiration, but was merely a corollary of the ordinary lay psychology of the time and place."[4] It

---

3. James Frazer, *Belief in Immortality and the Worship of the Dead*, Vol. I, p. 468.
4. John Baillie, *And The Life Everlasting* (New York: Charles Scribner's Sons, 1933), p. 91.

is later that the concept of immortality becomes integrally related to ancient religion; and, even later, becomes an acceptable concept of ancient philosophy.

The Destiny of Man in the Ancient Religions

The first great civilized states were established in Egypt and Mesopotamia during the fourth millennium before Christ. Both of these ancient civilizations have revealed their evaluation of human life and destiny through archeological remains and literary texts.

The *Pyramid Texts,* which come from the fifth and sixth dynasties (about 2425-2300 B.C.), were inscribed on the interior walls of the pyramids. They are concerned with securing a safe passage of the dead Pharaoh into the next world and with his proper state in that world. These texts reflect an eloquent concern of the Egyptians (at least those of the upper classes) with the awful problem of death. "They reveal," says Brandon, "the terror that was felt about the physical phenomena of death, and they bear witness to a deep-rooted belief that these horrors could be prevented or overcome by practical (i.e. magical) means and a new and more glorious life with the gods attained."[5]

It is clear from the evidence that comes from ancient Egypt that the after-life somehow involves the survival of the body. The Egyptian could not imagine any future mode of existence apart from the body. Though the *Pyramid Texts* do not contain an exposition of the Osiris legend, yet they allude to it frequently, leading one to believe that this cultic legend with its dying-rising god is in the background of much

5. Brandon, pp. 38-39.

9

within the texts. The legend, as it is reconstructed by Egyptologists from various sources, pictures Osiris as an ancient ruler of Egypt. He had been killed by his brother Set, the reason or motive unknown. His body, apparently in a state of decomposition, is rescued from the Nile by Isis and Nephthys, who mourn over him. The body is reconstituted and revived by the agencies of one or all of the deities, Isis, Nephthys, Anubis, Horus and Re. Osiris, restored to life, is vindicated and his brother is vanquished after a long struggle by Horus, the son of Osiris. Osiris though revived does not return to his former life, but becomes the lord of the realm of the dead.

In *The Book of the Dead* various magical compositions or "spells" are found that embody or allude to this Osirian drama.[6] These spells take various forms: "hymns, prayers, myths, guidebooks, incantations, even threats against the gods."[7] By 1500 B.C., such spells had so multiplied that many of them were written on a papyrus scroll and laid within the coffins of the dead, hence the term "the book of the dead."

One might suppose that this concentration on death and after-life was a denial of this world and reflected a morbid pessimism pervading ancient Egypt. This is not true. One could say, in fact, that they abhorred death and were preoccupied with death *because* they loved life so much. Wilson says: "They did spend an extraordinary amount of time and energy in denying and circumventing death, but the spirit was not one of the gloomy foreboding. On the contrary, it was a spirit of hopeful triumph, a vigorous relish

---

6. Thomas George Allen, translator, *The Book of the Dead or Going Forth by Day: Ideas of the Ancient Egyptians Concerning the Hereafter as Expressed in Their Own Terms* (Chicago: The University of Chicago Press, 1974).

7. Ibid, p. 1.

of life, and an expectant assertion of continued future life as over against the finality and gloom of death."[8]

But this rather happy approach to life and death did not survive in ancient Egypt. Sometime around 1200 B.C. there arose an entirely different attitude toward death, accompanied by a general skepticism about the hereafter. It is, as Wilson notes, as if "the shadow of an uncertain eternity had dropped over the sunny gaiety of Egypt."[9]

When one passes from considering man and his destiny in ancient Egypt to a similar consideration in Mesopotamia in that same period, the contrast is most notable. Some have tried to explain this difference on the basis of environmental circumstances, but whatever the explanation the Mesopotamians (Sumerians and ancient Assyrians) reveal an "unrelievedly gloomy evaluation of human destiny . . . when contrasted with the Egyptian view."[10]

The sources for this study of the ancient Mesopotamian concept of human destiny form three groups which generally corroborate and shed light upon each other. These are: (1) archeological data coming from the excavation of ancient tombs; (2) ritual texts designed to offset various kinds of misfortune; and (3) longer texts which set forth views about man, the cosmos, man's relation to the gods, and the nature of the netherworld.

The excavations of ancient tombs show that even in the earliest Sumer there was a clear expectation that the dead survived the grave in that the dead were provided with various kinds of equipment to meet physical needs. This

---

8. A. Wilson, *The Culture of Ancient Egypt* (Chicago: The University of Chicago Press, 1958), p. 78.

9. Ibid, p. 297.

10. Brandon, p. 71.

11

view continues to be reflected in the funerary practices of later times among the Akkadians and Assyrians. This expectation and belief is given dramatic underpinning by an inscription of King Ashurbanipal in which he boasts that he had taken his revenge upon the Elamites even beyond this life by casting the bones of their dead rulers out of their tombs so that, "Upon their spirits I imposed restlessness (and) cut them off from food offerings (and) libations of water."[11]

What is indicated by the archeological evidence is also confirmed in the various ritual texts. These texts reveal not only belief in life after death but a kind of horror regarding death and the dead. The dead, if not properly cared for by the family at the time of death, were considered a potential menace. Many of the ritual texts refer to the "ghosts of a nobody," (that is, one who had no one to bury him properly) that have afflicted or could afflict the living. Apparently, the dead were endowed with demonic power to take revenge for any neglect toward their mortuary preparation.

Longer, more mythic texts, tend to confirm this dread and horror of the living toward the living dead. *The Descent of Ishtar to the Underworld*, a well-known Sumerian myth, dating from about 2000 B.C., tells about the goddess Ishtar's descent into "the land of no-return." Even the celestial goddess surrenders all dignity and splendor before the queen of the underworld. In reacting to this she is smitten by sixty diseases and dies. Dire consequences come upon the world above since the goddess of fertility is dead. The wise god Ea secures Ishtar's revivification and she returns to the real world.

---

11. Quoted by Brandon, pp. 72-73.

The Epic of Gilgamesh also contains passages about the state of the dead and the underworld. This myth has been described by Heidel as "a meditation on death in the form of a tragedy."[12] It is perhaps the best representation of the Mesopotamian world view, which is filled with the spirit of pessimism with reference to death and the grave. The Mesopotamians, like the Egyptians, apparently believed in a dying-rising god. There is a healing-ritual text which intimates that Tammuz, the god of vegetation, dies and is revived. In this text certain rituals are to be carried out so that the ill person will be identified with Tammuz and will also be reanimated. The difference between this and the Osirian mortuary rites of Egypt are apparent. In Egypt the rite is performed upon the dead so that he may rise to a continued life beyond death; in Mesopotamia it is designed to restore a sick man to health.

The ancient Mesopotamians believed in life after death but their view is more pessimistic than the views of the Egyptians. This pessimism is not unique for it represents "a more realistic estimate of the experience common to man."[13] What is unique is that aggravated form of pessimism which invested this belief with a grim picture of subsequent demonic consequences for the living.

Man's destiny in pre-Christian Eastern religious thought is inextricably interwoven with the doctrine or belief in "transmigration of souls." This is the presumption which underlies Buddhism, Jainism and the whole of Hinduism. Present existence is but one of the infinite series reaching backward and forward in endless sequences. Each living creature, from highest to lowest is an incarnate soul doing penance for sins committed in some previous existence.

---

12. See Brandon, p. 89.
13. Ibid, p. 104.

Theoretically, there is nothing in this doctrine which necessarily makes it an object of dread; but, practically, in the ancient Hindu system, transmigration was seen within a context of pessimistic gloom. "The thought of wandering perpetually through the bodies of men, animals, and plants, and of being compelled in each existence to experience more pain than joy,"[14] says R. Garbe, must have been dreadful for the ancient Hindu. Even the gods are involved in this cycle of existence and must descend to lower forms of existence "when the power of former merit is exhausted through the enjoyment of divine position and honors."[15]

Later, in the *Upanishads*, a release from this endless cycle of existence is seen as possible through self-knowledge. This "way of knowledge" could be trodden only by a few. This saving knowledge consists "in the recognition of the sole existence of the Brahman, the soul, of the universe, of the illusory nature of the phenomenal world, and especially of the identity of the individual soul, the *atman*, with the Brahman."[16]

Buddhism carried this one step farther by showing that it is the *desire* for existence that creates misery for man. Consequently the Buddhist scheme of training was designed to free disciples from these innate desires and emphasized renunciation. The process is thus described in the Samanna-phala-sutra:

> With his mind thus concentrated, purified, and cleansed, without lust, free from the depravities, subtle, ready to act, firm, and impassible, he turns and directs his mind to the

---

14. R. Garbe, "Transmigration (Indian)," in *Hastings Encyclopedia of Religion and Ethics* (New York: Charles Scribner's Sons, 1951) Vol. III, p. 435.
15. Ibid, p. 435.
16. Ibid, p. 435.

knowledge of the destruction of the asavas. He duly understands 'this is pain'; he duly understands, 'this is the cessation
of pain'; he duly understands, 'this is the path that leads to
the cessaton of pain'; he duly understands, 'these are the
asavas'; he duly understands, 'this is the cause of the asavas';
he duly understands, 'this is the path that leads to the destruction of the asavas'. As he thus knows and thus perceives, his
mind is released from the asava of sensual desire, from the
asava of desire for existence, from the asava of ignorance. In
the released is the knowledge of his release: ignorance is
destroyed, the religious life has been led, done is what was
to be done, there is nothing further for this world.[17]

The Buddhist goal is to reach or attain Nirvana. The ultimate state of one who has attained Nirvana is difficult to
explain. It is certainly not annihilation, but it is difficult to
speak positively of what it is. Various positive epithets which
were used to describe Nirvana by those who had attained
it during their lifetime have been collected by Rhys Davids.[18]
Whether these can be regarded as valid with reference to
those attaining Nirvana at death may be questioned. At any
rate Nirvana is possible for the elite who have "laid down
the burden . . . in whom the fetter of desire for existence is
destroyed, and who are released with complete knowledge."[19] Others must return to a series of rebirths, some in
an unhappy, others in a happy state.

Immortality in Ancient Philosophy

It is sometimes difficult to draw the line between religion
and philosophy in the ancient world, for implicit in most

---

17. quoted by Brandon, p. 340.

18. These include such statements as the harbor of refuge, the cool cave,
the island amidst the floods, the place of bliss, the calm, emancipation, liberation,
the tranquil, the home of ease, the end of suffering, the medicine of all evil,
the abiding, the detachment and the holy city. Brandon, p. 345.

19. Brandon, p. 347.

religions is a philosophy, a world view. But, it will be particularly instructive to view the doctrine of immortality developed in the Western world prior to the beginnings of Christianity. These views developed contemporaneously with, yet distinct from, some of the Old Testament literature. These views also influence the literary developments of Jewish thought in the intertestamental period, and they will come to have a profound influence on later Christian thought.

The literature on the philosophical problem of immortality begins with Plato (or Socrates, Plato's mentor) in the fifth century before Christ. In the dialogue *Phaedo*,[20] Plato puts forth a demonstration of the immortality of the soul. The agruments advanced in this work are:[21]

1. The soul existed before birth. This pre-existence is drawn from the argument that all real knowledge is recollection.
2. There are eternal and immutable "forms" or "ideas."Since the soul is capable of knowing these it, too, must be eternal and divine, for "nothing mortal knows what is immortal."[22]
3. The soul rules the body, and therein, resembles the immortal gods.
4. The soul is simple, uncompounded, incapable of dissolution. Anything so constituted cannot change and is eternal.
5. The soul's essence is life, the opposite of death. It cannot be conceived of as dying any more than a fire can be conceived of as being cold.[23]

---

20. *Phaedo* in *Plato's Dialogues*, Jowett translation, (New York: Random House, 1937).

21. This summary is seen in Jacques Choron, *Death and Western Thought* *(New York: Macmillan, 1962) p. 48.*

22. *Phaedo, 78a-84b.*

23. *An additional proof is given in the dialogue, Phaedrus, where the soul* is seen as self-moved and the source of life and motion; therefore, it can never cease to move and live.

Having heard, and apparently accepting, these arguments put into the mouth of Socrates just prior to his death, Crito asks:

"But how shall we bury you?" "However you please," Socrates replied, "if you can catch me and I do not get away from you." And he laughed gently, and looking towards us said: "I cannot persuade Crito, my friends, that the Socrates who is now conversing and arranging the details of his argument is really I: he thinks I am the one whom he will presently see as a corpse, and he asks how to bury me. And though I have been saying at great length that after I drink the poison I shall no longer be with you, but shall go away to the joys of the blessed, he seems to think that was idle talk uttered to encourage you and myself."[24]

Here in Plato (or Socrates) is the first genuine attempt to think seriously about the problem of death and to try to present rational arguments for what John Wisdom calls "these logically unique expectations" relative to personal survival. The argument attempts to show mind and knowledge as transcending physiological or bodily processes and to identify this transcendental quality with that which is essentially personal. In popular parlance, the body becomes the "prison house" of the soul. When the prison house is destroyed, the soul flies forth untrammeled and free.

Such argument and subsequent doctrine is seen in bolder relief when viewed against the back-drop of pre-Christian Greek culture and life. There, says Brandon, we see only "a pessimistic estimate of man's nature and fate" characterizing "the main stream of Greek thought from the seventh

---

24. Phaedo, 115 c, d. It is this episode that Dr. Cullman contrasts with the attitude of Jesus in his lecture *Resurrection of the Dead or Immortality of the Soul?* See Appendix.

century B.C. down to the exponents of Stoic and Epicurean thought."[25] Even more distinguishing, says this same scholar, is the absence of any eschatology "since it tacitly conceived of human life as virtually limited to existence in this present world."[26] Some have even suggested that Plato's belief in immortality came not from inexorable reasons forcing him to such a position but because he feared death.[27]

Later Greek thought does not reach this high level seen in Plato relative to personal survival. Aristotle in *De Anima* sees reason alone as immortal. Such reason (*nous*) comes to man "from the outside"; it is the divine element in man distinguishing him from animal life. It alone does not perish at death. He says:

> When mind is set free from its present conditions[28] it appears as just what it is and nothing more; this alone is immortal and eternal (we do not, however, remember its former activity because, while mind in this sense is impossible, mind as possible is destructible), and without it nothing thinks.[29]

Aristotle sees death as this "most terrible of all things," but it must be faced with courage and virtue, not through some mythology of an eternal soul surviving or transmigrating. Aristotle's wonder and amazement at the universe drove him to a life-long study of all things. He believed that there was a plan—reason—pervading it all. And, says Choron, "although there is no providence that cares for the

---

25. Brandon, p. 168.

26. Ibid.

27. See William Barrett, *Irrational Man* (New York: Anchor Books, 1958), p. 82.

28. This phrase reminds us of Plato's view of the liberation of the soul.

29. De Anima, 430a, 14, 23.

well-being of each single individual being, and man's personality does not survive death, Aristotle felt very strongly that human existence is meaningful and important in this cosmic plan. Death may be evil, but not yet absurd."[30]

As one moves closer to the Christian era, the two philosophical positions that held sway among the intelligentsia were Epicureanism and Stoicism. Both were reactions to Platonic dualism; both denied the continuation of personal existence beyond death. The specific patterns of their reactions were quite different. Stoicism emphasized living "according to the practical acquaintance with the processes of nature," to follow nature. Hence, death is a part of Nature, disagreeable perhaps, but necessary. Since Nature teaches nothing of personal survival it is a notion that cannot be held with any firmness. Concerns should be with this life and its conformity to the laws of Nature.

Epicureanism is essentially materialistic and hedonistic or pleasure-oriented. Such hedonism is not that of sensualists and profligates but that which seeks freedom from "pain in the body and from trouble in the mind."[31] The basic obstacle to peace of mind, to Epicurus and his followers, was the fear of death. This fear is totally unfounded and can be eliminated, since at death we no longer exist.[32] If one has "no craving for immortality,"[33] then death is nothing and,

---

30. Choron. p. 57.

31. Quoted by Choron, p. 60. The famous, or infamous, "eat, drink, and be merry, for tomorrow we die" is a pseudo-epicurean slogan and a distortion of Epicurus' teaching.

32. Ibid, p. 60.

33. Epicurus wrote: "A right understanding that death is nothing to us makes the mortality of life enjoyable, not by adding to life an illimitable time, but by taking away the yearning after immortality."

understanding this the "mortality of life" can become "enjoyable." In light of this Lucretius, a later disciple, advances some seventy-eight arguments against the idea of the immortality of the soul.[34]

Conclusion

In this brief survey of the idea of immortality in the ancient world—both in the religious idea and philosophical notions propounded—an undercurrent of hope and hopelessness appears. There is hopelessness tinged with vague hopes. As history moves out of that time of general superstition and mythology, the hopelessness increases by virtue of the application (and limitations) of human reason. The ancient world indeed is characterized correctly by the Apostle as "having no hope and without God" (Eph. 2:12). How little do the gifted men of ancient times speak of hope. It is there in their vocabularies, but lacking Israel's conception of a creative God who is faithful and steadfast towards His people, they lacked also the conception of hope as steadfast confidence. The highest ethic of the ancient world is characterized by the "Cosmic resignation in Stoicism."[35]

Paul Tillich sees the ancient world as burdened by the "anxiety of fate and death," but, as Tillich points out, much of the modern world is hopelessly caught up in the "anxiety of emptiness and meaninglessness."[36] The existentialism of Unamuno and Sartre, the "death of God theology," the bankruptcy of liberal theology, the engulfment of a scientific humanism—all these have continued to undermine any genuine hopefulness. Can the answer that Corliss Lamont gives satisfy?

34. *De Rerum Natura*, Book III.
35. Paul Tillich, *Being and Courage*, p. 10.
36. Ibid, p. 41.

Finally, the knowledge that immortality is an illusion frees us from any sort of preoccupation with the subject of death. It makes death, in a sense, unimportant. It liberates all our energy and time for the realization and extension of the happy potentialities of this good earth. It engenders a hearty and grateful acceptance of the rich experiences attainable in human living amid an abundant Nature. It is a knowledge that brings strength and depth and maturity, making possible a philosophy of life that is simple, understandable and inspiring. We do not ask to be born; and we do not ask to die. But born we are and die we must. We come into existence and we pass out of existence. And in neither case does high-handed fate await our ratification of its decree.

Yet between the birth and death we can live our lives, work for and enjoy the things that we hold dear. We can make our actions count and endow our days on earth with a scope and meaning that the finality of death cannot defeat. We can contribute our unique quality to the ongoing development of the nation and humanity; give of our best to the continuing affirmation of life on behalf of the greater glory of man.[37]

Others would express this hopeless faith differently. James Thomason, in his *City of the Dreadful Night*, says:

> When Faith and Love and Hope are dead indeed,
> Can Life still live? By what does it proceed?
>
> . . . .
>
> This life itself holds nothing good for us,
> But it ends soon and nevermore can be;
> And we know nothing of it ere our birth,

---

37. *The Illusion of Immortality* (New York: Philosophical Library, 1959), pp. 277-278.

And shall know nothing when consigned to earth;
I ponder these thoughts and they comfort me.[38]

It is over against this bankruptcy of human thought that the Biblical revelation of a God who raises the dead is set. It is this revelation of an existence, the reality of which is beyond commonly accepted categories of life and death, that invites attention.

FOR FURTHER STUDY

Addison, James Thayer. *Life Beyond Death in the Beliefs of Mankind.* Boston: Houghton Mifflin, 1932.

Baillie, John. *And the Life Everlasting.* New York: Charles Scribner's Sons, 1933.

Brandon, S.G.F. *Man and His Destiny in the Great Religions.* Manchester: University of Manchester Press, 1962.

Brown, William Adams. *The Christian Hope: A Study in the Doctrine of Immortality.* New York: Charles Scribner's Sons, 1912.

Choron, Jacques. *Death and Western Thought.* New York: Macmillan, 1963.

Flew, Anthony. "Immortality," *The Encyclopedia of Religion,* Volume IV.

Holck, Frederick H. *Death and Eastern Thought.* Nashville: Abingdon Press, 1973.

Salmon, S.D.F. *The Christian Doctrine of Immortality.* New York: Scribner's, 1896.

---

38. *The City of the Dreadful Night,* XVI, quoted by Robert O. Fife, *Christ Our Hope* (Manhattan, Ks: Manhattan Bible College Press, 1964), p. 11.

QUESTIONS FOR DISCUSSION

1. Compare and contrast the ancient Egyptians and Mesopotamians' views on life after death.
2. Compare Plato's view of immortality with what you have
   been taught from Scripture. Read the Appendix by Cullman in this light and discuss its implications.
3. Discuss the view of Corliss Lamont. Do you believe that
   persons today are satisfied with this approach? Why?

Chapter Three

RESURRECTION IN THE OLD TESTAMENT

"Thus it is written, that the Christ (Messiah) should suffer and on the third day rise from the dead" (Luke 24:46).

In Paul's letters, particularly Ephesians and Colossians, he uses the term *mysterion,* mystery, in a distinct sense: it has the idea of a "sacred secret" (This is how J. B. Rotherham uniformly translates it in his *Emphasized Bible*). This is brought out in that closing benediction in Paul's letter to the Romans:

> Now to him that is able to strengthen and establish you according to my gospel, according to the revelation of the mystery (sacred secret) which was kept secret since the world began, but now is made manifest; and at the command of the eternal God made known through the writings of the prophets to all the nations that lead them to obedience and faith; To the one wise God, be glory forever through Jesus Christ. Amen" (Rom. 16:25-27).

Or, as Paul phrases it in the Ephesian letter:

> And, by reading what I have written you will be able to judge how far I understand this hidden purpose of God in Christ (the mystery of Christ—KJV), which in former generations was not made known to mankind as it has now been revealed unto his holy apostles and prophets by the Spirit (Eph. 3:4-5).

Recognizing the meaning of this term we can see why Paul uses it in that great Resurrection chapter—I Corinthians 15. There, Paul says:

> Behold, I show you a mystery (a sacred secret): We shall not all sleep, but we shall all be changed, in a moment, in the twinkling of an eye, at the last trump. For the trumpet shall sound and the dead shall be raised beyond the reach

of corruption, and we who are still alive shall be transformed into new bodies as well" (I Cor. 15:51-52).

Paul is pointing out that the resurrection truth which he is revealing was partially, if not wholly, hidden to past generations. We must take this seriously and not read New Testament revelation back into the Old Testament accounts, pointing out how this Messianic passage or that allusion has within it a full-blown doctrine of resurrection.[1] In other words we should approach the Old Testament text cautiously as we determine what is clearly set forth concerning resurrection.

In offering this word of caution, we are not suggesting that there is nothing revealed in the Old Testament about the resurrection of the body. In fact, it will be shown that there is much in the Old Testament which speaks directly or indirectly to this idea which will be revealed so fully in later stages of God's revelatory Word.

In the Pentateuch and Historical Books of the Old Testament

It is generally conceived that there is little about resurrection or after-life in what the Jews called the Torah (the five books of Moses) and the Former Prophets (or historical books of the Old Testament). Death is seen as the end, the destruction of human existence. So we read in Genesis:

---

1. H. H. Rowley, in *The Faith of Israel* (Philadelphia: Westminster Press, 1956), sounds this same caution. Rather than reading back into the Old Testament record a "sure faith in the resurrection," one ought to see that there is "a less sure embrace of the hope of any satisfying life after death" (p. 153). The lack of such hope is not because of "the vacillating and uncertain mind of God, but the imperfect apprehension by men of the truth which is hidden in God's heart" (p. 158).

> In the sweat of your face you shall eat bread till you return to the ground, for out of it you were taken; you are dust, and to dust you shall return (Genesis 3:19, RSV).

This same thought is expressed in the book of Job:

> Yes, I know that thou wilt bring me to death, and to the house appointed for all living (Job 30:23, RSV).

Many feel that this general concept of death is not invalidated by those isolated accounts of individuals returning to life. In the cases of the widow's son in Zarephath (I Kings 17:17-22), the Shunammite's son (II Kings 4:18-37), and the man thrown hurriedly into Elisha's grave (II Kings 13:20f.), one sees the extension of physical life beyond death, but in terms of miraculous power mediated through the prophet of God. Death is still final, and, presumably, these (like Lazarus and others in the New Testament) experienced physical death again.

The translations of Enoch (Gen. 5:24) and Elijah (II Kings 2:11) indicate that these two Biblical characters did not die but were taken from the earth before their deaths. Of Enoch, the Scripture says, "Enoch walked with God; and he was not, for God took him" (Gen. 5:24, RSV). The passage about Elijah in II Kings says:

> When they had crossed [the Jordan river] Elijah said to Elisha, "Ask what I shall do for you, before I am taken from you." And Elisha said, "I pray you, let me inherit a double share of your spirit." And he said, "You have asked a hard thing; yet, if you see me as I am being taken from you, it shall be so for you; but if you do not see me, it shall not be so." And as they still went on, and talked, behold, a chariot of fire and horses of fire separated the two of them. And Elijah went up by a whirlwind into heaven. And Elisha saw it and he cried,

"My father, my father! The chariots of Israel and its horsemen!"
And he saw him no more (II Kings 2:9-12, RSV).

These two accounts are intriguing, particularly since both
are in those sections of Old Testament Scripture where little
else positively emphasizes life beyond the grave. The fact
that in Israel's pre-history God is revealed as "taking" one
of the Patriarchs from the earth to be with him may indirectly
suggest some kind of after-life. Why would God so act?
Why is such action related to "one who walked with God,"
one whose tenor of godly life seems to be extraordinary?

The taking of Elijah "up to heaven by a whirlwind" (II
Kings 2:11) is also an interesting passage. At the close of a
long life of faithful service, this, the greatest of the "oral
prophets," is rewarded in a special way. Unless we dismiss
this episode as mere legend or myth, it must be taken seriously
and its meaning sought. Whatever else may be noted, the
notion that Elijah lives on with God is strongly emphasized.

Both of these passages, in describing the end of the lives
of two of God's saints, suggest these conclusions: (1) They
entered the presence of the Living God at the conclusion of
their earthly lives; (2) They did not experience the normal
end of physical existence—death; and (3) God Himself
took the initiative and, by His power, accomplished this.[2]

A very interesting episode within the historical portions
of the Old Testament needs some consideration. In I Sam.
28, Saul, desiring to know God's will ("when Saul inquired
of the Lord, the Lord did not answer him, either by dreams,
or by Urim, or by prophets"—I Sam. 28:6, RSV), consulted

2. The passages in Deuteronomy 32 and 34 concerning the end of Moses'
life are different from these passages cited. There Moses' death is specifically
mentioned, with the Lord burying him and "no man knowing the place of his
burial" (Deut. 34:5-6).

the witch or medium at Endor. She conjures up the spirit of Samuel—the account is not in doubt about this reality— saying, "I see a god[3] coming up out of the earth" (I Sam. 28:13). As Saul bows in obedient awe, Samuel speaks to Saul, "Why have you disturbed me by bringing me up?" (I Sam. 28:15). Samuel continues to converse with Saul, confirming what Saul already knew, that the Lord had taken the kingdom from him and given it to David.

It is difficult to understand this passage without assuming that those in Sheol are conscious and therefore alive. One commentator sees the "disturbance" which Samuel speaks of, not as any "emotional disturbance" but "at having to leave Sheol to be involved in earthly affairs again."[4]

Before moving on to survey other areas of Old Testament Scripture, one must deal seriously with Jesus' hermeneutical approach to Exodus 3:9. In answering the question of the Sadducees relative to the resurrection hypothetically tied up in the concept of levirate marriage (the seven husbands of the one wife), Jesus emphasizes what is basic in the Old Testament (see Matt. 22:23-33; Mark 12:18-27; Luke 20:27-40): God is the living God who continues to rule over and relate to His people. But He is also the source of the ongoing life of those who belong to Him. He is not the God of the dead, but of the living. Therefore, when God speaks to Moses, hundreds of years after the death of Abraham, Isaac, and Jacob, He identifies Himself as the God of the Patriarchs, who still live. Dr. William L. Lane states it well:

---

3. Probably "god-like being" and best rendered as "spirit."

4. J. Mauchline, I & II Samuel, *New Century Bible* (Greenwood, SC: Attic Press, 1971), p. 182.

The concept "God of the dead" implies a blatant contradiction, especially in the context of the Sadduceean understanding of death as extinction, without the hope of resurrection. If God had assumed the task of protecting the patriarchs from misfortune during the course of their life, but fails to deliver them from that supreme misfortune which marks the definitive and absolute check upon their hopes, his protection is of little value. . . . In citing Exo. 3:6 Jesus showed how resurrection faith is attached in a profound way to the central concept of biblical revelation, the covenant, and how the salvation promised by God to the patriarchs and their descendants in virtue of the covenant contains implicitly the assurance of the resurrection. It was the failure to appreciate the essential link between God's covenant faithfulness and the resurrection which led the Sadducees into their grievous error.[5]

The Prophets

If there is a sense of progressiveness in God's revelation to His people, then we can expect God's more definite emphasis upon resurrection and/or life after death. This appears to be borne out as we survey the prophetic literature, where we find a number of passages relevant to the discussion.

Come, let us return to the Lord; for he has torn, that he may heal us; he has stricken, and he will bind us up. After two days he will revive us; on the third day he will raise us up, that we may live before him (Hosea 6:1-3, RSV).

The historical context is the Syro-Ephraimitish War of 735-734 B.C. The passage is a call to repentance and faith. God will renew if Israel but believes and obeys Him. This

---

5. W. L. Lane, *The Gospel According to Mark*, NICNT (Grand Rapids: Eerdmans, 1974), p. 430. It may well be that this helps us understand how Jesus could use the Old Testament to show that "everything written" about him in "the law of Moses and the prophets and the Psalms" was fulfilled (Luke 24:44).

national renewal is seen in personal terms as "health, healing, reviving of the spirit, resurrection." The term "raise us up" is undoubtedly figurative; but, within this context, it suggests the human hope of life beyond the grave.

Another passage in Hosea speaks more pointedly to this hope. Hosea 13:14 asks,

> Shall I ransom them from the power of Sheol? Shall I redeem them from Death? O Death where are your plagues? O Sheol where is your destruction?[6]

This passage should not necessarily be understood as predicting the downfall of death by the risen Christ (as Luther and other older commentators have viewed it), but as a reference to the coming judgment of the nation of Israel. Israel, historically, faces death and destruction; but the extraordinary power of God can defeat death and the grave.

But the very notion that God has power over death and the grave is significant. Even admitting that the passage refers to Israel's existence, one must also conclude that the very application of individual ends (death and the grave) to a corporate situation reflects some kind of general hope in God's power to extend life beyond death.

Several passages in Isaiah seem to set out rather clearly a resurrection hope. In Isaiah 26:19 there is expressed confidence in Israel's resurrection:

> Thy dead shall live, their bodies shall rise.[7] O dwellers in the dust, awake and sing for joy! For thy dew is a dew of light, and on the land of the shades thou wilt let it fall (RSV).

---

6. The Septuagint version makes plagues and destruction "judgment" and "sting." It is the Septuagint which provides Paul the background for his celebration of the resurrection in I Cor. 15:55.

7. The Septuagint (LXX) phrase is this: "the dead shall rise and those in the tombs shall be raised."

God is apparently speaking. Resurrection will occur; life after death is more than a hope beyond the grave; it is coupled with "bodies arising, those in the tombs being raised."

Because this passage speaks so clearly to resurrection, some critics have suggested that it is an interpolation added at a later time when the doctrine of resurrection had become more dominant in Jewish thought. Isaiah 25:8 is also treated in this manner since it promises that

> He will swallow up death forever, and the Lord God will wipe away all tears from all faces, and the reproach of his people he will take away from all the earth; for the Lord has spoken (RSV).

The servant Songs of Isaiah (Isa. 52:13—53:12) have been variously interpreted as relating to Israel as a nation or to the Messiah. In light of later understanding, the personal interpretation seems most fitting. Throughout the passage the personal notion is stressed. "*He* was oppressed and *he* was afflicted, yet *he* opened not *his* mouth" (Isa. 53:7, RSV). There is no question about the "suffering" of the Servant, a "suffering unto death":

> . . . he was cut off out of the land of the living, stricken for the transgression of my people. And they made his grave with the wicked and with a rich man in his death (Isa. 53: 8, 9, RSV).

This vicarious suffering was within God's will. "Yet it was the will of the Lord to bruise him; he has put him to grief" (Isa. 53:10). But, it was also God's will that

> he shall see his offspring, he shall indeed prolong his days; the will of the Lord shall prosper in his hand; he shall see the fruit of the travail of his soul and be satisfied (Isa. 53:10, RSV).

31

One can conclude that the prophet is quite clear in informing the reader that the destiny of an individual and not of the nation is in view. Resurrection is presupposed as the exaltation of the Servant is underscored. The destiny of the humiliated and glorified Servant demands continuous life after death.

"The Writings"

It is in that segment of the Hebrew canon known as the Writings[8] that the clearest revelation of resurrection and after life are seen. Here, in Psalms, Ecclesiastes, Job, and particularly Daniel,[9] we have the richest material for our study.

Before looking at specific passages, one should survey the Old Testament understanding of Sheol, since this plays such a prominent role in many of these passages. Sheol is the place of the dead. In some respects it corresponds to the Greek Hades. It is "the house of meeting for all living" (Job 30:23), "the land of darkness, and of the shadow of death" (Job 10:21). Job's poetic description of it is quite graphic:

There the wicked cease from troubling, and there the weary are at rest. There the prisoners are at ease together; they hear not the voice of the taskmaster. The small and the great are there, and the slave is free from his master (Job 3:17-19, RSV).

Another vivid description is found in Isaiah's prophecy of the fall of some ancient tyranny.[10].

---

8. This is what the New Testament generally refers to as Psalms (see Luke 24:44).

9. Though Daniel is included in the prophets in modern arrangements of the bible, within Judaism Daniel, being apocalyptic, was included in the section known as "The Writings."

10. The "great fall" may be of a king (Nebuchadnezzar?), a nation (Babylon?), or a power (Persia?) whose fall would precede Israel's restoration.

> Sheol beneath is thrilled at thee,
>   Meeting thine advent;
> Arousing for thee the shades,
>   All the bell-wethers of Earth,
> Making rise up from their thrones.
>   All the kings of the nations.
> They shall all of them answer
>   And lay to thee,
> "*Thou*, too, art made weak as we
>   Unto us art made like."
> Brought down to Sheol is thy pomp,
>   The music of thy lutes;
> Beneath thee maggots are spread,
>   And of worms is thy coverlet.[11]

In Ezekiel 32, *Sheol* is seen as the repository of all the dead of all nations—Egypt, Assyria, Elam, Edom, etc. In introducing this lament, Ezekiel speaks "the word of the Lord" that came to him:

> Son of man, wail over the multitude of Egypt, and send them down, her and the daughters of majestic nations, to the nether world, to those who have gone down to the Pit: "Whom do you surpass in beauty? Get down and be laid with the uncircumcised." They shall fall amid those who are slain by the sword, and with her shall lie all her multitudes. The mighty chiefs shall speak of them, with their helpers, out of the midst of Sheol (Ezek. 32:18-21, RSV).

Sheol, then, is the place of the dead, the Pit, or destruction. In Hebrew thought man's death occurs when his spirit, his breath, is withdrawn ("when thou takest away their breath,

---

11. Isa. 14:9-11, Translation by G. B. Gray, *International Critical Commentary* (New York: Charles Scribner's Sons, 1912), p. 248.

they die and return to dust"—Ps. 104:29).[12] His soul—
his *nephesh*—may be said to die (Num. 23:10, Judg. 16:30)
or to depart to *Sheol* (Ps. 16:10; 30:3; 94:17). Here,
soul (*nephesh*) is "practically synonymous with the personal
pronoun; there is no thought of an immortal soul existing
after death [as in Greek philosophy]. In sum . . . man is
. . . an animated body rather than an incarnate soul."[13]

The dead exist in *Sheol* as "shades" (*rephaim*) not as
"souls" (*nephesh*). A shade is man himself, or rather, man
stripped of all vitality, a mere shadow of his earthly self, a
faint replica of man. The most shattering consequence of
death and *Sheol* is that the believer is cut off from fellowship with God. Listen to the Psalmist:

> For in death there is no remembrance of thee;
> in Sheol who can give praise? (Psa. 6:5, RSV)
> Dost thou work wonders for the dead?
> Do the shades rise up to praise thee? *Selah*.
> Is thy steadfast love declared in the grave,
> or thy faithfulness in Abaddon?[14]
> Are thy wonders known in the darkness,
> or thy saving help in the land of forgetfulness?
> (Ps. 88:10-12)
> The dead do not praise the Lord,
> nor do any that go down in silence. (Ps. 115:17)

But, this is not the last word. If God's people had trusted
Him in life and deep fellowship was enjoyed with God, then
death could not bring an end to that relationship. That relationship depended upon God's power, not upon man's
condition. So the Psalmist could ask:

12. So we must understand Ecclesiastes 12:7, "the dust returns to the earth
as it was, and the spirit returns to God who gave it." To read Christian implications into this passage is anachronistic and poor hermeneutics.

13. George E. Ladd, *I Believe in the Resurrection of Jesus* (Grand Rapids:
Eerdmans, 1975), p. 45.

14. *Abaddon* is another name for *Sheol*, meaning "place of destruction."

34

> Whither shall I go from thy Spirit?
> Or whither shall I flee from thy presence?
> If I ascend to heaven, thou art there!
> If I make my bed in Sheol, thou art there! (Ps. 139:8)

Several of the Psalms express the consequence of such a conviction about God's power and his steadfast love toward his people. Psalm 16, though extolling the blessings of fellowship with God, a salvation that is pre-eminently this-worldly, still looks to the other-worldly end. The key to the Psalm is verse 11:

> Thou dost show me the path of life; in thy presence there is fulness of joy, in thy right hand are pleasures for evermore.

And, verses nine and ten depend upon this divine presence:

> Therefore my heart is glad, and my soul rejoices; my body also dwells secure. For thou dost not give me up to Sheol, or let thy godly one see the Pit.[15]

The genuine question here is that of fellowship or communion with God. The Psalmist sees this as endless; Sheol, the place of the dead, the Pit, or bodily destruction, will have no genuine effect upon the continuance of this relationship. How this persistence is possible does not seem to trouble the Psalmist's mind. Why should it, since it depends solely upon God!

A more specific Psalm is Psalm 49, where we find this affirmation of faith,

> But God will ransom my soul from the power of Sheol, for he will receive me. (Ps. 49:15)

---

15. The older translations usually render this last phrase, "thy Holy One see corruption." This later became one of the texts Peter used to establish the resurrection of Jesus (see Acts 2:25-28, 31).

This affirmation follows this statement:

> This is the fate of those who have foolish confidence,
> the end of those who are pleased with their portion. *Selah*.
> Like sheep they are appointed for Sheol;
> Death shall be their Shepherd;
> Straight to the grave they descend,
> And their form shall waste away;
> Sheol shall be their home. (Ps. 49:13, 14)

Apparently the Psalmist sees the inequities of life being rectified after death. The wicked may have good fortune in this life but all they can hope for is *Sheol* as an eternal home. On the other hand, the righteous, as represented by the Psalmist himself, will be "ransomed from Sheol," taken by God to Himself, and blessed after his death.[16] Resurrection, as such, is not clearly seen, but an after life of bliss and the experience of God's presence is certainly underscored.

A similar context is found in Psalm 73. The evil seem to prosper, the righteous face many problems. The wicked are at ease and increased with riches; the righteous seem to be under discipline and chastening every day. The Psalmist then says:

> But when I thought how to understand this, it seemed to me a wearisome task, Until I went into the sanctuary of God; then I perceived their end (Ps. 73:16, 17).

This understanding leads the Psalmist to praise God for his continued goodness:

---

16. E. F. Sutcliffe (*The Old Testament and the Future Life,* p. 102) supposes that the author of this Psalm "half discerned the truth of a richer after life." H. H. Rowley, *The Faith of Israel* (Philadelphia: Westminster Press, 1956), p. 171.

Whom have I in heaven but thee?
And there is nothing upon earth that I
   desire besides thee.
My flesh and my heart may fail,
   but God is the strength of my heart and
   my portion forever.
For lo, those who are far from thee shall perish;
   thou dost put an end to those who are false to thee.
But for me it is good to be near God;
   I have made the Lord my refuge
   that I may tell of all thy words. (Ps. 73:25-28)

In such a context, the inspired writer affirms,

"Thou dost guide me with thy counsel, and afterward thou wilt receive me to glory" (Ps. 73:24).[17]

The Psalmist, within this context, could not be speaking of some material boon ("glory" or "honor") to be granted in this life. He already experiences fellowship with God and its consequent blessing. The Psalmist clearly is speaking of receiving glory and honor after death ("afterward," that is, after God has guided with His counsel throughout this life).

These passages from the Psalmists give us a glimpse of the hope of Israel of some blessed existence beyond the grave. This is based upon their belief that the living God who has called a people into covenant fellowship will not even allow death and the grave to break that fellowship. The living God who created man and decreed that because

---

17. The passage in Ps. 17:15 may also speak to a consciousness in the after life. "As for me, I shall behold Thy face in righteousness;/I shall be satisfied, when I awake, with beholding Thy form." This awakening is presented in opposition to the status of the wicked "whose portion is in this life" (v. 14). See J. Barton Payne, *The Theology of the Older Testament* (Grand Rapids: Zondervan, 1962), p. 450.

of man's sin he would die, is still sovereign over all things. He can overcome death and the grave and He will for those who serve Him.

As certain as this hope was, it still was not focused upon the resurrection of the body. Personal resurrection may have been entertained as a vague hope as early as the days of Abraham (cf. Gen. 22:5), but the resurrection of man is first seriously discussed in the book of Job, which cannot be dated any earlier than the days of Solomon Job, in his inspired pondering, says:

> For there is hope of a tree,
>   if it be cut down, that it will sprout again.
>
> . . . .
>
> If a man die, shall he live again? (Job 14:7, 14)

Job knew that man would not return from death to this present life. He says:

> "He that goeth down to the grave shall come up no more. He shall return no more to his house, Neither shall his place know him anymore." (Job 7:9, 10; also cf. 10:21; 16:22)

Yet, he also believes that "in his flesh" he will see God. Listen to his articulated faith in some kind of resurrection:

> For I know that my Redeemer (Vindicator) lives,
>   and at last he will stand upon the earth;
>   And after my skin, even this body is destroyed,
>   Yet in my flesh shall I see God;
> Whom I, even I, shall see on my side.
>   And my eyes shall behold and not another. (Job 19:25-27)[18]

---

18. There seems to be some textual corruption here, but this is perhaps the best way to translate this passage. Some, of course, see this as a later interpolation but there is no reason to hold this view.

Job, apparently, believes that he would be raised bodily sometime after his body is destroyed. This time is likened with the appearance of a living "Redeemer" or "Vindicator" upon the earth at some later period. He (Job) would then behold God, in his flesh and with his eyes.

Though some scholars would not interpret Job 19 as a clear reference to resurrection, all will agree that in Daniel 12 there is undisputed affirmation of a resurrection of both the righteous *and* the unrighteous.

The context speaks of a future tribulation such as had never been experienced in Israel's history. Michael, the great archangel ("the great prince who has charge of your people"), arises to deliver Israel, at least those whose names are "found written in the book." Resurrection is promised and the righteous who are raised appear as the sun and the stars. Daniel is to "shut up the words" and "seal the book" until "the time of the end." Within this eschatological or futuristic context this affirmation occurs:

> And many of those who sleep in the dust of the earth shall awake, some to everlasting life, and some to shame and everlasting contempt. And those who are wise shall shine like the brightness of the firmament; and those who turn many to righteousness, like the stars forever and ever (Dan. 12:2, 3).

To go beyond what is clearly stated would be unfruitfully conjectural. However, the idea of a general resurrection— of both good and evil—is certainly in view. The resurrection of the righteous issues in "everlasting life": and that of the unrighteous in "everlasting contempt." So, both general resurrection and ensuing rewards are clearly indicated.

Perhaps we could conclude this chapter by showing that the developing idea of the future life and resurrection seen in the Old Testament is consistent with the Hebrew view of man. Man's soul is primarily his vitality, his life, not some separate part of man that has independent existence and an immortal nature. God's spirit (His breath, His power) creates and sustains all living things (Ps. 33:6; 104:29-30), even the human spirit (Zech. 12:1), but never is man's soul or spirit seen as an immortal part of man surviving death. Man dies when his spirit is taken or withdrawn (Ps. 104:29; Eccl. 12:7); his soul is even said to "die" (Num. 23:10; Judg. 16:30) or depart to *Sheol* (Ps. 16:10; 30:3; 94:17). Life is bodily existence in fellowship with God (Deut. 30:15-20); death means the end of life, but not necessarily the cessation of *existence*. The dead *exist* in *Sheol* as "shades." But *Sheol* cannot be the end. The righteous will continue to know fellowship with God, even in spite of death and the grave. This conviction gradually emerged and finally led to the belief that in the future death would be destroyed and bodies ("in the dust") would be raised. But, as George E. Ladd notes, "this belief *is* eschatological. It is resurrection on the last day. . . . Therefore we must pursue our search a step further. What was the belief in resurrection in Jesus' day?"[19]

The questions we now must answer are: What concepts of resurrection developed in the intertestamental period? What is the doctrine of resurrection found in Judaism and therefore current during Jesus' ministry? In answering these questions, we will be able to understand better what the Bible teaches about resurrection.

FOR FURTHER STUDY

J. Barton Payne, *The Theology of the Older Testament*. Grand Rapids: Zondervan Publishing Co., 1962.

---

19. Ladd, p. 49.

H. H. Rowley. *The Faith of Israel*. Philadelphia: Westminster Press, 1956.

Various commentaries on Old Testament passages, such as the New Century Bible, Anchor Bible, International Critical Commentary, etc.

QUESTIONS FOR DISCUSSION

1. Why should we be cautious about reading New Testament truth back into the Old Testament?
2. What is the Hebrew understanding of Death?
3. Define Sheol. What does Sheol have to do with death and resurrection?
4. What is the key to understanding after-life in the later "Writings"?
5. Discuss the revelation given in Daniel 12 in relation to later revelation in the New Testament.

Chapter Four

THE UNDERSTANDING OF RESURRECTION IN JEWISH THOUGHT IN THE INTERTESTAMENTAL PERIOD

*"I know that he will rise again in the resurrection
at the last day" (John 11:24).*

Intertestamental Jewish thought relative to resurrection reflects what is seen in the Old Testament canon. Taking its cues from the Psalms, it too affirms that *Sheol* cannot separate the chosen ones from God. Jewish thought also reiterates and expands on Daniel's assertion that those "lying in the dust shall be raised," some to everlasting life and some to everlasting contempt (Dan. 12:1, 2). Frequently these Old Testament assertions and expectations are couched in eschatological and apocalyptic terms, sometimes with bizarre elaborations.

Sometimes it is assumed that there was little literary development in Judaism during that period between Malachi and the Gospels. These years are often called the "four hundred silent years," but they were not silent at all. Some of the finest products of Jewish religious zeal were written during this time. There are, of course, various reasons that this literature was not included in the Hebrew canon and, therefore, considered ultimately authoritative for Jewish life, but this does not detract from their character as genuinely religious literature.

Some of these works, known as the *Apocrypha*,[1] are recognized as authoritative by the Roman Church, since

---

1. The word comes from the Greek word, *apokryphos*, meaning "hidden" or "concealed." Some of these books were used by early heretical groups in Christianity, and these words were condemned by the orthodox. Hence, the name *Apocrypha,* hidden or secret. The term was later used to signify any book not included in either Old or New Testament canon.

they were incorporated into the Latin Vulgate version which was accepted as the authoritative version at the Council of Trent in the sixteenth century. However, neither the Jews nor the Christians of the first four centuries considered them in this manner. Though not considered canonical, or authoritative, the apocryphal books provide us with significant information about the life and thought of the Jews during an important period of their history—the period just prior to the inauguration of Christianity.

It is difficult to set limits to the number of books in the Old Testament Apocrypha, but there are fourteen books generally accepted as belonging to the Apocrypha, ten separate books,[2] one addition to Esther, and three additions to Daniel.[3]

In addition to the Apocrypha, there is a larger group of Jewish literature known as the *Pseudepigrapha*. This term is a Greek term meaning "a writing under an assumed name" (literally, "false writings"). Most of these literary works have the name of some important Biblical character attached to them as presumed author or are the the wisdom or account of activities of some Old Testament character (e.g., *The Assumption of Moses*).[4] To explain this, Dana suggests that "no longer was there sufficient courage or religious leadership for one to raise his voice as being himself a spokesman for Jehovah. Consequently, they wrote under the names of the celebrated and influential leaders of the past, such as Enoch, Noah, Elijah, Baruch, Ezra, and so forth."[5] These

---

2. *I and II Maccabees, I and II Esdras, Tobit, Judith, Wisdom of Sirach (Ecclesiasticus), Wisdom of Solomon, I Baruch,* and *The Prayer of Manasseh.*

3. *Prayer of Azariah and Songs of the Three Children, Susanna,* and *Bel and the Dragon.*

4. Some of the Apocryphal works are technically *Pseudepigrapha.*

5. H. E. Dana, *The New Testament World* (Nashville: Broadman Press, 1937), p. 46.

writings were not as widely accepted and used as were the Apocrypha, since they often represent and present the thinking of one of the sectarian emphases within Judaism of this period.

The following chart gives a picture of the time slot in which these works were probably written.

Apocalyptic Literature		Other Writings	
B.C.		B.C.	
		250ff.	Greek translations of O.T. (LXX)
		190-170	Tobit
		185	Sirach = Ecclesiasticus
170	I Enoch 1-36 (Visions and Journeys)		
166	I Enoch 83-90 (History of Israel)	168-163	Prayer of Azariah
		150	Song of the Three Young Men
		150	Judith
		150-100	I Baruch (Greek) Letter of Jeremiah (= Bar. 6)
		150-50	I Esdras (Greek)
140	Sibylline Oracles, Proem and Book III (Greek)		
		132	Translation of Sirach (Greek)
		114	Additions to Esther
110	I Enoch 72-82 (Astronomical Secrets)	104-100	I Maccabees
109-106	Testaments of the XII Patriarchs		
105	Book of Jubilees		
104-95	I Enoch 91-108 (Apocl. of Weeks)	100	Epistle of Aristeas

Apocalyptic Literature		Other Writings	
B.C.		B.C.	
100 (?)	Joseph and Asenath	100	Jason of Cyrene (abr. in II Macc.)
		100-50	Prayer of Manasseh
		100	Susanna
		100 (?)	Zadokite Fragments
		100 (?)	Dead Sea Manual of Discipline
94-64	(or later) I Enoch 37-71 (Parables)	100	Bel and the Dragon
		65	II Maccabees
		63-40	Psalms of Solomon
		50	III Maccabees
31	Sibylline Oracles, 3:1-62	50	Wisdom of Solomon
7 B.C.	A.D. 29 Assumption of Moses		
1-50	Martyrdom of Isaiah	A.D. 1-50	IV Maccabees
1-50	Secrets of Enoch (II Enoch)	30-50	Writings of Philo
70ff.	II Baruch ("Syriac Baruch")		
80	Sibylline Oracles, Book IV	75-110	Writings of Josephus
		80	Revision of Shemoneh Esreh
90	II Esdras (= IV Ezra) with additions (ch. 1-2, ca. A.D. 150; ch. 15-16, ca. A.D. 250)		
90-100	Apocalypse of Abraham	100 (?)	Books of Adam and Eve
After 100	Sibylline Oracles, Book V	After 100	III Baruch (Greek)
		210	The Mishnah

Using F. C. Grant's basic distinction—apocalyptic and non-apocalyptic—we shall survey Apocryphal and Pseudepigraphal literature for testimony to Jewish belief in (or lack of belief in) the resurrection. Following that, we shall investigate what the Qumran literature (Dead Sea Scrolls) reflects about resurrection.

The Resurrection as Seen in
Non-Apocalyptic Literature of Judaism

Belief in resurrection was by no means commonly accepted in this period between the testaments. In the work known as *Ecclesiasticus,* or *The Wisdom of Ben Sirach,* we do not see any doctrine of resurrection. What is reflected is that which is commonly emphasized in the Wisdom literature of the Old Testament, rewards and punishment occur in this life only. In 11:14, 26-28, Ben Sirach writes:

> Good and evil, life and death,
>   Poverty and wealth come from Jahveh.
> . . . .
> For it is easy in Jahveh's sight
>   At the end to requite a man according to his deeds.
> An evil time causeth forgetfulness of delights,
>   And the last end of a man will tell of him.
> Pronounce no man happy before his death;
>   For by his latter end a man shall be known.[6]

---

6. Translation in R. H. Charles, *Apocrypha and Pseudepigrapha,* Vol. I (London: Oxford University Press, 1913), pp. 354, 356. Charles comments on verse 28: "It is noticeable that the idea of a future life is entirely absent from this passage," p. 356.

This is an early and clear witness to a particular theology (or lack of it) that developed during this period. This will be manifested later by the Sadducees of the New Testament (see Acts 23:8). This reticence about expressing belief in a future life hardens into disbelief and this type of thinking will persist among Jews throughout the intertestamental period and on into the Christian era.

The other current of thinking relative to resurrection which we see in this period is expressed generously in II Maccabees.[7] In chapter VII where the martyrdom of seven brothers and their mother is recorded, the second brother, undergoing torture, "at the last gasp," said: "Thou cursed miscreant! Thou dost despatch us from this life, but the King of the world shall raise us up, who have died for his laws, and revive us to life everlasting" (verse 9).[8] When the third son was asked to put out his tongue, he does so, holding out his hands as well. He says: "These I had from heaven; for His name's sake I count them naught; from Him I hope to get them back again" (VII, 11). The fourth brother, prior to his death, says: "Tis meet for those who perish at men's hands to cherish hope divine that they shall be raised up by God again, but thou—thou shalt have no resurrection to life" (VII, 14). The mother who watched the torture and death of her sons, encouraging them in their martyrdom, says: "Twas not I who gave you the breath of life or fashioned

---

7. II Maccabees is not a continuation of I Maccabees, but a second work upon the Maccabean struggle against the Seleucids. It covers much of the same material in the Maccabees, but is a much later work and perhaps not as historically trustworthy. It is probably written by one who belonged to the Pharisaic party.

8. All quotations from Charles, p. 141ff.

the elements of each! Twas the Creator of the world who fashioned men and deviseth the generating of all things, and he it is who in mercy will restore to you the breath of life even as you now count yourselves naught for his laws' sake" (VII, 22-23). As her last son is martyred, she says: "Fear not this butcher, but show thyself worthy of thy brothers, and accept thy death, that by God's mercy I may receive thee again together with thy brothers" (VII, 29). This brother then confesses that his martyred brothers, after enduring brief pain, have "now drunk of everflowing life" (VII, 36).

In recording some of the activities of Judas Maccabeus the author notes that in expiation of the sin of idolatry, Judas collected a sum of money from the guilty and sent it to Jerusalem as a sin-offering. He adds, "In this he acted quite rightly and properly, bearing in mind the resurrection—for if he had not expected the fallen to rise again, it would have been superfluous and silly to pray for the dead—and having regard to the splendour of the gracious reward which is reserved for those who have fallen asleep in godliness— a holy and pious consideration! Hence he made propitiation for the dead, that they might be released from their sin" (XII, 43-45).

This resurrection belief not only assumes glorious life after death and reunion with loved ones (as above), it seems to include the restoration of the body[9] as well. In telling the story of Nicanor, the Syrian governor of Judea, the author of II Maccabees relates that the governor attempted to capture Razis, a patriotic and highly esteemed Jew. Rather than allowing himself to be captured and tortured, Razis fell on his sword, and, sorely wounded, ran through the crowds

---

9. See II Maccabees, VII, 11 as quoted above.

to a steep rock. Here, as his blood flowed from him, "he tore out his bowels, taking both in his hands to them, and flung them at the crowd. So he died, calling on Him who is lord of life and spent to restore them to him again" (XIV, 46).

The Wisdom of Solomon, another non-apocalyptic work, has long "enjoyed the reputation of being the most attractive and interesting book in the Apocrypha."[10] It is variously dated from 145 to 50 B.C., with the weight of scholarship suggesting a date closer to 50 B.C. The author may well have been an Alexandrian Jew, since the work uses the Septuagint (Greek) version of the Old Testament exclusively and reflects other vocabulary usage that was common to Alexandrian Judaism (as in Philo). It is of that genre known as Wisdom literature and resembles (and perhaps is a polemic against) the book of Ecclesiastes in the Old Testament.[11]

In this book there is a clear emphasis upon the after life and resurrection. The author says:

Because God created man for incorruption,
And made him an image of his own proper being;
But by the envy of the devil death entered into the world,
And they that belong to his realm experience it.
But the souls of the righteous are in the hand of God,
And no torment shall touch them.
In the eyes of fools they seemed to die;
And their departure was accounted *to be their* hurt,
And their going from us *to be their* ruin:
But they are in peace.
For though in the sight of men they be punished.
Their hope is full of immortality;
. . . .

10. Charles, Vol. I, p. 518.
11. See Charles, Vol. I, p. 525.

And in the time of their visitation[12] they shall shine forth,
And like sparks among stubble they shall run to and fro.
They shall judge nations, and have dominion over peoples;
And the Lord shall reign over them for evermore.
They that trust in him shall understand truth,
And the faithful shall abide with him in love; (2:22—3:4, 7-9)

Here, and elsewhere, there is a clear affirmation of an after-life and generous intimations of resurrection, at least of continued activity of the person in and after the time of visitation (deliverance). As some have suggested, there may be a reflection of the influence of Platonic immortality (a view which was commonly held in later Alexandrian Judaism), but it is not a thoroughgoing Platonism.[13]

The book known as *The Fourth Book of Maccabees* is a treatise on the supremacy of wisdom.[14] It appears to have been written during the first Christian century, sometime prior to the destruction of the Temple in A.D. 70.[15] In emphasizing the supremacy of reason to steel his Jewish brethren for the coming persecution, the author combines stoic virtues and the historical heroism of the Maccabean martyrs.

The doctrine of immortality is strongly enunciated within this work. Martyrs are seen as hastening to their death "as if running the road to immortality" (14:5). Pious souls are

---

12. The term "visitation" seems to connote the end-time consummation which includes resurrecton and judgment.

13. See Metzger, *An Introduction to the Apocrypha* (New York: Oxford University Press, 1957), p. 74.

14. It is cited by Eusebius and Jerome under this title and appears among the works of Josephus (some believing he wrote it) under this title as well.

15. R. H. Charles suggests a date between B.C. 63 and A.D. 38. He also supposes that it was written in response to the deification of the Roman emperor and therefore would date it in the reign of Caligula. Vol. II, p. 653, 654.

spoken of as achieving "the prize of victory in incorruption in everlasting life" (17:12); standing "beside the throne of God" and living in "the blessed age" (17:18). The closing statement may well epitomize the author's belief in immortality: "But the sons of Abraham, with their victorious mother, are gathered together unto the place of their ancestors, having received pure and immortal souls from God, to whom be glory for ever and ever. Amen" (18:24). On the other hand, eternal torment is the lot of the wicked (9:9; 10:11, 15, 21; 12:12).

Again, we see the Platonic influence of the immortality of the soul, but the doctrine of immortality seen here is not an inherent quality of soul or spirit but the result of God's intervention (7:19; 17:17-21; 18:23).

The Resurrection and Afterlife Seen in the Apocalyptic Literature of Judaism

In the two centuries preceding Christ's birth, eschatological ideas were prominent in Jewish preoccupations and speculations. Undoubtedly, the Roman domination heightened and sharpened these notions since the Jews lived in a constant state of anxiety. One of the results is seen in the apocalyptic literature of this period. Some of this literature is known to us only in fragments, sometimes in other languages than Aramaic, and frequently with Christian additions or, at least, edition.

These Apocalypses vary greatly in their descriptions of the "last things," but they are commonly bound together in their fundamental ideas. These seers "turned their eyes to the future and to a realization of the divine Promises which would be dependent on a complete transformation of the world and of the conditions of human life. This world was evil, therefore it must vanish, this life was wretched, hence it must be replaced by a better."[16]

In this literature the destruction of Israel's enemies by God (or by the Messiah in some works) passes over into the thought of a Last Judgment for all, including Israel, and this, along with its necessary association of ideas of Resurrection, becomes a dominating concept in Jewish eschatology.

The Book of Enoch (I Enoch) is perhaps the most important pseudepigraphical work of the first two centuries before Christ. It is a composite work, written by a number of anonymous authors over a period of a century. In the first section (1-36) known as "Visions and Journeys" the righteous dead are raised and, with the righteous who are living dwell in the seventh mountain, "whose summit . . . is His throne, where the Holy Great One, the Lord of Glory, the Eternal King will sit, when He shall come down to visit the earth with goodness" (25:3). The fragrant tree on this mountain is to "be given the righteous and holy. Its fruit shall be for food to the elect" (25:4, 5).

In the "Similitudes or Parables" of I Enoch (37-71), the lot of sinners is discussed:

> And into heaven they shall not ascend,
> And on the earth they shall not come:
> Such shall be the lot of the sinners (45:2).

The coming of "the Elect One to sit on the throne of glory" is promised (45:3ff.) along with the creation of a new heaven

---

16. Charles Guignebert, *The Jewish World in the Time of Jesus* (New Hyde Park, New York: University Books, 1959), p. 134.

and new earth (45:4, 5). In this connection the triumph of the righteous and the resurrection of the righteous dead are stated unequivocally:

> And in those days shall the earth also give back that which has been entrusted to it,
> And Sheol also shall give back that which it has received,
> And hell shall give back that which it owes,
> For in those days the Elect One shall arise,
> And he shall choose the righteous and holy from among them:
> For the day has drawn nigh that they should be saved (51:1, 2).

Again, the author states:

> And the righteous and elect shall have risen from the earth,
> And ceased to be of downcast countenance.
> And they shall have been clothed with garments of glory, (62:15).

This emphasis upon resurrection is also stated in the *Testament of the Twelve Patriarchs,* which seems to have been written about 109-105 B.C. In the Testament of Benjamin is this promise:

> And then shall ye see Enoch, Noah, and Shem, and Abraham and Isaac, and Jacob, rising on the right hand in gladness.
> Then shall we also rise, each one over our tribe, worshipping the King of Heaven. Then shall we all be changed, some into glory, and some into shame . . . (10:6, 7.)[17]

In the *Psalms of Solomon,* which may be dated sometime between B.C. 70-40, a similar picture of resurrection is

---

17. "This resurrection is usually interpreted as meaning a restoration of the body which has been laid in the grave, but there may be also a suggestion that the righteous will undergo a kind of spiritual transformation." Guignebert, p. 137.

portrayed, but within the context of a personal Messiah who will drive the heathen and sinners from Israel, gather the righteous and rule over them in holiness. This is a day of mercy,

> But they that fear the Lord shall rise to life eternal,
>> And then life (shall be) in the light of the Lord, and
>> shall come to an end no more (3:16).
>
> For the Lord spareth His pious ones,
>> And blotteth out their errors by His chastening.
> For the life of the righteous shall be for ever (13:9).

But, at the same time this day of mercy is a day of recompense for the wicked who receive Hades, the eternal abode for sinners (16:2), and experience darkness and destruction forever (3:13).

The *Apocalypse of Baruch*, or II Baruch as it is sometimes known, and *II Esdras* (often referred to as IV Ezra) appear to be affected by the destruction of Jerusalem and the Temple by the Romans. This cataclysmic event with all the suffering that followed produced a mood of despair, bewilderment and pessimism. Comfort could be found only in utopian dreams of a future Messianic Age preceded by Judgment. In chapters 49-51 of II Baruch, the nature of the resurrection body and the final destiny of all men is out. Baruch asks:

> In what shape will those live who live in the day?
> . . . .
> Will they then resume this form of the present? (49:2).

The answer is given poetically:

> For the earth shall then assuredly restore them,
> [which it now receives in order to preserve them].

It shall make no change in their form
But as it has received, so shall it restore them
And as I delivered them unto it, so also shall it raise them,
(50:1, 2).

The "Mighty One" adds: "For then it will be necessary to show the living that the dead have come to life again, and that those who had departed have returned (again)" (50:3). The wicked will then "see those, over whom they are now exalted, (but) who shall then be exalted and glorified more than they, they shall respectively be transformed, the latter into the splendour of angels, and the former shall yet more waste away in wonder at the visions and in the beholding of the forms. For they shall first behold and afterwards depart to be tormented" (51:5, 6).

In II Esdras (IV Ezra), where the revelation of God's Son, the Messiah,[18] and His kingdom is given, the resurrection is clearly portrayed as a general resurrection in which both righteous and wicked are raised:

And
 the earth shall restore those that sleep in her,
 and the dust those that are at rest therein,

. . . .

And then shall the pit of torment appear,
 and over against it the plate of refreshment;
The furnace of Gehenna shall be made manifest,
 and over against it the Paradise of delight, (7:32, 36).

F. C. Grant's statement on the resurrection as reflected in the apocalyptic literature of Judaism is an excellent summary:

---

18. This may reflect some Christian influence for this is not the typical Judaistic theology of Messianism. See later chapter.

The resurrection was either to precede, accompany, or follow the messianic era. It was to be a resurrection either of the martyrs, or of the righteous, or of all men. Various forms of the expectation are reflected in the literature: (a) If only the martyrs are to rise from the dead, it is because God in a sense owes it to them—they have laid down their lives in the battle, and must they not be present at the triumph? Men cannot claim this as their right; but God is just, and he will see that his servants are justly rewarded. (b) If all the righteous are to rise, it is for the same reason—the righteous have served God faithfully and cannot be allowed to perish, or to remain permanently in the dim and chilly halls of Sheol, (Hades). (c) If good and bad alike are to be raised, it is so that the former may be rewarded and the latter punished. God will not allow the wicked to escape their just penalties by an easy lapse into unconsciousness or extinction. Thus the religious motivation of the resurrection-hope, rather than any purely speculative interest, is clear wherever it appears in the older apocalyptic literature.

The departed are to rise up at the command of God, either out of their graves or out of the promptuaria or storerooms of souls (II Esdras 4:41). Considerable variety is found in the conception of the resurrection body. (a) Some believed that it would be simply a reanimation of the buried corpse, the bones acquiring a covering of flesh once more (as in Ezek. 37), and severed parts of the body being restored each to its proper place. (b) Others held, apparently, that the soul itself would need to be reanimated. Underlying this conception is the old, really primitive idea of the souls as a faint, ethereal copy of the body, both lifeless and powerless, not at all the Platonic philosophic conception of the soul as the center of power, vitality, and even intelligence. (c) Still others thought of the resurrection body as entirely new, comparable to fresh garments, prepared by God and given by him to deserving souls. (It is apparently with the third of these views that Paul's conception has the closest affinity—see I Cor. 15, II Cor. 5:1-10.) Quite obviously, the variety in these views of the resurrection reflects a variety in anthropological conceptions. The date of the resurrection and the precise point at which it was to be included in the eschatological drama was also subject to various interpretations or speculations.[19]

The Resurrection and Afterlife in
The Qumran Literature

The Qumran literature,[20] the majority of which was discovered in the mid-twentieth century in caves near the Dead Sea in Palestine, has been a great boon in helping us see what certain Essenes believed in that period preceding and following Christ's birth.[21] In addition to Biblical (Old Testament) manuscripts, this wonderful find included commentaries on the Biblical material, and various other works which apparently were manuals of discipline for the community, as well as works which expressed the faith and practice of the community.

Within these texts, eschatology (teachings relative to the end times) plays an important role. God's visitation in judgment of the wicked and vindication of the righteous is quite

---

19. Grant, pp. 72, 73.

20. The term Qumran comes from that ascetic (Essenic) community that lived near the Dead Sea and produced this literature.

21. This literature has been variously dated between 230 B.C. and 170 A.D. Such dating depends upon both carbon-dating procedures, archaeological discoveries at Qumran, and the characteristics both external and internal of the writings themselves. It is probable that the literature dates from about 130 B.C. to 70 A.D. For a historical overview see Millar Burrows, *The Dead Sea Scrolls*, (1955), J. Danielou, *The Dead Sea Scrolls and Primitive Christianity*, (1958), and F. F. Bruce, *Biblical Exegesis in the Qumran Texts*, (1959).

prominently portrayed in several of the texts (see *The Thanks-giving Psalm*). This will occur in connection with a great final battle (*War Scroll*). There is the suggestion in certain fragments from Caves 1, 4, and 5, that a new Jerusalem will be inaugurated following this time of conflict, with God being worshipped in a new Temple. At that time the "Anointed ones," the Messiahs, would appear.[22]

Did the Qumran sect believe in the resurrection of the dead? Although there is no statement that clearly teaches resurrection, there seems to be an allusion to the resurrrection from the dead in Thanksgiving Psalm, 6:29-35, which speaks of the last great battle against the powers of evil:

> Then shall God's sword speedily come at the appointed time
>   of judgment,
> and all the children of truth shall awaken
>
> . . . .
>
> For to God the Most High belongs [the power and strength,
> . . . .],
> and they who lie in the dust will raise a flagstaff
> and the worms of the dead will lift up an ensign[23] (1QH, 6:34).

Though this could be interpreted in a figurative sense, the context suggests (even as Daniel had indicated) that those "lying in the dust" are the dead now raised.

Another passage speaks of

> bodies gnawed by worms may be raised from the dust to the
>   counsel [of Thy truth],

----

22. The Qumran sectaries apparently believed in both a Messiah of Aaron and a Messiah of Israel (or Judah).

23. Quoted by Helmut Ringgren, *The Faith of Qumran: Theology of The Dead Sea Scrolls* (Philadelphia: Fortress Press, 1963), pp. 159-160.

and that the perverse spirit (may be lifted) to the understanding [which comes from Thee];
that he may stand before Thee with the everlasting host and
with [Thy] spirits [of holiness] to be renewed with all
the living and to rejoice together with them that know
(1QM, 11:12ff.).[24]

The *Manual of Discipline* speaks of "the Renewal," of
God choosing them "for an everlasting Covenant and all
the glory of Adam shall be theirs" (1QS, 4).[25] Again it says:

And as for the visitation of all who walk in this spirit, it shall
be healing, great peace in a long life, and fruitfulness, together
with every everlasting blessing and eternal joy in life without
end, a crown of glory and a garment of majesty in unending
light (1QS, 4:7f.).[26]

The literature of Judaism shows ample belief in a general
resurrection. This will come at the end of the age, accompanied, many believed, with some form of Messianic Judgment and Glory. This is reflected in the Judaism of Jesus'
day. Martha says to Jesus about her brother Lazarus, "I
know that he will rise again in the resurrection at the last
day" (John 11:24). Jesus does not deny this, but speaks
a more sure word to Martha: "I am the resurrection and
life!" (John 11:25). We must come to the Gospel records
to find this more "sure word" spoken by Him who has become
our final revelation of truth (Heb. 1:1-3).

---

24. Quoted by Colin Brown, "Resurrection" in Colin Brown, ed. *The New
International Dictionary of New Testament Theology*, vol. 3, p. 273 (Grand
Rapids: Zondervan, 1978).

25. *Ibid.*

26. *Ibid.*

FOR FURTHER STUDY

Metzger, Bruce. *An Introduction to the Apocrypha.* New York: Oxford University Press, 1957.

Pfeiffer, Robert H., *History of New Testament Times with an Introduction to the Apocrypha.* New York: Harpers Brother, 1949.

Ringgren, Helmut, *The Faith of Qumran.* Philadelphia: Fortress Press, 1963.

Rost, Leonard, *Judaism Outside the Hebrew Canon: An Introduction to the Documents.* Nashville: Abingdon Press, 1971.

Shürer, Emil, *The Literature of the Jewish People in the Time of Jesus.* New York: Schocker Books, 1972.

QUESTIONS FOR DISCUSSION

1. Define and discuss the term "Apocrypha."
2. Discuss the differences of thought concerning the afterlife as they developed during the intertestamental period.
3. Relate the Roman domination of the Jews to their changing views concerning resurrection of the dead.
4. Discuss the belief of the Qumran sect concerning resurrection of the dead. How does this compare to those of Judaism in Jesus' day?

Chapter Five

JESUS AS MESSIAH:
HIS TEACHINGS ABOUT RESURRECTION

"I am the Resurrection and life; he that believeth in me, though he were dead, yet shall he live" (John 11:25).

The New Testament era begins, as the Gospels testify, with the ministry of John the Immerser. A kinsman of Jesus (Luke 1:36ff.), whose birth is recorded by Luke as semi-miraculous (Luke 1:5-25), John suddenly appears in the wilderness of Judea, passionately preaching the coming kingdom. This flaming prophet came as did the ancient prophets with "the word of God" as his burden. He called God's people to repentance (as did the ancient prophets) and immersed them in the Jordan river "to obtain the forgiveness of sin" (Luke 3:3).[1]

The message, then, was simple and yet forthright: "Repent, the Kingdom of Heaven is near" (Matt. 3:2). He saw himself as fulfilling that prophetic note of Isaiah (Isaiah 40:3) that spoke of

> A voice of one calling in the desert,
> Prepare the way for the Lord,
>   make straight paths for him.
> Every valley shall be filled in,
>   and every mountain and hill leveled off.
> The crooked roads shall become straight,
>   and the rough ways smooth.
> And all mankind shall see God's salvation (Luke 3:4-6).

Yet, that eschatological message had ethical consequences; as crowds came to be immersed by John, he would cry out:

---

1. Acts 19 gives an inspired interpretation of the significance of this preparatory baptism of John.

"Oh generation of vipers, who has warned you to flee from the coming wrath? Bring forth fruit in harmony with your repentance" (Luke 3:7, 8). And there is in that message a playing down of Jewish nationalism: "Don't begin saying, 'We have Abraham as our father,' for I say that God is able to raise up children to Abraham from these very stones" (Luke 3:8). There is also a note of impending judgment as John speaks of "axes laid to the roots of trees" not bearing good fruit (Luke 3:9) and of the "winnowing fork" in the hands of the Coming One (Matt. 3:12).

The gospel record indicates that John was quite aware that he was not the Messiah; for as men were debating whether this Judean prophet could possibly be the Messiah, he quickly admitted that he was not. He was just a "voice," one preparing the way; there was one coming after him who was mightier than he "whose sandals he was not worthy to unfasten" (Luke 3:16). This Coming One would demonstrate his superiority (for he was "before me" both in existence and preeminence, John affirmed—John 1:30) by baptizing "with the Holy Spirit and with fire" (Luke 3:16).[2]

By the time that the Gospel accounts were written (probably in the seventh and eighth decades of the first century), it was understood that John's appearance indeed fulfills the last prophetic utterance in the Old Testament. In Malachi 4:5 we have this statement: "Behold, I will send you Elijah the prophet before the coming of the great and dreadful day of the Lord."

In Luke's Gospel, Zecharias is told by the angel of the Lord that this child to be born to Elizabeth (John) would be

---

2. He will begin the Messianic Age by pouring out His Spirit on all flesh (John 2:24-26; Acts 2:18ff.) and conclude that age—that day of God's visitation in judgment, a baptism of fire.

"filled with the Holy Spirit," that he would turn many of the children of Israel to the Lord, and that he would go before the Lord "in the spirit and power of Elijah" (Luke 1:15-17). Later, in Jesus' ministry, he makes clear that John fulfills this prophecy concerning Elijah. Coming down from the Mount of Transfiguration (probably Matt. Hermon), the three disciples who had witnessed Jesus in conversation with Moses and Elijah, asked, "Why do our scribes say that Elijah must come before the Messiah appears?" Jesus responds, "Elijah must come first and set everything in order, but Elijah has already come but he was not recognized and they have worked their will on him. And the Son of Man is destined to undergo a similar fate" (Matt. 17:10-12). Then, Matthew records, "The disciples understood that he was speaking of John the Baptist" (Matt. 17:13), thus identifying the "coming Elijah" with John.

Jesus comes from Nazareth to the Jordan, submitting himself to the baptism of John. There is something about his presence that causes John to hesitate. "I have need to be baptized by you," he says. Jesus responds: "You must baptize me for this is what God requires" (Matt. 3:14, 15). As Jesus is baptized, John is given assurance that this one is indeed the Coming One. John testifies: "I knew him not, but he that sent me to immerse in water, said unto me, 'Upon whom you see the Spirit descending and remaining on him, that same one is the One who shall immerse with the Holy Spirit'" (John 1:33).

But Jesus does not meet the current Messianic expectations. He gathers no armies; only a few disciples. He preaches no revolution; in fact, his message is pacifistic, speaking of "turning the other cheek," giving up our coat as well as our cloak, going "the second mile" (Matt. 6:39-41). No wonder, at a later time, that John, languishing in Herod's prison, could be perplexed. Sending two of his disciples, John asks through them, "Are you the Coming One, or must we keep on looking for another?" (Luke 7:19). Jesus sends them back saying: "Go tell John what you have seen and heard: the blind see, the lame walk, lepers are cleansed, the deaf hear, the dead are raised, poor men have good news preached to them" (Luke 7:22). Thus, Jesus was showing that his ministry was a ministry of compassion, a ministry which went to the heart of human need. He was also calling to John's mind that great Messianic passage in Isa. 61:

> The Spirit of the Sovereign Lord is on me
> because the Lord has annointed me
> to preach good tidings to the poor.
> He has sent me to bind up the brokenhearted,
> to proclaim freedom for the captives
> and release for the prisoners,
> to proclaim the year of the Lord's favor (Isa. 61:1, 2a).

Therefore, as the Christian era opens there is great Messianic expectation. Could John be that Messiah? Is Jesus, the prophet of Galilee, the Messiah?

Jesus, Confessed as Messiah

Jesus had not been involved in his public ministry of compassion long before he had called twelve men to be special disciples. He called them apostles, sending them out (the meaning of the term) to proclaim, even as he and John before him, that the "Kingdom of God is drawing near" (Matt. 10:1ff.). He began an intensive training program with them, in which direct teaching, modeling and on-the-job training

64

were involved. These men were being instructed by the Master Teacher.

But, examination time must eventually come and near Caesarea-Philippi, on one of his training trips with the twelve, Jesus poses that great question: "Whom do you believe that I, the Son of Man, am?" Peter's response is more than an impetuous reaction; it is a growing conviction now being publicly expressed. "Thou art the Christ, the Messiah, the Son of the Living God" (Matt. 16:16).

In response to this confession, Jesus blesses Peter, and promises that upon the rock-like truth of Himself confessed as Messiah he would build His new community. But, at the same time, he warned the twelve not to tell anyone that He was the Messiah. Presumably, this warning would help to avoid a wild Messianic enthusiasm developing among His followers, thus deterring him from his true Messianic mission. Later, following the Transfiguration of Christ and his conversation with Moses and Elijah, the inner three are warned: "Do not tell anyone what you have seen until after the Son of Man has been raised from the dead," (Matt. 17:9).

It is in connection with this confession of Messiahship that Jesus begins to teach about his impending death and subsequent resurrection. The first gospel states it in this manner:

> It was just after that that Jesus for the first time clearly taught His disciples that he had to go to Jerusalem and submit to many forms of suffering at the hands of the elders, high priests, and scribes; and be put to death and be raised again the third day (Matt. 16:21, Williams).

The idea of death could not be countenanced by Peter. Apparently, his confession of Messiah did not envisage the possibility of death. He "took him aside" and began to correct him. "Mercy on you, Lord! this shall never happen to you!"

65

(Matt. 16:22). But, Jesus interrupted Peter saying "Get behind me, Satan, for you look at things, not as God does, but as man does" (Matt. 16:23). Then, addressing all the disciples, Jesus puts his death into a larger perspective and indicates the kind of death he would undergo.

> If any man will come after me, let him leave self behind, take up his cross and follow me. For the man who tries to save his life shall lose it, but the man who loses his life for my sake will secure it; for what advantage does a man have if he gain the whole world and lose his life. What shall a man give in exchange for his life? (Matt. 16:24-26).

Jesus will return to this theme of death again and again. Not because of a morbid death wish, but undoubtedly to prepare these special envoys of his reality. As he comes down from the Mount of Transfiguration he speaks of his death and resurrection. The vision is not to be shared until he has been raised from the dead (Matt. 17:9). The Son of Man will suffer even as John, the Elijah to come, suffered (Matt. 17:12). Back in Galilee, Jesus again warns them: "The Son of Man is going to be delivered into the hands of men; and they will kill Him, and He will be raised again on the third day" (Matt. 17:22, 23). On the eve of entrance into Jerusalem he takes the twelve aside and says: "Listen! We are going up to Jerusalem and the Son of Man shall be betrayed and handed over to the chief priests and the scribes and they will sentence him to death, hand him over to pagans to mock, scourge and crucify, but on the third day he shall rise again" (Matt. 20:18, 19).

Later, John recalls that, while they were in Jerusalem, certain Greeks came seeking an audience with Jesus. This universalistic concern causes Jesus to speak of his true mission. "A kernel of wheat must die to bring forth fruit"

(John 12:24). "This is my hour, in spite of the distress of my heart. I cannot ask the Father to save me from this hour; for it is the hour of judgment upon the prince of this world and it is the hour in which many will be drawn to me in faith" (John 12:27, 31, 32). But, the hour must be endured; it involves a cross, death. "And I, if I be lifted up from the earth, will draw all men unto me" (John 12:32). The beloved disciple interprets: "This he said, indicating the manner of his coming death" (John 12:33).

Death and resurrection are always combined in those passages where Jesus speaks of the accomplishment of his mission in Jerusalem. These passages, emphasizing death and resurrection, occur after Jesus is confessed as Messiah. Frequently, the personal designation that Jesus uses in reference to such suffering, death and resurrection is that eschatological term, the "Son of Man." How can his statements be reconciled with that eschatological passage in Daniel 7?

> I kept looking in the night visions,
> And behold, with the clouds of heaven
> One like a Son of Man was coming,
> And He came up to the ancient of Days
> And was presented before Him.
> And to Him was given dominion,
> Glory and a kingdom,
> That all the peoples, nations, and men of every language
> Might serve Him.
> His dominion is an everlasting dominion
> Which will not pass away;
> And His kingdom is one
> Which will not be destroyed (Daniel 7:13, 14).

Apparently, Jesus is attempting to show his disciples that the redemptive ministry of the Messiah is twofold. He comes first to suffer and die and be raised from the dead—"to give his life a ransom for the many" (Mark 10:45). He will come a second time "in the glory of his Father with his angels" (Matt. 16:27). In both comings He is that Son of Man to whom an everlasting Kingdom has been given. Following his resurrection, Jesus will say to the two disciples he met on the way to Emmaus, "Ought not Messiah to have suffered these things and then enter into his glory?" (Luke 24:26). During this post-resurrection period He will continue to instruct the Twelve "that they might know the meaning of the Scriptures" (Luke 24:45). Opening their understanding, he shows how in the Torah, the prophets and the writings, are statements and predictions fulfilled in him. Scripture focuses upon his death and resurrection. "Thus it is written, Messiah must suffer and arise again from the dead on the third day" (Luke 24:46).

Death and resurrection are essential to Messiahship. This is clearly taught in the New Testament by Jesus Himself. Jesus also sets out the resurrection as a sign of his authority, a token of his Messiahship. Jews were always seeking signs (see Matt. 12:38, 39; I Cor. 1:22), but Jesus was unwilling to supply such signs or tokens of his authority. In fact, rather than giving a sign, he points to two historical events that demonstrate his Messiahship. The one event from the past prefigures the event of the future. "As Jonah was three days and three nights in the stomach of the great fish, so shall the Son of Man be three days and three nights in the heart of the earth" (Matt. 12:40).

The setting is somewhat different in John's Gospel. Jesus is in Jerusalem and he has driven the commercializers and their wares out of the Temple. The authority of the priests is thus brought into question. "What sign of authority do you show us for acting in this way?" Jesus replies: "Destroy this temple and in three days I will raise it up" (John 2:18, 19). John adds that personal word: "After his resurrection, his disciples remembered that he had said this to them, and they believed the Scripture, and the word which Jesus had spoken" (John 2:22).

Jesus and Current Messianic Expectation

As we have noted in the previous chapter, a general resurrection from the dead was expected within Judaism. Martha expresses this hope about her dead brother Lazarus as Jesus comes into Bethany: "I know he shall rise again in the resurrection at the last day" (John 11:24). The Jews, during the intertestamental period, also believed that a Messiah should appear. In fact, the literature of Judaism is rich with Messianism. Taking cues from the Old Testament this literature, particularly the apocalyptic literature, sees a Messiah coming who would be a king on the order of David. In such passages as Isaiah nine and eleven, such a king is predicted. Isaiah nine depicts one coming and reigning in a kingdom already established by God.

> For to us a child is born,
>   to us a Son is given,
>   and the government will be on his shoulders,
> And he will be called
>   Wonderful, Counselor, Mighty God, Everlasting Father,
>   Prince of Peace.
> Of the increase of his government and peace
>   there will be no end.
> He will reign on David's throne
>   and over his kingdom,
> establishing and upholding it

with justice and righteousness
from that time on and forever.
The zeal of the Lord Almighty
will accomplish this (Isa. 9:6, 7).

In Isaiah eleven a similar picture is presented. A new branch or shoot will come from "the root of Jesse" (David's father). God's Spirit will be upon him, giving wisdom, counsel, knowledge, reverence and power, so that his judgments may be righteous (verses 2, 3). He reigns as the Davidic King in God's Kingdom. "He will strike the earth with the rod of his mouth; with the breath of his lips will he slay the wicked" (verse 4). Peace will be the result over all the earth; violence and hostility will be banished. "For the earth will be full of the knowledge of the Lord as the waters cover the sea" (11:9). In that Day, under this Davidic King's "banner," nations will rally to him, Israel will be "reclaimed" from all the areas into which she had been dispersed (11:11), and this kingdom of peace will be triumphant.

This expectation of a mighty conquering Davidic King came over into pre-Christian Judaism. Sometime after the Roman legions under Pompey invaded Palestine, captured Jerusalem, defiled the altar and carried away captives, some unknown author penned the "Psalms of Solomon." In these Psalms, a prayer is addressed to God asking that He send to Israel "their king, the Son of David." He will be known as "the Lord's Christ" ("anointed one"), and his mission will be to "destroy the pride of the sinner as a potter's vessel, with a rod of iron he shall break in pieces all their substance. He shall slay the godless nations with the word of his mouth" (Psalm of Solomon, 17).[3]

---

3. See Charles, II, pp. 649-650.

Jesus was the Messiah, but not that kind of Messiah. We can understand, in light of this kind of expectation, why he cautioned his disciples to tell no one he was Messiah (Mark 8:30); why he forbade Peter, James, and John to tell anyone about the Transfiguration event; why he withdrew from that crowd, after the feeding of the five thousand, who desired to make him King (Messianic king?) (John 6:15).

A second, Messianic concept in the Old Testament that was emphasized and embellished by the pre-Christian apocalyptic writers of Judaism was that of "Son of Man" in Daniel 7 (see above). The book of Enoch, particularly, picks up this idea and enlarges it. To Enoch, the Son of Man is a pre-existent, supra-human (perhaps even divine) being who comes to the earth to destroy the wicked, raise the righteous dead, judge and reign forever in God's Kingdom. The Son of Man is an eschatological personage, for His coming will occur at the end of the age.[4]

But Jesus' use of the term, "Son of Man," does not fit into this eschatological expectation. This is his favorite expression. He, apparently, uses it as a personal designation in different ways; but all these distinctions find focal unity in one who has come to earth as man, to be identified with human experience, and to give his life for sinful man. That significant statement in Mark 10 underscores this, "For the Son of Man himself has not come to be served, but to serve and to give his life as a ransom for many" (Mark 10:45).

It is this "Son of Man" identifiable as Jesus of Nazareth, that must suffer and die (Mark 8:31; 9:12; 10:33) and be raised from the dead. Then he would come with the glory of His Father in Judgment and to establish an everlasting

---

4. See chapters 37-71 in Charles, *ibid*, pp. 208-236.

Kingdom, to bring in a New Age (Mark 8:38; 13:26). No wonder his disciples had difficulty in grasping their Master's revelations about his impending death. What he was saying ran counter to the current expectations which they had known from their childhood. They were interested in "chief seats of the Kingdom" (Mark 10:35f.); were hoping that "he would redeem Israel (Luke 24:21); and, even after his resurrection, were asking, "Are you now going to restore the kingdom to Israel?" (Acts 1:8).

Although the "Suffering Servant" passage in Isaiah 53 was interpreted as a significant Messianic text by the early church (Matt. 12:18-21; Acts 8:32f.), it apparently was never viewed in Jewish thought as such. A major authority in Jewish literature says, "In the whole Jewish Messianic literature of the Tannaite period before A.D. 200 this is no trace of the 'suffering Messiah.'"[5] In fact, it is only in the Jewish apocalyptic work known as 4 Ezra, written sometime after the fall of Jerusalem in A.D. 70, that we have any reference to Messiah's death.[6] But even in this work Messiah dies; he does not suffer.[7] His death seems to have no theological significance; he is no longer mentioned, although it could be assumed that he is raised as one of all the righteous to enjoy the Age to Come.

In light of these facts, what we find in the Gospel narratives is accurate as well as "psychologically sound."[8] Instead of offering swords and shields and victorious armies, Jesus offers his "body and blood" (John 6:53). Many of those who

5. Joseph Klausner, *The Messianic Idea in Israel,* p. 405, quoted by Ladd, *I Believe the Resurrection of Jesus,* p. 66.

6. And this may be in reaction to Christian preaching.

7. See Charles, II, pp. 542-624.

8. Ladd, p. 71.

had eaten their fill the day before and would have made him King "drew back and walked with him no longer" (John 6:66). Though the Twelve saw nowhere else to go (John 6:68) they too were undoubtedly perplexed and bewildered; only their deep commitment—"we believe and we are sure that you are the Messiah of God" (John 6:69)—kept them from trooping out of the synagogue as well.

Jesus, the Messiah Teaches About Resurrection

Jesus' Messianic mission was not primarily to teach yet his teachings are in harmony with his action. He makes possible a "new birth," a new life; and He gives directions for those who would live this new life. "He taught as one with authority not as the scribes" (Matt. 7:29), the people who heard him were "astonished at his teaching" (Matt. 7:28).

Much of his teaching centers in those ethical demands that his disciples must meet. Yet, he also teaches about heaven and hell, life and death, and other great theological themes. His teachings about resurrection fit into this pattern.

In addition to those revelations about his own resurrection, Jesus is recorded as committed to and teaching clearly that there *is* a resurrection of all men. In all three of the Synoptic Gospels, Jesus is approached by "some of the Sadducees, who maintain that there is no resurrection" (Luke 20:27; see also Matt. 22:23f.; Mark 12:23f.). They present that hypothetical problem based on the law of Levirate marriage, of the woman who had been wife successively to seven brothers. "Whose wife is she of these seven in the resurrection?" is their triumphant question. Jesus replies by showing that "that other world" is not like this one; therefore there is no marriage there and marriage relationships have no relevance.

73

Luke 20:34, 35). Those "counted worthy to find a place in that other world and in the resurrection from the dead" (Luke 20:35) are "as the angels, and, having shared in the resurrection, they are God's children" (Luke 20:36).

After explaining the nature of resurrection life, Jesus reinforces the reality of resurrection by relating it to Moses' experience near Horeb (recorded in Exodus 3). "But that the dead do rise, even Moses disclosed at the bush, when he refers to the Lord as the God of Abraham, the God of Isaac, and the God of Jacob" (Luke 20:37). In identifying Himself, Yahweh told Moses: "I am the God of your father, the God of Abraham, the God of Isaac and the God of Jacob" (Exod. 3:6). Jesus, emphasizing the tense of the verbal expression draws this conclusion: "He is not the God of the dead, but of the living; for to him all are alive" (Luke 20:38). Implied in Jesus' answer is that all men live and, at least some will participate as "children of the resurrection" in the blessings of that new age.

But the resurrection will include all men, not just those who are "counted worthy." In Luke 14, Jesus concludes that parabolic exhortation relative to choosing lower seats at a banquet so that the host may bid one come up higher by suggesting that his hearers invite only the poor, the maimed, and the blind, when giving a dinner. You will be blessed, he says, because they cannot repay you! (Luke 14:10-13). But, he adds, your repayment, your reward will come at "the resurrection of the just" (Luke 14:14). Implied is a general resurrection (as was currently believed) but divided into a "resurrection of the just: and a resurrection of the unjust."

That which is implied in this passage is clearly stated in the Fourth Gospel. The "beloved disciple" records Jesus' presence at a feast of the Jews. While there he heals an infirm man at the pool of Beth-zatha, near the Sheep gate. Since this cure was wrought on a Sabbath, Jesus is immediately embroiled in a controversy with certain Jews (Jewish leaders undoubtedly). In the process, Jesus refers to His Sonship to the Heavenly Father in a unique sense. His opponents do not misunderstand him. John notes: "This made the Jews all the more eager to kill him, since he not only had broken the Sabbath but was calling God his own Father, making himself equal with God" (John 5:18). In response to this attitude, Jesus repeats and expands this unique relationship:

> Then Jesus answered, Truly, I say to you that the Son can do nothing on his own; he does only what he sees the Father doing. Whatever the Father does the Son does in turn; for the Father loves the Son and shows him everything He is doing. He will show him still greater works than these to fill you with wonder (John 5:19-20).

As an example of these greater works, Jesus cites the resurrection.

> For as the Father raises the dead and makes them live, even so the Son also gives life to whom he will. For the Father, himself, judges no man, but he has entrusted all judgment to the Son; that all men may honor the Son equally with the Father. Whoever refuses to honor the Son does not honor the Father who sent him. Truly, truly, I say to you, He that hears my words and believes in Him who sent me, has eternal life and does not have to face judgment, but has already passed out of Death into Life (John 5:21-24).

Then follows that astonishing statement that links a general resurrection of both just and unjust directly to the ministry of the incarnate Son of God who is the eschatological "Son of Man" (John 5:27).

> Truly, truly, I say to you, The hour is coming, and now is, when the dead shall hear the voice of the Son of God; and all who hear shall come to life. For as the Father is the source of life, so also has he granted to the Son to have life in himself and has given him authority to execute judgment as well because He is the Son of Man.[9] Marvel not at this: for the hour is coming in which all that are in the grave shall hear his voice. And they shall come forth; those who have done good in the resurrection of life, and those who have practiced evil in a resurrection issuing in judgment and condemnation (John 5:25-29).

In a genuine sense, the eschatological age had dawned. The "end time" (the "latter days") would soon be upon men. This age will be under the authority of the Messiah, God's Son; and it will be consummated in a resurrection initiated by "his voice." Judgment will be executed by him; life or death will result in terms of the judgment.

But Jesus not only teaches the reality of the general resurrection and life after death, seeing himself as that Messiah and eschatological Son of Man who will be the instrument of coming Judgment and coming glory, he also speaks of himself as bringing resurrection life into human experience now. To some degree this is what he demonstrates in those "acted parables" in which he raised the dead—Jairus' daughter (Mark 5:39f,), the widow's son at Nain (Luke 7:12), and Lazarus (John 11:43-44).

As Jesus comes into Bethany, four days following the death of Lazarus, Martha meets him. She says: "Lord had

---

9. There is no question but that Jesus is here emphasizing the eschatological "Son of Man" motif of the book of Daniel and the intertestamental literature.

you been here, my brother would not have died" (John 1:21). To this Jesus replies that her brother will rise again. Martha, reflecting current Jewish thought, responds: "I know that he will rise again at the resurrection on the Last Day (John 11:24). Jesus then speaks emphatically: "I am the resurrection and the life. He that believes in me, even though he dies, shall live again. And whoever lives and believes in me shall never die" (John 11:25, 26). Jesus is not denying a final resurrection, but he is emphasizing the fact that faith in him brings men into a relationship to eternal life which death cannot destroy. Rather than seeing only an "end time" event in which the righteous will participate, Jesus affirms that eternity (the Kingdom of God) has broken into time in his person and one may experience that eternity now. As he says in his prayer in John 17: "This is eternal life, that they know thee the only true God and Jesus Christ, whom thou hast sent" (John 17:3).

QUESTIONS FOR DISCUSSION

1. Why was Jesus not greeted by the Jews as the expected Messiah? How does this affect John the baptizer later?
2. Why does Jesus caution His disciples to tell no one that He is the Christ?
3. How does the confession of His Messiahship lead into Jesus' teachings concerning resurrection?
4. How does Jesus indicate to His disciples that His redemptive ministry as Messiah is twofold?

Chapter Six

THE RESURRECTION FACT AS EXHIBITED IN THE GOSPELS

"He is not here, for He is risen even as He said. Come, see the place where He lay" (Matthew 28:5-6).

The records are clear. Jesus, in His ministry predicts His resurrection. He does this on several occasions and in different terminology. He also presents this foretold resurrection as a Messianic sign. This will be the only sign given substantiating His authority.

Did his predictions come true? Was the Messianic sign fulfilled? The testimony of the evangelists who composed the "Gospels" is uniformly positive. It is that testimony that is presented in this chapter.

The Testimony of the Resurrection of Jesus in Harmony

Quite early in the second century the four documents which we call Gospels were circulated together under the singular word, the Gospel.[1] Recognizing that these four records were varied, harmonies were developed so that all the information in the four could be presented as a continuous, integrated story. The earliest of these harmonies is that produced by Tatian, a Syrian Christian, somewhere around the middle of the second century. His work was in the Syriac translation and was called *Diatessaron* ("through the four").

---

1. Paul's epistles apparently were also gathered and circulated under the term, the Apostle.

Such a harmony of the resurrection accounts or narratives may prove to be helpful in setting out Resurrection fact.[2]

Risen Victorious

An Earth-shaking Dawn
(Mt. 28:1-15; Mk. 16:1-11; Lk. 23:56-24:12; Jn. 20:1-18)

Now when the Sabbath was past, Mary Magdalene, and the other Mary, the mother of James, and Salome, bought spices that they might come and anoint him. And on the first day of the week at early dawn they came, and certain others with them, to see the sepulchre, bringing the spices and ointments which they had prepared.

And behold, there was a great earthquake; for an angel of the Lord descended from Heaven, and came and rolled away the stone from the door, and sat upon it. His appearance was like lightning, and his raiment white as snow; and for fear of him those on guard trembled, and became like dead men.

(Now after Jesus rose, early on the first day of the week, he appeared first to Mary Magdalene, out of whom he had cast seven demons.) Mary came to the sepulchre while it was yet dark, and saw that the stone had been removed from the tomb. She ran therefore and came to Simon Peter, and to the other disciple, he whom Jesus loved, and said to them, "They took away the Lord from the sepulchre! And we know not where they laid him."

Peter therefore and the other disciple (arose, and) went forth and ran (toward the sepulchre). And they began to run together, but the other disciple outran Peter and reached the sepulchre first; and stooping down he saw the linen cloths lying there, but did not go in. Simon Peter therefore came following him, and he went into the sepulchre;

---

2. See Appendix 2 where the historical reliability of the New Testament documents is explored.

(and stooping down), he saw the linen cloths lying (by themselves), and the napkin, which had been about his head, not lying with the linen cloths but folded up in a place by itself.

Then therefore the other disciple also, who had reached the tomb first, went in, and he saw and believed; for as yet they did not understand the scripture, that he must rise from the dead. So the disciples departed again to their abode, (wondering at what had come to pass).

"Rabboni!"

But Mary kept standing outside near the sepulchre, weeping. While therefore she was weeping, she stooped and looked into the sepulchre; and she beheld two angels in white sitting, one at the head and the other at the feet, where the body of Jesus had lain.

And they asked her, "Woman, why are you weeping?" She said to them, "Because they took away my Lord, and I know not where they laid him." And when she had thus spoken, she turned around and saw Jesus standing, but did not know that it was Jesus.

Jesus said to her, "Woman, why are you weeping; whom are you seeking?" She, supposing him to be the gardener, said to him, "Sir, if you bore him away, tell me where you laid him, and I will take him away." Jesus said to her, "Mary." Turning about, she said to him, "Rabboni!" (which is to say, dear Teacher!).

Jesus said to her, "Do not hold me, for I have not yet ascended to my Father. But go to my brethren, and say to them, 'I am ascending to my Father and your Father, and to my God and your God.'"

Mary Magdalene went and told those who had been with him, as they mourned and wept, that she had seen the Lord and he had spoken these things to her; but they, though hearing that he was alive and had been seen by her, disbelieved it.

At the Tomb After Sunrise

Now Joanna and Mary the mother of James and the other women with them came to the sepulchre when the sun had risen. And they were saying among themselves, "Who will roll us away the stone from the door of the sepulchre?" (For it was very great). But when they looked up, they saw that the stone had been rolled away.

Then on entering the sepulchre they found not the body (of the Lord Jesus). But it came to pass that, as they were much perplexed about this, they saw a young man sitting at the right side, clothed in a long, white garment. And they were greatly amazed; behold, two men stood by them in dazzling garments.

And as they became terrified and bowed their faces to the ground, the angel answered and said to the women, "Do not fear; do not be amazed. For I know that you seek Jesus of Nazareth, who was crucified. Why seek the living among the dead? He is not here, for he has risen, as he said. Remember how he spoke to you, while he was yet in Galilee, saying, 'The Son of man must be delivered into the hands of sinful men, and be crucified, and the third day rise again.'"

And they remembered his words; and he said to them, "Come, see the place where the Lord lay. But go quickly and tell his disciples, and Peter, that 'He has risen from the dead, and behold, he is going before you into Galilee; there shall you see him, as he said to you, lo, I have told you.'"

"Rejoice!"

So they went out quickly and fled from the sepulchre, for trembling and astonishment possessed them. Neither said they anything to anyone, for they were afraid; and they started to run to tell his disciples.

But as they were on their way, behold, Jesus met them, saying, "Rejoice!" And they came and seized him by his feet, and worshiped him. Then said Jesus to them, "Fear not; go tell my brethren to go into Galilee, and there shall they see me."

And they returned with great joy and told all these things to the eleven apostles, and to all the rest. But these words seemed to them as idle tales, and they did not believe the women.

Bribery of the Guard

Now as they were going, behold, some of the guard came into the city, and reported to the chief priests all that had come to pass. And they, when they had assembled with the elders and counseled together, gave the soldiers a large sum of money, saying, "Say that 'His disciples came by night and stole him away while we slept.' And if this comes to the governor's ears, we will 'persuade' him and free you from trouble."

So they took the money and did as they were told, and this report is spread abroad among the Jews to the present day.

Jesus and Two on the Emmaus Road
(Mk. 16:12-13; Lk. 24:13-35)

(Then after these things he was revealed in another manner.) And behold, that same day two of them (were walking into the country), to a village called Emmaus, about seven miles from Jerusalem; and they were talking together about all these things that had taken place. And it came to pass that, as they conversed and reasoned, Jesus himself drew near and walked with them; but their eyes were held from recognizing him.

And he said to them, "What are these things which you are discussing with each other, as you walk with sad faces?" And one, whose name was Cleopas, answered and said to him, "Are you the only sojourner in Jerusalem who has not known the things that have happened there in recent days?"

And he asked of them, "What things?" And they said to him, "The things concerning Jesus of Nazareth, a man who was a prophet mighty in deed and word before God and all the people; and how the chief priests and our rulers delivered him up to be condemned to death, and crucified him. Now we were trusting that it was he who would redeem Israel.

"But to top it all, this is the third day since these things happened. And besides, certain women from among us astonished us, who were at the sepulchre early in the morning and did not find his body; and they came saying that they had even seen a vision of angels, who said that he was alive! And some of those who were with us went to the sepulchre and found it so, as the women had said, but him they did not see."

"Believe the Prophets!"

Then said he to them, "O foolish ones, and slow of heart to believe all the things which the prophets uttered! Was it not needful that the Messiah should suffer these things and enter into his glory?" And beginning from Moses and all the prophets he expounded to them in all the Scriptures the things concerning himself.

Then they drew near to the village where they were going, and he made as though he would go farther; but they constrained him, saying, "Lodge with us, for it is toward evening and the day is now far spent." So he went in to lodge with them.

And it came to pass, as he reclined at table with them, that he took the bread and blessed and broke it, and began to give it to them. And their eyes were opened and they knew him; and he vanished out of their sight. Then said they to each other, "Did not our hearts burn within us, as he talked with us on the road and kept opening up to us the Scriptures?"

His Appearance to Peter Convinces

And rising up that same hour they returned to Jerusalem; and they found the eleven and those with them assembled together, saying, "The Lord has risen indeed! And he appeared to Simon!"

So they told the things that had happened on the road, and how he was known by them in the breaking of the bread; (but they did not believe them).

Sunday Evening with the Disciples
(Luke 24:36-43; Jn. 20:19-23)

But as they were speaking these things, it being therefore evening of that first day of the week, the doors being shut where the disciples were assembled, for fear of the Jews, Jesus himself came and stood in their midst and said to them, "Peace to you!"

Yet they were shocked and were filled with fear, and thought that they were beholding a spirit. But he said to them, "Why are you troubled? And why do doubtings arise in your hearts? Behold my hands and my feet, that it is I myself. Handle me, and see; for a spirit does not have flesh and bones, as you see I have." And when he had said this, he showed them his hands and feet, and his side.

Then did the disciples rejoice at seeing the Lord. And while they were still disbelieving for joy and were filled with wonder, he said to them, "Have you anything here to eat?" And they gave him a piece of broiled fish and of a honeycomb, and he took and ate it before them.

Jesus therefore said again to them, "Peace to you! As the Father has sent Me forth, so am I sending you." And when he had said this, he breathed on them, and said to them, "Take the Holy Spirit. Anyone's sins which you forgive, they have been forgiven them, and anyone's sins which you retain, they have been retained."

The Convincing of Thomas
(John 20:24-29)

Now Thomas, called Didymus, one of the twelve, was not with them when Jesus came. The other disciples therefore said to him, "We have seen the Lord!" But he said to them, "Unless I see in his hands the imprint of the nails, and press my finger into the mark of the nails, and my hand into his side, I will not at all believe."

Then after eight days his disciples were again indoors, and Thomas with them. Though the doors had been shut, Jesus came and stood in their midst, and said, "Peace to you!"

Then said he to Thomas, "Bring here your finger and look at my hands, and bring your hand and press it into my side, and be not unbelieving but believing." And Thomas answered and said to him, "My Lord and my God!" Jesus said to him, "Because you have seen me, Thomas, you have believed; blessed are they who have not seen and yet have believed."

With Seven Disciples in Galilee
(John 21:1-24)

After these things Jesus revealed himself to the disciples again, this time at the Sea of Tiberias, and he did so in this way.

There were together Simon Peter and Thomas called Didymus and Nathanael of Cana of Galilee, and the sons of Zebedee and two others of his disciples. Simon Peter said to them, "I am going fishing." They said to him, "We also are going with you." They went out at once and climbed into the boat. But that night they caught nothing.

But when morning had now come, Jesus was standing on the shore, though the disciples did not know that it was Jesus. So Jesus said to them, "Children, have you anything to eat?" They replied to him, "No." And he said to them,

"Cast out the net on the right side of the boat, and you will find some." So they cast it, and now they could not draw it in for the size of the haul.

That disciple whom Jesus loved said therefore to Peter, "It is the Lord!" So when Simon Peter heard that it was the Lord, he thrust his coat around him, for he was naked, and flung himself into the sea. And the other disciples came in the small ship (for they were not far from shore, perhaps a hundred yards) dragging the net filled with fish.

"Come to Breakfast"

When therefore they got out on shore, they saw a fire of coals that had been laid there, and fish placed upon it, and bread. Jesus said to them, "Bring some of the fish you have just caught." Simon Peter went on board and drew the net to shore, filled with one hundred fifty-three large fish. And in spite of there being so many the net was not torn.

Jesus said to them, "Come; have breakfast." But not one of the disciples dared ask him, "Who are you?" For they knew that it was the Lord. Jesus therefore came and took the bread and gave to them, and likewise of the fish. This was now the third time that Jesus was revealed to his disciples after he was raised from the dead.

"Do You Love Me, Simon?"

When therefore they had eaten breakfast. Jesus said to Simon Peter, "Simon, son of John, do you love me, more than these?" He said to him, "Yes, Lord; You Know my affection for You." He said to him, "Feed My lambs."

Again a second time he said to him, "Simon, son of John, do you love me?" He said to him, "Yes, Lord! You know my affection for You." He said to him, "Shepherd my sheep."

He said to him the third time, "Simon, son of John, do you have affection for me?" Peter was grieved because of the third question, "Do you have affection for me?" and he said to him, "Lord, You know all things; You know that I have affection for You!"

Jesus said to him, "Feed My Sheep! Verily, verily, I say to you, when you were younger, you girded yourself and walked where you desired; but when you are old, you will stretch out your hands and another will gird you and carry you where you would not go." Now this he said to signify by what death he would glorify God. And when he had spoken this, he said to him, "Follow Me."

The Story Told by John Closes

But Peter turned about and saw following them the disciple whom Jesus loved, who also at the supper had leaned against his breast and said, "Lord, who is he that betrays You?" At seeing him Peter said to Jesus, "But what of this man, Lord?" Jesus said to him, "If I desire that he remain till I come, what is it to you? Follow Me!"

Therefore the saying spread abroad among the brethren that that disciple would not die; yet Jesus did not tell him that he would not die, but said, "If I desire that he remain till I come, what is it to you?" He is the disciple who testifies of these things and wrote these things, and we know that his testimony is true.

On a Mountain of Galilee
(Mt. 28:16-20)

Then the eleven disciples proceeded into Galilee to the mountain to which Jesus had directed them. And when they saw him, they worshiped him, though some doubted.

And Jesus came to them and addressed them, saying, "All authority has been given unto Me in heaven and upon earth. Go therefore and disciple all the nations, baptizing them in the name of the Father and of the Son and of the Holy Spirit, teaching them to observe everything I commanded you. And lo, I am with you alway, until the consummation of the age.

His Final Appearing and Ascension
  (Mk. 16:14-20b; Lk. 24:44-53)

(Afterward he was manifested to the eleven as they were reclining at table, and he reproached their unbelief and hardness of heart, because they had not believed those who saw him after he had risen.

And he said to them, "Go into all the world and proclaim the Glad News to the whole creation. He who believes and is baptized shall be saved, but he who disbelieves shall be condemned.

"And these miraculous signs will accompany those who believe: in My name will they cast out demons; they will speak in new tongues; they will pick up serpents; and if they drink any deadly thing, it will not in any way hurt them; they will lay hands on the sick and they will recover.")

Parting Words to the Eleven

And he said to them, "These are the words which I spoke to you while I was yet with you: that all things must be fulfilled which have been written in the law of Moses and the prophets and the psalms concerning me."

Then opened he their understanding that they might comprehend the Scriptures, and said to them, "Thus it has been written, and so it was needful, that the Messiah should suffer and rise from the dead on the third day; and that repentance and remission of sins should be proclaimed in his name to all the nations, beginning at Jerusalem.

"And you are witnesses of these things. And behold, I am sending forth the promise of my Father upon you. But remain in the city of Jerusalem till you are clothed with power from on high."

He Ascends from the Mount of Olives

So then the Lord Jesus, after speaking thus to them, led them out as far as to Bethany; and he lifted up his hands and blessed them. And it came to pass that, as he was blessing them, he was parted from them (and was carried up into heaven, and sat at the right hand of God).

And they (worshiped him, and) returned to Jerusalem with great joy and were continually in the temple, praising and blessing God. (And they went forth and preached everywhere, the Lord working with them and confirming the message by the miraculous signs that followed.)

That You May Have Life
(Jn. 21:25; 20:30-31)

Now Jesus also wrought in the presence of his disciples many other miraculous signs which are not written in this book; if they were written one by one, I suppose that not even the world itself could contain the books that would be written (John 20:31). "But these have been written that you may believe that Jesus is the Christ, the Son of God; and that believing you may have life in His name."[3]

The Certainty of Jesus' Death and Burial in the Gospel Narrative

The Gospel narratives are quite explicit about the death of Jesus. They record Jesus' prediction that he would die (see

---

3. A harmony produced by Johnston M. Cheney, edited by Stanley A. Ellisen, *The Life of Christ in Stereo* (Portland, Oregon: Western Bantist Senia Press, 1969), pp. 204-213.

Mark 8:31, etc.). In fact, Matthew shows that Jesus revealed his death at different times with increasing concreteness and intensity as He drew closer to Jerusalem. In Chapter 16, following Peter's confession near Caesarea, Philippi, Jesus began to "show his disciples that he must go to Jerusalem and suffer many things . . . and be killed, and on the third day be raised" (16:21). Later, back in Galilee, Jesus says that "the Son of Man is to be delivered into the hands of men, and they will kill him, and he will be raised on the third day" (17:22, 23). Even later, on the way to Jerusalem, Jesus says: "Behold we are going up to Jerusalem; and the Son of man will be delivered to the chief priests and Scribes, and they will condemn him to death, and deliver him to the Gentiles to be mocked and scourged and crucified, and he will be raised on the third day" (20:18, 19).

The Passion narrative unequivocally states that he was crucified. All four Gospels show that Jesus was aware of his fate (see Matt. 26:21ff.; Mark 14:18ff.; Luke 22:21ff.; John 13:21-33), and revealed something of this awareness at the final Supper at which he instituted the symbolic feast of bread and wine. Not only does he speak of his "body given" and the "blood of a new covenant" symbolized in that act of giving those simple elements, he actually says "This is my body . . . this is my blood." Within this same context, he warns that one of his trusted disciples would betray him (see John 13:21ff. and parallel passages). This betrayal, as portrayed in the Gospel of John, will lead to his "going . . . to prepare a place for them" (John 13:36 - John 14:6), and his going necessitates the sending of "another helper" (John 14:15f.) through which he would come to them and be with them.

Following these preliminaries, the narratives tell of the company leaving the upper room, going out toward the Mt.

of Olives and waiting (and sleeping) with Jesus through the Gethsemane experience. All four accounts testify to Judas' betrayal, Jesus' arrest, and the eventual flight of the disciples (Matt. 26:30ff.; Mark 14:26ff.; Luke 22:35ff.; John 18:1ff.). The trials of Jesus before Annas and Caiaphas, his denial by Peter; the confirmation of the verdict of death by the Sanhedrin, after dawn, follow (Matt. 26:57ff.; Mark 14:53ff.; Luke 22:54ff.; John 18:12ff.). Jesus is taken before Pilate so that the death verdict could be granted Roman approval, shuttled between Pilate and Herod Antipas (Luke 23:4-12), and finally given over to be crucified (Matt. 27:11ff.; Mark 15:2ff.; Luke 23:2ff.; John 18:28ff.).

Jesus is taken to the place of execution known as Golgotha, the place of the skull. There with two criminals, he is nailed to a cross and for six hours suffers excruciating agony, at which time he expires. Each of the Gospels devotes at least two full paragraphs to the fact of His death and subsequent burial. They vary as to the accompanying events and the actual words that Jesus speaks from the Cross, but they agree in almost identical words that he actually died on the Cross. Mark says that he "gave up the ghost" (Mark 15:37); Matthew that he "yielded up his spirit" (27:50); Luke that "he gave up the ghost" (23:46); and John that "he . . . gave up his spirit" (19:30). To these can be added those numerous declarations in the Acts and Epistles that "Christ died. . . ." There is unanimous agreement by the earliest witnesses that Jesus died.

But not only do these witnesses speak to the certainty of Jesus death, they also share other testimonies supporting this certitude. The centurian is seen by Mark as gazing up at the lifeless body of Jesus and saying, "Truly this man was the Son of God" (Mark 15:39). The very tense of the verb *was* indicates that this hardened Roman officer, who had witnessed death before, believed Jesus to be dead.

John's account preserves that eye-witness account of the piercing of Jesus' side. Since the bodies, according to Jewish custom, could not continue to hang during the Sabbath which would begin at sundown, the Roman soldiers were ordered to break the legs of those on the crosses to hasten their death. Coming to Jesus, they find that he is already dead. To make sure they pierce his side with a spear and "straightway there came out blood and water" (John 19:34). Here John is emphasizing the certainty of Christ's death.

Matthew and Mark both recount Joseph of Arimathea's request of the body of Jesus for burial (Matt. 26:57-58; Mark 15:43, 44). Pilate's surprise that Jesus is already dead is understood in light of the fact that death by crucifixion may have extended to as much as two or three full days. Ascertaining from the centurion that the Galilean is dead, Pilate grants Joseph's request. Mark's account clearly implies that Pilate would not have relinquished the body of Jesus if there had been the slightest doubt about the reality of death.

The burial party is another testimony to the certainty of death. Joseph of Arimathea and Nicodemus, both disciples of Jesus, both members of the Jewish Council, prepared his body for burial (Luke 23:50-53; John 19:38-42). These men (and their servants who undoubtedly assisted them) would have known if Jesus were really dead. They could hardly take the body down from the cross, and carry it to the nearby tomb, embalm it in spices and prepare it with grave cloths, without realizing that it was genuinely a corpse.

This testimony, both direct and indirect, leaves no room for doubt about the certitude of Jesus' death. Illusion and deceit, are clearly eliminated. The question that remains is, what became of the body? It could not have been brought out of a coma or revived by the deceitful action of disciples; it did not remain long enough in the tomb to decay and disintegrate into dust; and yet "it can be traced by the continuity of observation from the cross to the last resting place in the garden."[4] The only conclusion that is adequate is that something unique, mysterious and magnificent "happened on the morning of the third day to cancel the work of death and to transform the fleshly organism into the instrument of glory."[5]

The Evidence of the Resurrection in the Gospel Narratives

The Gospel narratives are just as clear about the actual resurrection of Jesus as they are about the certainty of his death. The evidence seen in these narratives is twofold. There are the material *facts* of the displaced stone, the empty tomb and the grave clothes. There are those witnesses who actually saw Jesus in person following his death. These taken together constitute such evidence that one can hardly accept any other alternative but that Jesus literally arose from the dead.

The Material Evidence

The new tomb of Joseph is described in the first gospel as having been "hewn out in the rock" with a great stone as the door (Matt. 27:60). This great stone would be circular, set on edge within a narrow groove paralleling the outer

4. Merrill C. Tenney, *The Reality of the Resurrection* (New York: Harper and Row, 1963), p. 108.
5. *Ibid.*

wall of the tomb. This stone, weighing hundreds of pounds, would be rolled across the entrance to the tomb after the body was prepared and placed on the ledge within. Because of its weight it could be rolled back, uncovering the entrance to the tomb, only with great difficulty.

It is no wonder that those women who had seen where Jesus' body was laid (Mark 15:47), were "saying to one another 'who will roll away the stone for us from the door of the tomb?' (Mark 16:2), as on that early Sunday morning they came with spices to anoint the body. But when they arrived the stone 'was rolled back' and they were amazed because 'it was very large'" (Mark 16:4). All four gospels make note of this. The stone was rolled back (see Luke 24:2; Matt. 28:2; John 20:1).

Matthew sees this as the result of an earthquake (Matt. 28:2), and prefaces it by showing that the chief priests and scribes petitioned Pilate to make the tomb secure, so that Jesus' disciples could not steal the body away and then tell the people that he had risen from the dead. Pilate tells them to use their guard and make it as secure as they could. Matthew reports: "So they went and made the sepulchre secure by sealing the stone and setting a guard" (Matthew 27:62-66).

But guard and seal were insufficient, and the stone is rolled back. To presume that a handful of discouraged, fearful, disorganized disciples or a small group of timid women could somehow overcome the guards or, given the myth perpetuated that the guards slept, could roll back the stone is preposterous. Added to that is the complete surprise of these women at the displaced stone and the empty tomb. John records that one of these women, Mary Magdalene, is broken-hearted, weeping profusely before the open tomb (John 20:11ff.). She apparently had no knowledge of someone coming to roll the stone back and steal away the corpse.

The excuse of the guards, "His disciples came by night and stole him away while we slept" (Matthew 28:13) is clearly false. How could they know this, if asleep? If their accusation could be proved, why were not the disciples of Jesus questioned? Why was Joseph not interrogated since he was responsible for placing the body in his own tomb? If they could locate the displaced body, why did they not produce it to prove the guards' accusation? The answers to all these questions are apparent. This charge was only a smokescreen to cover their own confusion and anger. The stone was displaced not by man but by divine power. Here is mute testimony to the reality of resurrection. The displaced stone "cries out" even as Jesus had promised (Luke 19:40)! Who moved that stone? is an important question and points to material evidence substantiating the resurrection of Jesus.

In addition to the displaced stone, the empty tomb is material witness to the actuality of Jesus' resurrection. Contrary to the thinking of some modern scholars, who claim that "the empty tomb . . . plays no part whatsoever in the New Testament as the foundation for faith in the Resurrection,"[6] the empty tomb is distinctly material evidence for Jesus' resurrection.

The four Gospels are unanimous in their testimony that when the women came to the tomb (and at least two of them had carefully watched where the body was buried (Mark 15:47) they found it empty (Matthew 28:6; Mark 16:6; Luke 24:3; John 20:1-10). Of course there is variety

---

6. Emil Brunner, *The Mediator*, (Philadelphia: The Westminster Press), p. 576. Or as Kirsopp Lake says in *The Historical Evidence for the Resurrection of Jesus Christ* (New York: G. P. Putnam's Sons, 1907), "The empty tomb is for us doctrinally indefensible and historically insufficiently accredited." (p. 253).

in the testimony as we would expect from independent witnesses. Matthew speaks of the earthquake, the catatonic state of the guards, the angel's appearance, and the announcement by the angel to the women that the one they sought was not there. "He has risen, as he said." The angel invites them to "come see the place where he lay" (Matthew 28:2-6). Apparently, the angel sees some significance in the emptiness of Joseph's tomb!

Mark's testimony is similar to Matthew's. The women enter the empty tomb and are amazed to see a young man, dressed in a white robe, sitting on the right side (apparently on the rock shelf where the body had formerly lain). This young man says to them: "Do not be amazed; you seek Jesus of Nazareth, who was crucified. He has risen; he is not here; see the place where they laid him" (Mark 16:4-6).

Luke's account reveals that the women, finding the stone rolled away from the door of the tomb, went in but found no corpse there. In their perplexity, they were additionally surprised and frightened by two men (angels) who suddenly stood before them in dazzling array. These messengers say to them: "Why do you seek the living among the dead? Remember how he told you, while he was still in Galilee, that the Son of Man must be delivered into the hands of sinful men, and be crucified, and on the third day rise." Believing, the women return to tell the eleven and the other disciples, but their report seemed like an "idle tale" to the apostles and they were unable to believe (Luke 24:3-11).

John's testimony is ever more extensive than that of the Synoptics. Mary Magdalene comes to the tomb while it is still dark. She finds the stone rolled back and the tomb empty. She rushes back into the city and finds Peter and John. "They have taken the Lord out of the tomb, and we do not know where they have laid him," she sobs.[7] Peter and John run to the tomb, John outrunning Peter. John peers in but does not enter; Peter arriving, enters the tomb and John follows. They both see the grave clothes, with the head cloth rolled up lying separate from the rest. They believe what Mary has reported about the empty tomb, but John relates that they do not as yet believe that he had been raised from the dead. The fourth Gospel indicates that Mary Magdalene has followed Peter and John and as she weeps beside the empty tomb, two angels ask her why she is weeping. "Because they have taken away my Lord, and I do not know where they have laid him," she cries. To the similar question of that one whom she supposed to be the gardener, she says, "Sir, if you have carried him away, tell me where you have laid him, and I will take him away." This supposed gardener, who is in reality the risen Jesus, reveals himself to Mary by speaking her name and she is overjoyed (John 20:1-16).

Here in this extensive testimony is a simple, irrefutable fact. The tomb is empty. Not just any tomb, but the one that enclosed the body of the crucified Nazarene. How is this to be explained? Modern thinkers have racked their brains to explain away this stubborn bit of historical fact, but these ingenious theories run counter to the evidence set out in the only adequate testimony that we have of this sequence of events. The only possible explanation, other than that given in the Gospels, is the one given by Jewish authorities. The disciples of Jesus stole the body! But even this counter-argument is put forth because of the stubborn fact of an empty tomb. *There was nobody there.*

---

7. It is ironic that here Mary is wondering why anyone would take the body, even seeing this as perhaps the work of Jesus' enemies. There is no inkling that Jesus' friends would do this.

Frank Morrison, in his interesting book *Who Moved the Stone?*, points out how strange it is that there is no trace in any extant Christian literature from the first few centuries of anyone going to Jerusalem to pay homage at the shrine of Jesus. The grave or tomb of Jesus simply fades out of later history, which is a complete reversal of religious customs seen in ancient religions, and, even later, in Christendom. Islam has its Mecca, but there is not even a whisper in early tradition of pilgrims visiting the grotto where Jesus was laid. The reason is quite clear; the tomb is empty, unoccupied, there was nothing to see or revere.

In the testimony given by John, the disciple whom Jesus loved, the graveclothes also are material evidence of the resurrection of Jesus. The synoptic gospels, as well as the Gospel of John, speak about the hastily prepared corpse. It is "wrapped in a clear linen cloth" (Matt. 27:59, 60; Luke 23:53); or, as Mark phrases it, "they wound him in the linen cloth" (Mark 15:46). John says that Joseph and Nicodemus "bound" his body in "swathes" or "bandages" using spices which Nicodemus furnished (John 19:38, 40). Apparently, the usual customs were followed in preparing the Nazarene's body for burial. He is bound in linen,[8] with aromatic spices placed between the folds. These served both as a partial preservative and as a kind of cement to form the wrappings into a solid covering. A piece of cloth was then wrapped around the head and tied under the chin to keep the jaw from sagging.

On that Sunday morning following the burial of Jesus, the body was gone, the tomb was empty but these grave clothes were still there. Perhaps the angels were referring to

---

8. See the account of the raising of Lazarus, (John 11:44).

these when they said, "Come, see the place where he lay" (Matthew 28:6; Mark 16:6), since a plain stone shelf would carry no visible impression. John is quite explicit. The beloved disciple, outrunning Peter, peers into the tomb and sees the "linen cloths lying there" (John 20:5). Peter, rushing up, enters the tomb and also sees the linen cloths lying there. Both are struck by the fact that the "head napkin" was "not lying with the linen cloths but rolled up in a place by itself" (John 20:7). Why should this arrangement have seemed strange enough to relate? Dr. M. C. Tenney suggests:

> There is a strong hint that the clothes were not folded as if Jesus had unwound them and then deposited them in two neat piles on the shelf. The word used to describe the napkin or head cloth does not connote a flat folded square like a table napkin, but a ball of cloth bearing the appearance of being rolled around an object that was no longer there. The wrappings were in position where the body had lain, and the head cloth was where the head had been, separated from the others by the distance from armpits to neck. The shape of the body was still apparent in them, but the flesh and bone had disappeared.
>
> If this hypothesis be correct, and it seems to follow the facts, how was the corpse extricated from the wrapping, since they would not slip over the curves of the body when tightly wound around it? No robbers would ever have rewound the wrappings in their original shape, for there would not have been time to do so. They would have flung the cloths down in disorder and fled with the body. Fear of detection would have made them act as hastily as possible.
>
> The answer to the enigma was that Jesus had risen, passing through the graveclothes, which He left undisturbed as a silent proof that death could not hold Him, nor material bonds restrain Him.[9]

9. Tenney, p. 119.

Here are stubborn facts; phenomena that must be explained. The theories propounded by critics, beginning with the "theft theory" of the Jewish Sanhedrin (Matt. 28:11-15), have neither proved adequately satisfactory. The conclusion drawn by those early eyewitnesses is the only adequate explanation: "The Lord has risen indeed" (Luke 24:34).

The Personal Appearances

But it was not news about an empty tomb, a displaced stone, and graveclothes left behind in unusual fashion that convinced these disciples of Jesus that he had risen indeed. Such news could be dismissed as "idle tales" told by silly women (Luke 24:12). Cleopas and his friend, as they journeyed toward Emmaus, could say to the stranger who joined them: "certain women from among us astonished us, who were at the sepulchre early in the morning and did not find his body; and they came saying that they had even seen a vision of angels, who said that he was alive. And some of those who were with us went to the sepulchre and found it so, as the women had said, but him they did not see" (Luke 24:22-25). Yet these two were downcast, saying, "we had hoped that he was the one to redeem Israel" (Luke 24:21).

The personal appearances of Jesus, risen from the dead, real and recognizable, were what caused faith to shine forth in the darkness of despair. Not just glimpses of his revived, resuscitated, resurrection body; but a renewal of his personal presence and a continuation, for a time, of former loving relationships and person-to-person interactions.

Those nine or ten appearances related in the four Gospels (see above), are not just visual reactions to visible phenomena. As A. M. Ramsay rightly points out: "There was the gradual impact of the risen Jesus upon the minds and consciences

100

of these disciples, and "there was the unfolding of the Scriptures so that what they heard and saw became integrated with their faith in God and His righteous purpose for mankind."[10]

Jesus appears to Mary Magdalene. She sees a figure but supposes it to be the gardener or caretaker of this tomb garden, but when Jesus speaks her name, "Mary," she recognizes his voice and knows that it is he, and that he knows her by name just as he had previous to his death (John 20:15-16). "Rabboni, Dear Teacher," she exclaims with joy and runs to tell the others that she had seen him.

Those other women, who had come to complete his burial, saw the empty tomb, heard the testimony of the angel about his resurrection and fled to tell the other disciples. Jesus meets them on the way saying, "Hail." They come up to him and fall at his feet in worship. "Don't be afraid," he says, "go tell my brethren to go to Galilee and there they will see me" (Matt. 28:1-10). It is not mere sight of him that produced the great joy that filled their hearts; it was touching him, hearing him, knowing through his word that this was the same one who had been with them in Galilee and would be with them again.

Cleopas and his companion spent some time in the actual presence of Jesus as they journeyed to Emmaus. They were avidly listening to the way the stranger was interpreting the Messianic message of the Old Testament Scriptures. It was only at supper time that they genuinely came to know as well as see that this was the risen Lord (Luke 24:13-35). He vanishes from their sight; but they were aware of his reality as companion ("as he talked with us on the road"),

---

10. A. M. Ramsay, *The Resurrection of Christ* (London: Geoffrey Bles, 1945), p. 37.

as interpreter of Scripture, and as the one who by his continuous life incorporated them into the "fellowship of the burning heart" ("did not our hearts burn within us"). Upon returning with haste to Jerusalem, they find that Peter has also seen the Lord.

But, one, even two or three, could be mistaken. Personal bias, (maybe Peter's remorse made him want to envision the Denied as alive) excitable nature (after all, women couldn't be trusted as rational) or hallucination could possibly explain away these appearances. But Jesus is suddenly there in their midst. There are at least twelve or thirteen men present; there may have been more, for both Luke and John use the more inclusive term disciples. He appears, speaks, allays their fears of some ghostly apparition by presenting his hands and feet with the evident nail scars. He invites them to handle him and experience the fact that he is indeed substantial ("flesh and bone"). He even eats a piece of broiled fish and some honeycomb in their presence.

Both Luke and John link this appearance with Jesus' commissioning of them for the continued task. "As the Father hath sent me, so send I you" John reports (John 20:21). He breathes upon them the Holy Spirit, promising the retention and remission of sins through them (John 20:22-23). Luke also, speaks of a continuing commission in this same context—"that repentance and remission of sins should be preached in his name to all nations beginning at Jerusalem, You are witnesses of these things" (Luke 24:47, 48). Luke also records the promise of power that the Father will give them (Luke 24:49), which presumably will empower them for their mission of witness and proclamation.

Eight days later (another first day of the week!), Jesus appears to the eleven again. This time that absent member, Thomas, is present. He had persisted in his doubt against all the testimony of these others. "I'll not believe," he says, "until I see in his hands the imprint of the nails, feel with my finger the mark those nails made, and put my hand into that side wound" (John 20:24ff.). Again the doors are shut and Jesus suddenly appears and offers to Thomas his hands and side. "Be a believer, not a doubter," Jesus says. Thomas, overwhelmed in the presence of the risen Lord, exclaims "My Lord and My God!" Then, Jesus says: "You have seen me, Thomas, and you have believed; but true happiness belongs to those who have not had such visual evidence and yet will believe."[11]

The last appearance that John records is that detailed and graphic account found in the epilogue to his gospel (John 21). Seven of the disciples met at the Sea of Galilee, perhaps to engage in some familiar activity to relax and restore them. At Peter's suggestion they go out for a night of fishing on the sea. Their labors are fruitless as dawn comes. A voice cries from the seaside: "Have you caught any fish?" they shout back, "No." The reply came back: "Cast the net on the right side of the boat and you will find some." They did so and were unable to haul the net in because of the abundance of the catch. The "beloved disciple" perceived this as miraculous and said to Peter: "That's the Lord!" Peter, in his haste, desiring to be the first to greet the Lord, put on his clothes and jumped into the sea; the remainder of the disciples brought the boat to shore dragging the net filled with fish behind them.

But John is not as concerned about this miraculous event as he is about the risen Lord's encounter with Peter, occurring after breakfast. Here, genuine love reflected by

---

11. John may not have had in mind those of our day who must have everything verified by sense experience, but his account certainly speaks to their limited experience.

103

service to the good Shepherd's potential flock ("So you love me?" Feed my sheep") is the message of the risen Lord. His final word to men is that given to Peter, "Follow me." Jesus has been raised to become the great Shepherd of His sheep and in following Him one testifies to being a part of his flock.

The final appearances that the Gospels record are also more than just visual sightings. On a mountain in Galilee Jesus appears (Matt. 28:16-20) to the apostles,[12] not just to be seen, but to give them continuing, perpetual commission, grounded in his authority guaranteed by his resurrection and involving the twofold pattern of discipleship-baptizing and teaching. The final appearance recorded in Luke's gospel sets the stage for the evangelist's continuation of the story of Christian origins in that second volume entitled, the "Acts of the Apostles" (Luke 24:50-52). This appearance is his parting farewell. In Acts 1 it is linked with Jesus' ascension and a reiterated and reinforced commission to be carried out as his witnesses following their empowerment (Acts 1:1-8).

So at different times of day; on different days during a period of forty days; in different areas ranging over several hundred square miles; in different circumstances; and for different purposes; Jesus appeared to varying groups of disciples, ranging from one or two to more than five hundred. This visual and audial evidence, coupled with the material facts, is probably the most cumulative evidence for any event recorded or accepted in all of human history.

---

12. Some scholars link this appearance with Paul's reference to an appearance to more than five hundred brethren at one time recorded in I Corinthians 15:6. There is no Scriptural evidence for this; it is suggested on the basis that no other Gospel appearances would accommodate this reference other than this one.

But one cannot see the Resurrection as some isolated well attested event. The resurrection of Jesus gives validity to Jesus' ministry disclosing the unity of his words and deeds, endorsing his promises and provision. Even more, the resurrection becomes the touchstone for understanding the Messianic message of the Old Testament, and the continuity and purpose of understanding a people of God through the centuries.

The resurrection of Jesus is the center of the Gospel. By its power a new people came into existence. That historic reality that we call Christianity can be understood only through faith in an actual resurrection, and, in turn, that historic existence of Church is, in itself, a proof of the reality of Jesus' resurrection.

FOR FURTHER STUDY

Green, Michael. *Man Alive!* London: InterVarsity Press, 1967.

Milligan, William. *The Resurrection of Our Lord.* New York: The Macmillan Co., 1917.

Beasley-Murray, G. R. *Christ is Alive.* London: Lutterworth Press, 1947.

Orr, James. *The Resurrection of Jesus Christ.* Cincinnati: Jennys and Graham, n.d.

Ramsay, A. M. *The Resurrection of Christ.* London: Geoffrey Bles, 1945.

QUESTIONS FOR DISCUSSION

1. Discuss Jesus' awareness of His impending death. Why is this significant to the resurrection account?

105

2. Why is the empty tomb important as material evidence for Christ's resurrection?
3. What custom concerning ancient and even current religions is lacking in early Christianity which by its absence supports the resurrection?
4. Did the empty tomb convince the disciples that Jesus had risen from the dead? Explain.
5. What is the significance of Jesus' suggestion to his disciples to touch Him?
6. Discuss the statement that the resurrection of Jesus is the center of the Gospel message.

Chapter Seven

PROCLAIMING THE RESURRECTION AS REFLECTED IN THE ACTS OF THE APOSTLES

"And we are witnesses to these things (crucifixion and resurrection of Jesus), and so also is the Holy Spirit . . ." (Acts 5:32).

Gospel, "good news," is to be preached! So John came into the wilderness of Judea, "preaching a baptism of repentance for the forgiveness of sin" (Mark 1:4). This "preaching in the wilderness" had a peculiar but meaningful message for Jewish auditors: "Repent for the kingdom of heaven is at hand" (Matthew 3:2). The kingdom, associated with the Messiah, was drawing near. John was quick to deny that he was the Messiah or any other special Messianic figure. He was just "a voice of one crying in the wilderness; prepare the way of the Lord" (Mark 1:3). There was one coming after him, mightier than he; "this one would baptize, not just in water but with the Holy Spirit and fire" (Matthew 3:11).

Jesus came from Nazareth to be baptized by John, thus "fulfilling all righteousness" (Matthew 3:15), by identifying himself with a sinful, needy people. God identified him as His "beloved Son" at his baptism (Matthew 3:16). Following a period of intense temptation, Jesus began his ministry. Mark says that "Jesus came into Galilee, preaching the gospel of God" and continuing to announce, as John had done, "the time is fulfilled, and the kingdom of God is at hand" (Mark 1:14, 15).

As the Gospels unfold we see that "the Gospel preached by Jesus became merged into the Gospel that *is* Jesus."[1]

---

1. A. M. Ramsay, p. 10.

It is still the Gospel of God (Romans 1:1, 2; II Corinthians 4:4); it is still the Gospel of the Kingdom (Acts 8:12; 28:23); but following the resurrection, the content is Jesus. That striking, almost redundant, phrase "to gospel Jesus" (*evangelidzomenoi ton Christon Jēsoun*) appears three different times in the book of Acts (Acts 5:42; 8:35; 9:20). The emphasis in each of these passages is that gospel preaching in the post-resurrection age is the proclamation of Jesus' life, death and resurrection. This constitutes the "drama of the mighty acts of God who came to deliver and to reign."[2]

Paul could later introduce that marvelous summary of Christian truth which he sent to the church at Rome by saying: "For I am not ashamed of the gospel: it is the power of God for salvation to everyone who believes, to the Jew first and also to the Greek" (Romans 1:16). The gospel, of which he speaks, is the "gospel of God, which he promised beforehand through his prophets in the holy scriptures, the gospel concerning his Son, who was descended from David according to the flesh and designated Son of God in power according to the Spirit of holiness by his resurrection from the dead, Jesus Christ our Lord . . ." (Romans 1:1-4).

The proclamation of this Gospel is unfolded in that second volume of Luke's work on the origins of Christianity which is termed the Acts of the Apostles. The first ("former treatise") volume was concluded with a summary of that post-resurrection period climaxed by an original reference to Jesus' ascension ("he parted from them"). This second volume, says Luke, picks up the story following "all that Jesus began to do and teach" (Acts 1:1). It tells of the continued action of the risen Jesus ("he presented himself alive after his passion by many proofs appearing to them during forty

---

2. *Ibid*, p. 10.

days" Acts 1:3) through the promised Spirit. This is why they must remain in Jerusalem (Acts 1:4-5). When such power is experienced *then* they will bear witness to Jesus, "in Jerusalem and all Judea, in Samaria and to the end of the earth" (Acts 1:8). As Luke recounts the story, this pattern is apparent. Gospel preaching begins in Jerusalem, it moves into Samaria, and, through the agency of that great gospel preacher, Paul, it moves toward the ends of the earth.

The Beginning: "To the Jew First"

It was during the Pentecost feast in the year A.D. 30 that the Gospel was first proclaimed in fulness. The outpouring (baptism) of Holy Spirit promised both in the Old Testament and by the forerunner John (Matthew 3:11), becomes reality even as the risen Jesus had told the eleven apostles just before ascending (Acts 1:5). Such power allowed these men "to speak in different dialects (different native languages)." This, along with other sights ("tongues of fire resting upon each one") and sounds ("a sound like the rush of a mighty wind"), drew a great multitude together (Acts 2:1-7). In their amazed bewilderment they cry out, "What does this mean?" Peter, countering the answer of drunkenness or insanity, points out that this is the fulfillment of that Messianic prophecy found in Joel (Acts 2:12-16). God had promised through Joel that in the last days he would pour out his Spirit upon all flesh and that he would show wonders and signs in the heavens "before the terrible day of the Lord came" (Acts 2:17-20).

But, before that terrible day of judgment, there is a day of grace. "Whoever calls upon the name of the Lord shall be saved" (Acts 2:21). It is this salvation Peter offers as he proclaims Jesus of Nazareth as God's Messianic Deliverer and Savior. Involved in the proclamation is the presentation of the humanity and miracle ministry of Jesus; his murder at the hands of lawless men; and his resurrection from the dead (Acts 2:22-24).

This resurrection, which Peter attributes to God ("God raised him up, having loosed the pangs of death because it was not possible for him to be held by it"), is foreseen by David. Speaking prophetically in Psalm 16, David had said:

> I saw the Lord always before me,
> for he is at my right hand that I may not be shaken;
> therefore my heart was glad, and my tongue rejoiced;
> moreover my flesh will dwell in hope
> For thou wilt not abandon my soul to Hades,
> nor let thy Holy One see corruption.
> Thou hast made known to me the ways of life;
> thou wilt make me full of gladness with thy presence.

Peter sees this as clear evidence of a promised resurrection (Acts 2:25-28). Since David died, was buried and his resting place was known to all, David must have been speaking of his Messianic Son whom God had promised to set upon the Davidic throne (Psalm 132:11). Jesus of Nazareth, therefore, is this resurrected Messiah, for he has been raised fulfilling the prophetic word. Peter adds that it is this same Jesus, who is exalted to God's righthand, who has poured

---

3. The very fact that Peter would speak of David's tomb still being occupied suggests that the "unoccupied tomb of Joseph" in which Jesus was laid is stark witness to Jesus' resurrection. The empty tomb is not unimportant in the proclamation of the early Church, and what is clearly viewed as material evidence in the Gospels is, at least, obliquely seen as evidence in the preaching recorded in the book of Acts (see also Acts 13:35-37). For further discussion see G. R. Beasley-Murray, p. 39f.

out his Spirit, producing these spectacular events (Acts 2:33). This, too, is in keeping with prophetic truth for, says Peter, David also said:

> "The Lord said to my Lord, Sit at my right hand, till I make thy enemies a stool for thy feet" (Acts 2:34).

What is the conclusion of the matter? Peter announces boldly: "Let all the house of Israel know assuredly that God has made this Jesus whom you crucified both Lord and Christ" (Acts 2:36). Upon this 3,000 Jews responded in faith, repentance and baptism (Acts 2:37-41), and became a part of that community of the risen Nazarene.

What is seen in the initial proclamation recorded by Luke in Acts 2, is repeated in Peter's address to the crowd that had gathered in the temple area following a notable healing miracle (Acts 3:1ff.). Peter declared that this healing act was not accomplished by him but through God's glorified servant, Jesus, who had been delivered up, denied and killed. When Pilate would have released him, Peter charges, "you denied the Holy and Righteous One, and asked for a murderer to be granted to you, and killed the Author of life, whom God raised from the dead" (Acts 3:14, 15). Peter not only sees himself and the other apostles as witnesses of the resurrection, but he also affirms that miracles wrought by them are done in the name of, through the power of, this risen Jesus.

In this message Peter is recorded as proclaiming the resurrection fact not only as fulfillment of prophetic hope (Acts 3:18, 22-24), but also as the ground for refreshing and renewal both now and in the future. How does God bless "all the families of the earth" as he promised Abraham? By raising up "his servant" and sending him "to you first, to bless you in turning everyone of you from your wickedness" (Acts 3:25-26). So, response to the call to repentance— "Repent, therefore, and turn again" (Acts 3:19a)—brings the "blotting out of sins" and "times of refreshing from the presence of the Lord" (Acts 3:19b). But such repentance and continued response in faith brings one into vital relation with the resurrected Lord who is the key to future renewal. Peter says: "And that he may send the Christ appointed for you, Jesus, whom heaven must receive until the time for establishing all that God spoke by the mouth of his holy prophets from of old" (Acts 3:20-21).

The resurrection is not only God's answer for human sin (Acts 2:38; 3:19, 26), but it is also God's mighty answer to murderous rebels. This is what Luke implies in Acts 4 and 5 as he records the conflict between the Apostles and the Sanhedrin. The priests, and Sadducee party generally, were greatly displeased that Peter and John were using the Temple precincts to proclaim "in Jesus the resurrection from the dead" (Acts 4:2). So, they arrest Peter and John and set a hearing on the morrow. Rather than being intimidated at the subsequent hearing before this prestigious, ruling body, Peter boldly emphasizes what he had previously stated in Solomon's portico. "Be it known to you all, and to all the people of Israel, that by the name of Jesus Christ of Nazareth, whom you crucified, whom God raised from the dead, by him this man is standing before you well" (Acts 4:10).

Peter, however, is not content merely to justify the healing act of the day before. He continues to show that this risen Jesus, to whom he gives witness, is that "Stone, rejected by you[4] builders, but which has become the head of the

---

4. He, thus, personally applies the Old Testament prophecy, showing that these leaders were indeed the rejecting ones.

corner" (Acts 4:11). Then, without hesitation, Peter dogmatically affirms: "And there is salvation in no one else, for there is no other name under heaven given among men by which we must be saved" (Acts 4:12). This is not just a question of power and authority, relating to healing acts and sacred places; it is a matter of life and death, salvation or damnation. It is only through the risen Jesus' name and power that Salvation can now be secured.

The Sanhedrin is perplexed. How can they do anything to these men in light of the notable miracle that had been performed by them in the presence of so many? Yet, they want to curb the spread of this new movement; so they decide to "warn them to speak no more to anyone in this name" (Acts 4:16, 17). The response to this warning and implied threat is that bold answers: "Whether it is right in the sight of God to listen to you rather than God, you must judge, for we cannot but speak of what we have seen and heard" (Acts 4:19, 20).

Upon returning to their brethren, Peter and John report on this confrontation. Immediately that great Messianic passage of Psalm 2 comes to mind.

> Why did the Gentiles rage,
> and the people imagine vain things?
> The kings of earth set themselves in array,
> and the rulers were gathered together,
> against the Lord and against his Anointed [Christ]
> (Psalm 2:1-2).

And that passage is interpreted as speaking of the opposition against God's "holy servant, Jesus" which had led to his death, but had been overcome in resurrection power. Such opposition would continue, but God is entreated, to grant boldness in speech as He continues to demonstrate

His power through miracles and signs performed through the name of his risen Son (Acts 4:29-31).

This opposition continues since the results of bold proclamation grow (Acts 5:14). The party of the Sadducees, under the leadership of the High Priest, arrest all the apostles, putting them in prison, intending to bring them before the Sanhedrin on the next day. Miraculously released, they are found early in the morning preaching "the words of this life" (Acts 5:17-21). Escorted to the council chamber, they are questioned by the high priest. His exasperation and frustration is apparent! "We strictly charged you not to teach in this name, yet here you have filled Jerusalem with your teaching and you intend to bring this man's blood upon us" (Acts 5:27, 28).[5]

The apostles' answer is "We must obey God rather than men." But, in addition, they take the offensive: "The God of your fathers raised Jesus whom you killed by hanging him on a tree.[6] God exalted him at his right hand as Leader and Savior, to give repentance to Israel and forgiveness of sins." Here, amidst the trappings of earthly authority, Jesus is presented as King (Leader), and through his resurrection "God confounds and ridicules the sin, the revolt, the foolishness of his adversaries."[7] But, at the same time, repentance and forgiveness of sins are distinct possibilities even for these who stand in opposition to the risen Lord. Luke may even be underscoring this truth in that later summary of

---

5. Apparently, he had forgotten that he had joined in the cry, at the time of Jesus' trial before Pilate, "his blood be upon us and on our children"(Mt. 27:25).

6. The ultimate insult to a Jew was to be executed by being "hung on a tree." Such a man is "accursed of God" (Deut. 21:23).

7. Markus Barth and Verne H. Fletcher, *Acquittal by Resurrection* (New York: Holt, Rinehart and Winston) 1964, p. 69.

numerical growth: "And the word of God increased; and the number of the disciples multiplied greatly in Jerusalem, and a great many of the priests were obedient to the faith" (Acts 6:7).

All these speeches which Luke records give a rather clear picture of the preaching (*kerygma*) of the Apostles. Several themes constantly recur. They can be summarized in this manner: (1) The messianic age has come. The things which God foretold by the prophets has been fulfilled. (2) This age comes through the ministry, death and resurrection of the Messiah. He came as heir of David, and his death was not a defeat but within God's foreordained purpose for man's ultimate redemption. In resurrection God identifies and indicates his Messiah, Jesus of Nazareth. (3) Jesus has been exalted at God's right hand. He is Lord, sharing in full sovereignty with the Father. (4) That sovereignty is demonstrated in the outpouring and indwelling presence of the Holy Spirit. The gift comes from the risen and exalted Jesus himself. (5) The end is at hand, and Jesus will return to renew all things and judge the living and the dead.[8] As A. M. Ramsay says:

> "This is the drama wrought by God in the events in Jerusalem whereof the Apostles are witnesses. It implies the

---

8. See C. H. Dodd, *The Apostolic Preaching and Its Development* (New York: Harper & Row, 1964), p. 17ff. These three lectures, first delivered in 1935 set out clearly that the New Testament shows that preaching and teaching are two distinct tasks of the early church. Leaders in the Nineteenth Century Reformation were spelling this out almost 100 years prior to Dodd's significant book, e.g., B. A. Hinsdale, in 1895, was writing: "Christianity consists of a Gospel and a discipline. Out of this fundamental distinction arises the two distinct functions of Christian ministry. . . . These two functions, which we constantly tend to blend and confuse, the New Testament as constantly keeps distinct and separate." *Jesus As Teacher* (St. Louis, Christian Publishing Co., 1895), p. 1.

coming of the new age, the breaking into history of the powers of the world to come. It impells the Apostles to summon men to repent and to be baptized into the name of Jesus.[9]

The Continuation: "Also to the Greek"

In Luke's account of the growth and development of the early Christian community, it is the Apostle Paul, or Saul of Tarsus, who is set forth as the major instrument of gospel proclamation to the Gentiles. Luke, wisely, gives attention to the way in which this Jew, Saul of Tarsus, comes to embrace the Christian faith and becomes the great missioner of the risen Jesus. In this narrative, the reality of resurrection looms large.

Saul appears on the scene in connection with the martyrdom of Stephen. Stephen began an impassioned but inflaming defense before the Sanhedrin in which he attempts to show that his preaching of Jesus is nothing more than the fulfillment of his Hebrew heritage (Acts 7:2-50). His witness reaches a bold crescendo: "You stiffnecked people, uncircumcised in heart and ears, you always resist the Holy Spirit. As your fathers did, so do you. Which of the prophets did not your fathers persecute? And they killed those who announced beforehand the coming of the Righteous One, whom you have now betrayed and murdered, you who received the law as delivered by angels and did not keep it" (Acts 7:51-53).

The anger of the Sanhedrin is outwardly apparent; but Stephen is not dissuaded. Full of the Spirit, he gazed into heaven and seeing the "glory of God, and Jesus standing

---

9. Ramsay, pp. 10-11.

at the right hand of God," he exclaimed: "Behold I see the heavens opened, and the Son of man standing at the right hand of God" (Acts 7:55, 56). His opponents, shocked by what they consider blasphemy, rush upon him, drag him out of the city and stone him. Those witnesses who according to Jewish law must actually cast the stones upon the one accused, lay their outer garments at the feet of a young man named Saul (Acts 7:58-59). And, this Saul (says Luke), "was consenting to his death" (Acts 8:1).

But Saul is no impartial, neutral bystander. He not only consents to Stephen's death, but, himself, became actively engaged in persecuting the Christians. He later testifies: "I persecuted this way unto the death" (Acts 22:4). Or, as he says to King Agrippa: "I thought that I ought to do many things against the name of Jesus of Nazareth. I did this, first, in Jerusalem, putting many of the saints in prison; and, when they were put to death, I gave my voice against them. I punished them frequently in every synogogue, compelling them to blaspheme. I was so filled with persecuting zeal against them, I even persecuted them in foreign cities" (Acts 26:9-11, free translation). He "made" havoc of—literally, "he was ravaging"—the church (Acts 8:3). This strong metaphor occurs only here in the New Testament and refers to such action as wild boars uprooting vineyards.

Saul's conversion from a persecutor of Christians to a preacher of Christ is given careful attention by Luke. In Chapter 9, Luke gives a general narrative of those elements involved in this crucial experience. In Chapter 22, and again in Chapter 26, Luke records (are these stenographic shorthand reports?) Paul's own recitals of this event. These three accounts, when taken together give a clear picture of the impact of this cluster of events upon Paul.

Securing letters of authority from the high priest, he begins his journey to Damascus. He will search out the Jewish community and any who may have come to faith in the impostor Jesus, he will bind and bring back to Jerusalem for trial, judgment, and punishment. As he nears Damascus about mid-day, a dazzling light shone around him and his companions. He fell to the ground and he heard a voice saying: "Saul, Saul, why are you persecuting me? Don't you know that it is hard to kick against the ox goad?" Saul replies: "Who are you?" The answer comes back: "I am Jesus of Nazareth whom you are persecuting."

Jesus of Nazareth, the crucified Galilean prophet is alive! Saul had met him in the dusty road outside Damascus. But, even more, he was guilty of persecuting him since he was persecuting those who were His body, His Church. Their message centering in a crucified, risen Savior and Lord was not false but true. Jesus was no impostor, but the very Son of God. Trembling and astonished, Saul can only say, "Lord what will you have me do?" Blinded, he is led into the city, where, said the risen Lord, "you shall be told what you must do."

As Saul waited in the house of Judas on the street called Straight, one of the Christians of Damascus is prepared by the Lord to be the instrument of his initial conversion (Acts 9:10-16). Ananias comes to Saul who has been engaged in penitential prayer. "I have come, brother Saul," Ananias says, "so that you may receive your sight and know the fulness of the Holy Spirit. There is no need to wait; rise up and be baptized. As you do so, you can know your sins are washed away and you can continue to call upon his name" (Acts 9:17-19; 22:16).

118

Even from this beginning stage of his Christian experience, Saul knows that he has been specifically chosen as an envoy of this risen Jesus. This Jesus told him that he had appeared for a definite purpose: "to make you a minister and a witness both of those things which you have seen, and of those things which you shall see later as I appear to you . . . to open the eyes of the Gentiles—to whom I am sending you—and to turn them from darkness to light, from the power of Satan to God; that they may receive forgiveness of sins, and an inheritance among those who are sanctified by faith in Me" (Acts 26:16-18). Or, as the Lord said to Ananias, "he is a chosen vessel unto me, to bear my name before the Gentiles, and kings, and the children of Israel. For I will show him how great things he must suffer for my name's sake" (Acts 9:15, 16).

In Paul's experience, the resurrection of Jesus is stark reality. He has seen him, heard him, conversed with him! This is Jesus of Nazareth, raised from the dead, exalted to God's right hand! What Stephen had seen and expressed was true. But, even more, this special manifestation of the risen Christ to him—"as of one born out of due time" (I Corinthians 15:7)—qualifies him as an eyewitness, a special apostle of Jesus. "Am I not an apostle?" He asks the Corinthians. "Have I not seen Jesus Christ our Lord?" (I Corinthians 9:1). To him is given a special apostleship to the Gentiles (Eph. 3:6-8), which will be his special burden the remainder of his life. He would refer to himself as "least of all the Saints" (Eph. 3:8) and as "chief of sinners" (I Timothy 1:15), because he had been a "blasphemer, a persecutor and injurious" of the church (I Timothy 1:13), but he would revel in the "grace given him" so that he could "preach the unsearchable riches of Christ" (Eph. 3:8).

Luke continues the narrative of Saul's subsequent career. Almost immediately, after his baptism, he is preaching Christ in the synagogues of Damascus. Luke describes the content of his preaching as showing that Christ "is the Son of God" (Acts 9:20) and "proving that this (Jesus) is the very Christ" (Acts 9:22). Saul is so fervent and powerful in his preaching that certain of the Damascene Jews plot to kill him. Knowing of this conspiracy Paul is aided by the disciples in Damascus and escapes to Jerusalem.

Suspicion and opposition at Jerusalem was so strong, in spite of Barnabas' mediatorial attempt to eliminate it (Acts 9:26-28), that Saul was encouraged to return to his home city of Tarsus in Cilicia.[10] Removing to Cilicia Saul does not come back into Luke's account until later when Barnabas seeks him out and brings him to Antioch to share with him in a ministry of evangelism and teaching (Acts 11:25ff.). It is from Antioch that the Gentile mission is launched (Acts 13:1-3), as Barnabas and Saul are separated and sent out by the Church as directed by the Holy Spirit.

Paul's preaching, on this first missionary journey and subsequent journeys, is continuous with that which was proclaimed in Jerusalem. The pattern is somewhat different. It is "to the Jews first, but also to the Greek" (Romans 1:16). Wherever Paul went, he would go to the synagogue if there was one in that city. There, he would reason with them, showing by Scripture that Jesus of Nazareth is the long-awaited Messiah, proven by his resurrection, offering salvation to all. If the Jewish community would not accept his message, he would then turn to the Gentiles. Such pattern would be repeated again and again (see Acts 13, 14, 17, 18).

---

10. The time spent in this area occupied about four or five years. Paul apparently is not inactive, for Acts 15:4 indicates that Paul and Silas went through Syria and Cilicia confirming the Churches.

An excellent example of this is given by Luke in Acts 13, not long after Barnabas and Saul began their missionary labors. The party has moved into the Asia Minor interior and has come to Pisidian Antioch. They enter the synagogue on the Sabbath, and, following the usual preliminary lectionary readings, the rulers of the synagogue ask them to give some word of explanation if they care to do so (Acts 13:14, 15). Paul[11] uses this as an opportunity to proclaim Jesus as Messiah. He begins his message with a recital of key events of Old Testament history (what some call the Old Testament kerygma)—God's call to Abraham, the exodus from Egypt by God's mighty hand, the forty years of trial in the wilderness, the possessing of the land, the judges, and the beginning of the kingdom under Samuel and Saul (Acts 13:17-21). In this brief recital Paul speaks of God's choice of David to be King in Saul's stead. From this historical perspective he moves to the promised Messiah. "Of this man's [David] seed God has raised up for Israel, according to his promise, a Savior, Jesus" (Acts 13:23). This Jesus, was preceded by John the baptizer, who testified to his greatness. This Jesus, condemned and crucified, fulfills those prophetic voices "read every Sabbath" (Acts 13:27). They took him "down from the tree," continues Paul, "and laid him in a tomb. But God raised him from the dead, and he was seen by those who had come up with him from Galilee over a period of many days. They have become witnesses unto the people" (Acts 13:29-32).

On the basis of this resurrection, "glad tidings" about the fulfillment of the promises made to the fathers can be declared. Paul says: "God has fulfilled these promises to us

---

11. By this time Luke is now referring to Saul as Paul and he has assumed the leadership of the mission party. At Antioch of Syria it was Barnabas and Saul, from Antioch of Pisidia on it is Paul and Barnabas.

who are their children by raising Jesus; as it is written in the second psalm: Thou art my Son, today I have begotten thee! And as for the fact that he raised him from the dead, no more to return to corruption, he spoke in this way, 'I will give you the holy and sure blessings of David.' And, in another psalm, he says: 'Thou wilt not let thy Holy One see corruption. David, after he had served his own generation by God's will, fell asleep, was laid with his fathers, and saw corruption. But he whom God raised up saw no corruption" (Acts 13:33-37). Forgiveness of sin, freedom from bondage, is now proclaimed through this risen Jesus.

The Jewish community in Antioch desired to hear more so they invited Paul to address them again the following Sabbath. The next Sabbath saw not only Jews and devout proselytes in attendance but Gentiles as well. Upon this, certain Jews, out of jealousy and envy, began to oppose, revile and contradict Paul (Acts 13:42ff.). In response to this Paul and Barnabas speak out boldly, saying, "It was necessary that the Word of God should be spoken *first* to you. Since you reject it, judging yourselves unworthy of eternal life, we turn to the Gentiles" (Acts 13:46). They see this move within the prophetic will of God as well, saying: "For so the Lord has commanded us, saying, 'I have set you to be a light for the Gentiles, that you may bring salvation to the uttermost parts of the earth' " (Acts 12:47, quoting Isa. 49:6).

Paul's preaching centers in the crucified, risen Lord through whom Salvation is now offered to all. His pattern of evangelism is "to the Jew first, but also the Greek." To the Jew, he would explain and prove "that it was necessary for Messiah (Christ) to suffer and to rise from the dead" (Acts 17:3a). He would then show that "this Jesus whom I proclaim to you is the Messiah [Christ]" (Acts 17:b). Skillfully using the Old Testament Scriptures, he would demonstrate that the hope of Israel centers in a Deliverer, the Messiah; and that this hope is fulfilled in resurrection. Later in his ministry when he stands before the Sanhedrin in Jerusalem, he will boldly proclaim: "with respect to the hope of the resurrection of the dead I am on trial" (Acts 23:6). And, before Felix in Caesarea, he defends his faith and life as but the fulfillment of his heritage. "This I admit," he says, "that according the Way, which they [his opponents] call a sect, I worship the God of our fathers, believing everything laid down by the law written in the prophets, having a hope in God which these themselves accept, that there will be a resurrection of both the just and the unjust" (Acts 24:14-15). It was in Jesus, risen from the dead, proved God's Messiah, that this hope finds its fulfillment.

Paul's approach to Gentile audiences, however, was different. The message is the same—the risen Jesus—but he does not come to this central preachment through Jewish Scripture. Early in Paul's ministry this difference is seen. On that first missionary journey, Paul and Barnabas arrive in the Phrygian-Galactic region of Asia Minor. At Lystra, Paul heals a crippled man. The inhabitants of Lystra interpret this as a special appearance of the gods; supposing Barnabas to be their patron god, Zeus or Jupiter, and Paul, because he was the chief speaker or "interpreter," Hermes or Mercury[12] (Acts 14:8-13). Upon discovering that these citizens are about to sacrifice to them as deities, Paul and Barnabas rush among them, showing that they are men of flesh, "men of like nature," not gods. This gives Paul opportunity to

---

12. These are Greek and Roman designation, respectively of these ancient mythological deities. F. F. Bruce notes that there is archaeological evidence that Zeus and Hermes were dually worshiped in this area. *The Acts of the Apostles* (Grand Rapids: Wm. B. Eerdmans, 1951), pp. 281-282.

witness to these pagan Gentiles about the true God who alone is to be worshiped and served. He says, in effect, "Our purpose in coming is to bring you good news about this living God. This living God who made the heavens, the earth and sea, would have you turn from these vain idols to Him. He also allowed you to walk in your own ways all these past generations; but he has not left you without a witness of his power and goodness for he has given you rain from heaven and fruitful seasons, satisfying your hearts with food and gladness" (Acts 14:15-18, freely translated).

This approach to Gentiles is best seen in Paul's ministry in Athens. He had come to Athens from Macedonia. He had left Macedonia because of intense persecution by unbelieving Jews (Acts 17:13-15). Christian brethren had escorted him as far as Athens and he was waiting for Silas and Timothy to join him here in this ancient city described by the poet as:

> Athens, the eye of Greece, Mother of Arts
> And Eloquence, native to famous wits
> Or hospitable, in her sweet recess,
> City or Suburban, studious walks and shades.[13]

Lovely as this ancient city was, Paul could not just sit about waiting. In fact, Luke says (using as strong a words as possible) Paul's spirit was "provoked" ("enraged") as he saw evidence—beautiful though it may be—of the violation of that Second Commandment. Wherever he looked he saw some idol, deific image or shrine. So he joined battle; first, with Jews and devout persons[14] in the synagogue, and also with the Greeks in the marketplace.

---

13. Quoted by Bruce, p. 331.

14. This phrase is used by Luke almost technically to refer to those Gentiles who were "proselytes at the Gate," that is, committed to Jewish faith but failing to go through the ritual acts to make them actual proselytes.

Some of these Greek philosophers—both from the Stoic and Epicurean schools—were amused and perplexed. Amused, for Paul appeared to be like a gutter-sparrow, a "seed-picker,"[15] who had picked up bits of knowledge here and there and was intent upon telling others. Perplexed, because he seemed to them to set forth "strange deities," as he spoke of Jesus and the resurrection (Acts 17:18). Apparently, they assumed that the feminine word, *anastasis*, "resurrection," was the female counterpart to the male, Jesus, and that these were new gods being proclaimed. Since, the Council of the Aeropagus, which met on the Hill of Ares (or Mars), west of Acropolis, still had jurisdiction over religious matters, these philosophers bring Paul before the Council to present his strange teachings (Acts 17:19-20).

Here in the midst of the Council of the Aeropagus, Paul presents his masterful address, or at least the introduction to an intended address. He begins by faintly praising the Athenians: "I see that you are excessively religious" (Acts 17:22). An example of that religious fervor is cited. "As I passed along and observed the objects of your worship, I found an altar with this inscription, 'To the Unknown God' "[16] (Acts 17:23). This is Paul's point of contact; his starting point. "It is this unknown God [unknown to you but known to me] that I proclaim," Paul states boldly. "Furthermore," says Paul, "He made the universe and all within it, thus being Lord of heaven and earth. He does not need a human-made shrine to live in, nor does He need to be served by human hands as if He needed something that humans could

---

15. This is what the word, *spermalogos*, originally meant (Acts 17:18).

16. It would not be out of order to translate this inscription (which is recorded in Luke without a definite article) "To any unknown God." Apparently, such altars were common in the ancient world to allow for any deity overlooked or unnamed. Bruce, p. 336.

give. On the contrary, He gives life and breath and every other thing to man, since He made all nations of men that live all over the earth; He determines their allotted times; He fixes the boundaries of their national existence. Furthermore, He desires that they should seek Him, though He is not far from any one of us for 'in him we live and move and have our being' and 'we are indeed his offspring' even as your poets have indicated [though they certainly did not know the full reality of what they were saying]. Since this is how we should think of ourselves—as this sovereign God's offspring—we ought not think of Deity as like gold, silver, or stone, or in the fashion of the representations created by the art and imagination of man" (Acts 17:24-29, free translation).

Now Paul is ready to move to the central core of his proclamation. "This God" Paul says by way of transition, "is a gracious God, willing to overlook these times of ignorance. But now He commands all men, everywhere, to repent" (Acts 17:30, see also Acts 26:20). Why now? Why was judgment suspended until now? Because this is the "fulness of the times" (Gal. 4:4) and God has set forth a man, His Son, "by whom he will now judge the world in righteousness" (Acts 17:31a). This man appointed has every right to judge and that judgment's assurance is guaranteed in that God has raised him from the dead (Acts 17:31b). Here is what Paul meant when he spoke of Jesus and the resurrection!

Undoubtedly Paul intended to go into a detailed narrative about Jesus' historical appearance, his life and ministry, his death, burial, and resurrection, but at his reference to "the resurrection of dead men" he is stopped by derisive laughter (Acts 17:32). The idea of the immortality of the soul had long been known in Greek thinking, but Greek philosophy

126

had no room for the resuscitation of dead bodies. In fact, Aeschylus, the Greek poet, represents the god, Apollo, as saying, on the occasion of the inauguration of the very court where Paul was pleading his religious case, to the city's patron goddess Athene:

> "Once a man dies and the earth drinks up his blood, there is no resurrection (*Anastasis*)."[17]

Christian proclamation centers in the resurrection of Jesus Christ from the dead. His death as atonement and ransom, the deliverance promised to captive Israel, judgment of dead works and licentious practice,[18] all revolve around this attested event. Therefore, whether the audience is Jew or Gentile, this is the heart of proclamation. Gentiles may need to be shown who the God of Salvation is that sent Jesus and raised him from the dead, but the message to them comes around to this central event.

The book of Acts is the book of witness. Those twelve Galileans had all seen Jesus following his death and burial. "He is alive," they exulted! There is no question in their mind. "This same Jesus, whom you crucified" (Acts 2:36) is the one who was raised. This is the testimony of Peter. When Paul came to Damascus he saw no vague Heavenly Being, no impersonal Messiah, but that same Jesus, "the Person of whom he had heard so much, whose life and character and lineaments had become well known to him through his persecuting contacts with the new sect." To have seen some sort of heavenly Messiah, like that spoken of in the apocalyptic Jewish literature which he had pored over in his studies

---

17. See Bruce, p. 340. See also Appendix, which sets out this distinction between Greek philosophy and Biblical thought.

18. Thus, we can understand Paul's witness before Felix (Acts 24:24-25).

at the College in Jerusalem, would never have changed Paul so radically. It might only have strengthened his pride and confirmed him in his continued hatred of these followers of a crucified Nazarene. Dr. James Stewart does not over-state the case: "We cannot therefore too strongly underline the fact that it was Jesus, and none other, the Jesus who had been crucified, who appeared to Paul in the way. So came the great discovery that Jesus was alive. Then His followers had been right after all! Then the faith on which they had staked their lives was really true! Then Stephen's dying declaration that he saw Jesus on the right hand of God had been, not blasphemy, but sober, literal fact! Then all that those persecuted men and women had said about having their Leader with them still, about holding daily intimate communion with Him, had been no fabricated, preposterous story, as it had seemed, but strictly accurate and genuine! It was a staggering discovery."[19]

And this discovery would continue its impact on Paul's life. More than any other of those whom the Spirit used to strengthen and encourage the churches through an inspired literature, Paul would see the implications of the Resurrection of Jesus in their depth and breadth and heighth. Subsequent chapters will explore these implications.

QUESTIONS FOR DISCUSSION

1. Define "gospel." Compare and contrast "gospel preaching" as carried out by John the Baptist, Jesus, and the Apostles.

---

19. James S. Stewart, *A Man In Christ* (New York: Harper & Row, n.d.), p. 134.

2. Why would the gospel be proclaimed "to the Jew first"? Discuss the approach taken by the Apostles when their audiences were largely Jewish.
3. Define *kerygma*.
4. Show *how* the gospel was preached to the Gentiles. Compare this to the *way* it came to Jews.
5. Read carefully and discuss Paul's address at Athens recorded in Acts 17.
6. Show how Jesus and His redemptive action are the center of the Gospel, no matter to whom it was addressed.

Chapter Eight

RESURRECTION AND CHRISTIAN BAPTISM

"And you were buried with him in baptism, in which you were also raised with him through faith in the working of God, who raised him from the dead" (*Col. 2:12*).

There is no question but that baptism is significant. The New Testament revelation begins with a picture of God's prophet, John, proclaiming a "baptism leading to repentance and remission of sins" (Matt. 3:1-12; Mark 1:1-8; Luke 3:3-7). It reveals that this John was immersing these penitents in the Jordan River as a preparatory step to the coming of the Kingdom. Even, Jesus, God's Messiah, sees his own baptism at John's hand as that which "fulfills all righteousness," though certainly this sinless one had no need for penitence.

According to John's gospel Jesus and his disciples continue and extend this preparatory work begun by John the Baptist (John 3:22); though the evangelist John is careful to point out that Jesus himself, unlike John, did not personally perform any baptismal acts (John 4:1-2). Though there is nothing more said about baptism as related to the continued proclamation of the coming Kingdom, it may be inferred that this practice continued at least in the earlier, more popular stage of Jesus' ministry.

It is quite clear that the risen Jesus included baptism as a vital function in his final commission to those specially chosen apostles. As Matthew states it quite clearly: "Now the eleven disciples went to Galilee to the mountain to which Jesus had directed them . . . and Jesus came and said to them, "All authority in heaven and earth has been given to me. When you have gone, make disciples of all nations, by (initially) baptizing them in the name of the Father and of

130

the Son and of the Holy Spirit, and by continuing to teach them all that I have commanded you. I will be with you always even to the end of the age" (Matt. 28:16, 18-20, free translation).

Even though the longer ending of Mark may not have been part of the original, the significance of baptism in the ongoing evangelistic outreach of the church is nonetheless emphasized. It is apparent that Mark 16:9-20 is a summary added to the Gospel, for it summarized resurrection appearances found in both Matthew and Luke. Yet, this passage reflects what was currently accepted in the early church relative to baptism's place in response to Gospel preaching. This unknown editor writes: "Go into all the world and preach the Gospel to the whole creation. He who believes and is baptized shall be saved; he who is unwilling to believe will be condemned" (Mark 16:15-16).

What is preparatory in the Gospels becomes permanent in the book of Acts. Preparatory baptism (whether administered by John or Jesus' disciples) is superseded. In Acts 19 Luke records that Paul encountered certain disciples "who knew only the baptism of John" and, therefore, had not received nor knew about the Holy Spirit (Acts 19:1-3). Paul explains the nature of John's preparatory baptism: "John baptized with the baptism of repentance, telling the people to believe in the one who was to come after him, that is, Jesus" (Acts 19:4). Upon this these twelve disciples were baptized in the name of the Lord Jesus and were recipients of a special endowment of the Holy Spirit through the imposition of Paul's hands.[1]

---

1. I take it that this unique situation was to give them immediate awareness of the Spirit's presence, through the resultant *glossolalia* (tongue-speaking) and prophetic utterance.

The linking of baptism to the salvation coming through Jesus and the subsequent reception of the Holy Spirit as abiding presence is clearly seen in Acts. Following Peter's Spirit-directed presentation of the Gospel on the day of Pentecost, in which the death and resurrection of Jesus are so focal, the multitudes are convicted of their involvement in this great, tragic crime and cry out "Brethren, what must we do?" (Acts 2:24-37). In answer Peter says: "All of you must repent, and each one of you must be baptized in the name of Jesus Christ in order to be forgiven and receive the Holy Spirit as God's gift" (Acts 2:38, free translation). In Acts 22, where Paul recounts his own conversion to Christ, he also links baptism with cleansing or "washing" away of one's sins and the reception of the Holy Spirit (Acts 22:12-16; see also Acts 9:17).

In these passages, and others, baptism is the immersion of a penitent believer in water, by the authority (in the name of) Jesus Christ, so that such a believer may know that his sins are remitted and may experience the personal presence of Jesus Christ through His indwelling Spirit. By this means, such a penitent was added to the community of faith (Acts 2:41, 47), born into the family or kingdom of God (John 3:3-5), and became a member of the Body of Christ (I Corinthians 12:13f.). Every actual conversion recorded in this inspired volume involves this action.

Some have tried to draw some antagonistic distinction between what they call "spirit-baptism" and "water-baptism." In Acts one and two these two concepts are linked together but not set off in opposition. F. F. Bruce points out that in these passages there is "no suggestion that water baptism is to be superseded by Spirit-baptism. . . . The baptism of the Spirit which it was our Lord's prerogative to bestow was, strictly speaking, something that took place once for all on the day of Pentecost when He poured forth "the promise of the Father" on His disciples and thus constituted them the new people of God; baptism in water continued to be the external sign by which individuals who believed the gospel message, repented of their sins, and acknowledged Jesus as Lord, were publicly incorporated into the Spirit-baptized fellowship of the new people of God."[2] Bruce also affirms that "the idea of an unbaptized Christian is simply not entertained in the New Testament."[3]

But the significance of baptism transcends the idea of incorporation. It is, indeed, the "rite of initiation" into the Christian community; but it is much more. This much more is closely tied to the resurrection.

Baptism, Salvation, and Resurrection

Adolf Schlatter declares that "there is no gift or power which the Apostolic documents do not ascribe to baptism."[4] What he meant was that as a consequence of Christ's redemption guaranteed by His resurrection, baptism is the occasion of available grace. So forgiveness of sin (Acts 2:38); cleansing from sin (Acts 22:16; I Corinthians 6:11); union with Christ (Galatians 3:27), particulary in his death, burial, and resurrection (Romans 6:3ff.; Col. 2:11f.); participation in Christ's sonship (Galatians 3:28ff.); membership in the Church, Christ's spiritual body (I Cor. 12:13; Gal. 3:27-29);

---

2. F. F. Bruce, *The Book of Acts,* (NLCNT) (Grand Rapids: Wm. B. Eerdmans, 1945), pp. 76-77. See also I Corinthians 12:13.

3. *Ibid,* p. 78.

4. Quoted by G. R. Beasley-Murray, *Baptism in the New Testament* (Grand Rapids: Wm. B. Eerdmans, 1962), p. 263.

possession of new life in the Spirit (Acts 2:38; I Cor. 12:13); regeneration (John 3:5; Titus 3:5); the pledge of the resurrection of the body (Eph. 1:3; 4:30); and inheritance of the kingdom (John 3:5) are all vitally linked with baptism.

How can this be? How can an outward act like baptism have such cosmic significance? It is because baptism is sacramental in the highest sense. Just as in the redemptive act of Jesus' death, burial and resurrection God was at work, so in baptism God's gracious action continues. This is brought out clearly in I Peter 3:21. The salvation of Noah and his family is set out as prefiguring the salvation the Christian knows through baptism. Just as God, in gracious action, warned Noah (Genesis 6:13f.), instructed him as to the particulars of the ark, the instrument of his safety (Genesis 6:14f.), and "shut the door" (Genesis 7:16), so God's gracious action comes through baptism. But there is nothing magical in the water, for saving baptism is not "the removal of dirt from the body," but "a pledge to God proceeding from a good conscience"[5] through the resurrection of Christ. The power of baptism is in the resurrection of Christ; it has no meaning apart from that; it has no efficacy divorced from Jesus and His obedience. Baptism, properly understood, is that supreme occasion—that focal place and definite time —where God, through Jesus Christ, "deals with a man who comes to Him through Christ on the basis of his redemption acts."[6]

This high sacramentalism is born out by that passage in Hebrews 10:22, 23. Reflecting the ritual of the Day of Atonement the writer within this context is showing that

5. Beasley-Murray, "The baptismal candidate answers affirmatively to God's request for faith and obedience," p. 261.

6. *Ibid*, p. 262.

Jesus, the great High Priest, has entered the heavenly sanctuary with His own blood. In so doing this great High Priest opens the way to God for all who would approach Him with a "true heart." The exhortation follows: "Let us draw near with a true heart in full assurance of faith, having our hearts sprinkled clean from an evil conscience and having our bodies washed with pure water." It is evident that a contrast is being made between an internal and external act. The external sprinkling of blood as a symbolic act of the Old Testament is here internalized. The blood sprinkling our hearts clean is that blood which our High Priest presents in our behalf. At that time outwardly our bodies are washed—we are being baptized.

The cleansing power is not water but precious blood; but it is through obedience in baptism that such saving power is known. All of this because the one who died overcame death, was glorified in resurrection power, and sits at God's right hand as great High Priest, "saving to the uttermost those that draw near to God through Him, since He ever lives to make intercession for them" (Hebrews 7:25).

Salvation is offered on the basis of what Christ (Romans 4:25) accomplished. He "was put to death for our trespasses" says Paul; but this is known only because of that inseparable divine event of resurrection. He "was raised for our justification" (Romans 4:25). Such justification is a free gift to be appropriated by faith (Romans 5:1f.). But faith is demonstrated in baptism, which not only symbolizes His death and resurrection (Romans 6:3f.), but is a sacramental sign of God's gracious action. The baptized are "new creatures" (II Cor. 5:17), "rising to walk in newness of life" (Rom. 6:4), anticipating that time when God's glory "shall burst upon us" in the future (Romans 8:18).

135

Is baptism, then, necessary to Salvation? To the early Christians this would be almost tantamount to asking, Is becoming a Christian necessary to salvation? Since baptism brings persons "into Christ" (Romans 6:3, 4; I Cor. 12:13), and, at baptism, these persons are "added to" the church, the body of the faithful (Acts 2:41, 47), it follows that baptism is necessary. It is questionable, then, that saving faith can exist apart from baptism, for such faith, in the New Testament, is inseparably linked to baptism. Alan Richardson, the Anglican scholar, is emphatic upon this point: "To regard sincere faith as adequate to salvation apart from baptismal incorporation into Christ's Body is sheer 'Christian Science' by the standards of New Testament theology; by ignoring the reality of the Body it makes salvation a subjective affair, a disembodied soul-salvation of individuals who have 'enjoyed' a certain 'experience'. . . . Believing while dispensing with the act of obedience, with the act of baptism, is a kind of docetism, and is thus not belief in the New Testament sense at all. . . . The actual historical baptism of the individual Christian is important precisely in the sense in which the actual historical death of Christ is important. Both are *ephapax,* unrepeatable."[7]

Baptism and Jesus' Resurrection

Perhaps the relation of baptism to salvation can be seen more clearly as those passages are explored which point up baptism's symbolic nature. In the Roman letter, Paul sets this out beautifully. "How shall we who are dead to sin live any longer in sin? Do you not know that all of us who have been baptized into Jesus Christ were baptized into his

---

7. *Introduction to the Theology of the New Testament* (London: 1958), p. 348.

death? We were buried, therefore, with him by baptism into death, so that as Christ was raised from the dead by the glory of the Father, we too might walk in newness of life. For if we have been united with him in a death like his, we shall certainly be united with him in a resurrection like his. We know that our old self was crucified with him so that the sinful body may be destroyed and that we may no longer be enslaved to sin. For he who has died is freed from sin. But if we have died with Christ, we believe that we shall also live with him. For we know that since Christ has been raised from the dead, he will never die again for death no longer has any power over him. The death he died, he died to sin once for all, but the life he lives, he lives to God. So you also must consider yourselves dead to sin and alive to God in Christ Jesus" (Romans 6:2-11).

This passage, and its continuation, is primarily concerned with the process of sanctification, of living in that manner which demonstrates that sin's hold over the Christian's life is broken. However, it also speaks to the place and significance of baptism in God's economy of salvation, linking it closely with those saving events culminating in Jesus' resurrection. J. S. Lamar believes that this great passage proves and illustrates this distinct proposition: *"What the Lord did and suffered in order to enter into His glory must, in some sense, be done and suffered by everyone who is to participate in that glory."*[8]

Salvation response, Lamar is saying, is a re-enactment of the history out of which the glory of Christ sprang. That

---

8. J. S. Lamar. "The History of Redemption Reproduced in the Redeemed," in Z.T. Sweeney, ed., *New Testament Christianity*, Vol. I (Columbus, Ind.: privately published, 1923), p. 158.

response reaches its climax and summarization in the baptismal process. There is the threat of death, the spiritual crucifixion paralleling his death on the cross. "I have been crucified with Christ" Paul declares (Galatians 2:20a). Here in the baptismal act is seen that poignant picture of His dead, lifeless body, placed in a borrowed tomb. "We are buried with him by baptism." But that tomb, solid as it was could not contain Him, and, in the baptismal act, the penitent believer is raised "like as Christ" to live anew, even as did Jesus. This baptismal act, this obedient response, is also a pledge to us of coming glory. "Our citizenship is in heaven" Paul declares (Philippians 3:20). "Whom he justified, them he also glorified," he adds (Romans 8:30); but the fulness of that glory will "be revealed" in the future (Romans 8:18). "We are in this respect like the Savior in His humiliation—*our glory is not manifested. . . .* It is 'the *manifestation* of the sons of God,' for which the earnest 'expectation of the creature waiteth'; and this is not the *impartation* of glory, but 'the *revelation* of glory that is *in* us.'"[9]

Paul in other passages, links together baptism, Jesus' resurrection and regeneration. Regeneration is "quickening," making alive what was once dead. Christ "makes alive" those "dead in trespasses and sins" and causes them to "be seated in heavenly places" (Eph. 2:1-10). The resurrection power of God that, literally and physically, made the dead corpse of Jesus of Nazareth to live eternally is the power that makes possible this spiritual regeneration. It is at baptism that such an enactment occurs. Listen to the Apostle! "You were buried with him in baptism, in which you also were raised with him through faith in the power

9. J. S. Lamar, *ibid*, p. 168.

of God, who raised him from the dead. And you, who were dead in trespasses and the uncircumcision of your flesh God made alive together with him, having forgiven us all our trespasses, having canceled the bond which stood against us with its legal demands; this he set aside, nailing it to the cross" (Col. 2:12-14).

One may not go as far as Alexander Campbell who said "Baptism is regeneration"; but one cannot escape the clear implication that baptism, in its original mode of immersion, is that place where the individual "existentially participates" in Jesus' death and resurrection. By the power displayed at that first resurrection, the individual is made alive and can consider himself to be "risen with Christ" seated with Christ in heavenlies (Col. 3:1; Eph. 2:4, 5).

Karl Barth, the great Swiss theologian stresses the significance of this "existential participation" that baptism provides. He says, "it is impossible to understand the meaning of baptism, unless one keeps in mind that it implies a threat of death and a deliverance to life; not that, generally speaking, the custom followed in baptism is to be called good or bad as it more or less adequately represents such a process.

"What baptism portrays, according to the basic passage in Romans vi. 1f., is a supremely critical happening, —a real event whose light and shade fall upon the candidate in the course of his baptism. This happening is his participation in the death and resurrection of Jesus Christ: that is, the fact that at a particular time and place in the year A.D. 30 outside Jerusalem on the cross at Golgotha, not Jesus Christ alone, but with Him also this particular individual died eternally, and that, in the garden of Joseph of Arimathea, not Jesus Christ alone, but with Him also this particular individual rose from the dead for evermore. Not only his

139

sins and he not only in his character as sinner—but really he himself as subject, met his death then and there, was then and there buried, so that, although he is still in existence, he is in effect now no more. And not only did God's grace begin for him then and there, but also his real life in God's eternal Kingdom and therefore in its glory; so that he can now no more die, but can only live, even though he will one day die. Therefore, according to Romans vi. he is now dead to sin, but has become alive unto God for an existence in His Service.

"This is what happens for him and to him in the death and resurrection of Jesus Christ; in very truth for him and to him, in the power of the Holy Spirit which is poured out upon him. For it is the Holy Spirit, proceeding from Jesus Christ and moving this particular man, which unites him to Jesus Christ like a body to its head, making him belong to Jesus Christ and making everything that Jesus Christ is and does belong to him. This happens in such a manner that he can no more be without Jesus Christ because Jesus Christ can no more be without him; he is no more outside but in Jesus Christ and with Him to the end of all things, standing with Him at the dawn of a new heaven and a new earth. 'Wherefore if any man is in Christ, he is a new creature: the old things are passed away: behold they are become new' (II Cor. 5:17)."[10]

Baptism, Resurrection and Purity of Life

These passages which are so crucial in our understanding of how baptism is related to salvation, are also significant in

---

10. Karl Barth, *The Teaching of the Church Regarding Baptism* (London: SCM Press, 1948), pp. 11-12.

emphasizing the ethical demands of the Gospel. Baptism is a moral-religious act as well as an existential spiritual event. As Dr. Beasley-Murray notes: "The basic significance of baptism is participation in the death and resurrection of Christ, with the tremendous consequences that involves a new life in the Holy Spirit orientated towards the all holy God. The death of the baptized is a death *to sin,* and the life is a life *in* God, a life *after* God, a life *for* God."[11]

J. S. Lamar, after showing that the alien sinner comes to participate in those "acts of history out of which Christ's glory sprang" and by doing so is saved by and united with Christ, states that the Christian "is now remanded to the *example of Christ's life upon the earth,* to reproduce *that,* in order to his final glorification. In other words, being made *a son of God,* he is now to lead the life of *the* Son of God upon the earth."[12] This is what Paul implies in that great confession in Galatians: "I have been crucified with Christ [and, as he says in Colossians and Romans, "I am also buried and raised with Him"]; it is no longer I who live, but Christ who lives in me; and the life I now live in the flesh I live by faith in the Son of God, who loved me and gave himself for me" (Gal. 2:20).

The ethical demands of baptism, understood as spiritual resurrection, is clearly seen in those passages where the great Apostle to the Gentiles, uses those verbs that speak of spiritual growth figuratively as "putting off" and "putting on" clothing. It is striking that two of these passages are closely linked to baptism. In Galatians 3:27, Paul concludes his arguments for seeing justification as by faith not by law,

---

11. Beasley-Murray, *Baptism,* p. 286.
12. J. S. Lamar, *op. cit.,* p. 168.

since the law was only a temporary "custodian" until Christ came (Galatians 3:24). Now that faith has come, this temporary, yet important, measure is no longer necessary. All can become sons of God through faith in Christ, since "as many as were baptized have put on Christ" (Gal. 3:25-27). All distinctions are erased "in Christ": *racial* ("neither Jew nor Greek"), *sexual* ("neither male nor female"), *social* ("neither slave nor free"). All those who are baptized are clothed with Christ. They belong to Christ. They are Abraham's spiritual lineage. They are heirs according to the promise (Galatians 3:28-29).

In Colossians 3 Paul is more specific about the "clothing of Christ." "If you have been raised with Christ" (Col. 3:1), is the reason given for ensuing directions. 1) Seek heavenly things where Christ is seated at God's right hand (Col. 3:1). 2) Set your mind on things above, not on material or earthly affairs (Col. 3:2). 3) Put to death such earthly actions as immorality, evil desire, impure thoughts, idolatrous covetousness (Col. 3:5). 4) Put away, since you are spiritually dead to them, anger, wrath, malice, slander, foul talk (Col. 3:8). 5) Don't lie to one another, since this is a part of the old nature. You have put it off and have put on the new which is constantly renewed through knowledge of its creator (Col. 3:9, 10). 6) Put on that glorious apparel, reflecting God's choice as holy and beloved children. Such items as lowliness and meekness, patience, forbearance, compassion, forgiveness and, above all (like a girdle binding all together), love constitute this glorious dress. Throughout this tremendous passage Paul reminds his hearers that they *have been raised with Christ.* They have died and their old life is gone, hidden away with Christ in God (Col. 3:1-3). They have a new nature and must behave in a way reflecting that holy nature (Col. 3:9, 12). This new nature is Christ ("clothed with Christ"); and there can be no genuine distinctions (material, religious, social, or economic) for "Christ is all and in all" (Col. 3:11). It is at baptism that this union with Christ is clearly portrayed. Baptism is the sign and seal of incorporation into Christ; it is to be remembered as the touchstone of consequent moral action. The Christian must always confess: "I have been baptized and united with the crucified, risen Lord. I have been incorporated into His sacred body, His community of faith. I am a child of God, a member of God's new family. I now must behave in a manner that reflects this position to which my baptism witnesses!"

Just because baptism is so intimately and closely related to the risen Christ, it must therefore be seen as a very necessary and essential matter of faith. Here is the "trysting place of the sinner with His Savior."[13] Here is the experiential appropriation of sacrificial death. Here is the existential participation in glorious, powerful resurrection. Here, then, is ample motive for that holiness of life "without which no one will see the Lord" (Hebrews 12:15).

FOR FURTHER STUDY

N. J. Aylsworth. *Moral and Spiritual Aspects of Baptism* (St. Louis: Christian Publishing Co., 1902).

Karl Barth. *The Teaching of the Church Regarding Baptism.* Trans. by E. Payne (London: SCM Press, 1945).

G. R. Beasley-Murray. *Baptism in the New Testament* (Grand Rapids: Wm. B. Eerdmans Pub. Co., 1962).

Warren Carr. *Baptism: Conscience and Clue for the Church* (New York: Holt, Rinehart and Winston, 1964).

---

13. Beasley-Murray, *Baptism*, p. 305.

G. W. H. Lampe. *The Seal of the Spirit* (New York: Long-mans, Green and Co., Inc., 1951).

R. E. O. White. *The Biblical Doctrine of Initiation* (Grand Rapids: Wm. B. Eerdmans Pub. Co., 1960).

QUESTIONS FOR DISCUSSION

1. What Biblical evidence do we have that Jesus considered baptism important?
2. Is there any antagonism between "spirit-baptism" and "water-baptism"? What is the baptism of the Spirit?
3. Show how baptism is related to salvation? Link this to the reality of the resurrection.
4. Define "sacrament." How is baptism sacramental?
5. What is the symbolism of baptism? What does this symbolism suggest about the subsequent life of the Christian?

Chapter Nine

RESURRECTION AS POWER FOR CHRISTIAN LIVING

"That I may know Him and the power of His resurrection" (Phil. 3:10).

Baptism has tremendous theological meaning. Linked symbolically to the death and resurrection of Jesus Christ, it points back to those crucial events of sacred history. In its administration in the "name of the Father, and of the Son and of the Holy Spirit" (Matt. 28:18-28), it reflects a full-orbed theology not a truncated Christology ("Jesus only"). Warren Carr rightly sees baptism as reflecting an extensive Christian theology, for it "spells out personal faith and confession; the work of God in the atoning death and triumphant resurrection of Christ the Lord; death to sin and the newness of life to come; cleansing for ethical and moral life; identification with the death, burial and resurrection of Christ; and a community of faith as the arena of the Spirit's visitation upon the one whose faith has brought him to the water."[1]

Baptism's symbolism,[2] provided by its basic form, immersion, not only emphasizes "existential participation" with the saving history of the past, but speaks of a continued power that the risen Lord exerts in the present and will exert in the future. United with Christ in the likeness of his death and resurrection (Rom. 6:3-5), we are freed from the bondage of sin (Rom. 6:6), which was the cause of our spiritual

---

1. *Baptism: Conscience and Clue for the Church* (New York: Holt, Rinehart and Winston, 1964), p. 165.

2. Perhaps *symbol* is a better term to use for baptism than either *ordinance*, which can be interpreted rather woodenly and flatly, or *sacrament*, which often speaks of magic. Carr says: "The word 'sacrament,' popularly defined, harbors a magic which cannot be drowned or made obsolete, no matter what the protestations are to the contrary. The word 'ordinance' is bereft of mystery. It has no place for God or his work. It is man's obedience to Christ's memorandum, which He left behind, tacked on the bulletin board of scripture," p. 169.

death (Col. 2:13; Eph. 2:1-3), and are "made alive together with him" (Col. 2:13b). Since that is the *position* of each Christian, each Christian is urged to "work out their own salvation with fear and trembling" (Phil. 2:12), and come into full *possession* of that position. This is possible because it is "God who is at work in you, both to will and to work for his good pleasure" (Phil. 2:13). After all, Paul affirms elsewhere, since Christians are "made alive together with Christ and raised up to sit with him in heavenly places in Christ Jesus" (Eph. 2:5, 6) they are God's "workmanship, created in Christ Jesus for good works, which God prepared beforehand" (Eph. 2:10).

Resurrection power, then, provides the basis for dedicated Christian living, for an exemplary Christian life style. If a believer accepts at baptism the death of Christ as *his death* ("we are convinced that one has died for all; therefore all have died." II Cor. 5:14b), he must also accept that new kind of life which that saving death introduces ("And he died for all, that those who live might live no longer for themselves but for him who for their sakes died and was raised" II Cor. 5:15). This is the basic thrust of Romans 6 and Colossians 2 and 3. This is the Christian doctrine of sanctification for "sanctification is assent to the death that separates from sin, and appropriation of the vitality that empowers for righteousness."[3]

The Church, the Body of the Risen Lord: Context of Christian Living

The New Testament is not a manual for individualism. It developed *within* the community of faith and *for* the community of faith. Though one may speak of Christ dying for

---

3. Tenney, p. 159.

the sinner with personalistic, individualistic application; it is just that, application. Paul points out the more basic truth from which such application is derived: "Christ loved the church and gave himself up for her, that he might sanctify her, having cleansed her by the washing of water accompanied by the word, that he might present the church to himself in glorious splendor, without spot or wrinkle or any other kind of blemish, that she might be holy and without fault" (Eph. 5:25-27). Salvation is a family affair, with each individual receiving forgiveness and power. Baptism introduces one into a new family, a new people, joined together in love and fellowship (Eph. 5:23f.).

This church, is seen in the New Testament as bride (Eph. 5:23) and body of Christ (I Cor. 12:1ff.; Rom. 12:4f.; Eph. 1:22; Col. 1:18). In both metaphors resurrection is clearly implied. As Bride the Church awaits the Bridegroom (see Matt. 25:11-13) who has given Himself for her and promises to come again to receive her unto himself (John 14:1-4). At such a time the great nuptial feast will take place (Rev. 19:7f.) as the "bride has made herself ready," "clothed in fine linen, bright and clean; for such fine linen is the righteous acts of the saints" (Rev. 19:7, 8). This bride awaits a living Lord and Savior; she does not live in perpetual mourning over a crucified and buried prophet. Her hope is in One she knows is alive and continues to send word of His coming and give evidence of the truth of this word through His indwelling Spirit.

In that great analogy that Paul sets out in Ephesians 5, the most intimate union is depicted between Christ and His body, His bride. "Husband love your wives, even as Christ also loved the Church and gave Himself up for it" (Eph. 5:25). "The unity here pictured," say Beasley-Murray, "is

147

one created by mutual love, but deeper than its earthly counterpart, for the Lover is the Christ."[4] Paul goes on in that passage to quote that great maxim in Genesis: "For this cause shall a man leave his father and mother, and shall be joined to his wife, and the two shall become one flesh" (Eph. 5:31). Paul sees this divine direction for human propagation and intimacy as foreshadowing the spiritual union of Christ and His Church. "This mystery[5] is great: but I take it to refer to Christ and the Church" (Eph. 5:32). The greater reality, the antitype casting the shadow backward into history, is this spiritual union. From this "the kinship of man and wife is derivative. It is a reflection of the conviction that appears in many ways in the New Testament that the Church is not an afterthought, an accident of history, but was in the mind of God from the beginning and was the purpose of creation."[6]

A Body implies a head. A living body must have a living head! Paul is quite explicit on this point. In the Ephesian letter, he offers this prayer: "I pray that the eyes of your hearts may be enlightened, so that you may know what is the hope of His calling, what are the riches of the glory of His inheritance in the saints, and what is the surpassing greatness of His power toward us who believe. These are in accordance with the working of the strength of His might which He brought about in Christ, when He raised Him from the dead, and seated Him at His right hand in the heavenly places, far above all rule and authority and power and dominion, and every name that is named, not only in this age, but also in the one to come. And He put all things

---

4. *Christ is Alive!*, p. 130.

5. Paul uses this term uniformly as referring to a "sacred secret," hidden in the past, now revealed (See Eph. 3:9, 10; Col. 1:27; Rom. 16:25-27.).

6. Beasley-Murray, p. 131.

in subjection under His feet, and gave Him as Head over things to the Church, which is His body, the fullness of Him who fills all in all" (Ephesians 1:18-23). In this prayer, Paul not only links the Christian inheritance, inner power, and mental enlightenment, with that great power exerted by God in raising Jesus from the dead, but he sees this act of resurrection in cosmic perspective. Jesus is thus glorified, seated at God's right, given all authority, and made head of His Church, His body, which he enlivens fully.

In writing to the Church at Colossae, Paul emphasized this same truth within a different context. To counter that false teaching that had pervaded the Lycus Valley, Paul sets out the singular and unique greatness of Jesus Christ. In showing the incomparable Christ Paul emphasizes not only His redemptive work for man (Col. 1:13-14), but his eternal and cosmic power as well (Col. 1:15-16). Therefore, says Paul, "He is before all things, and in Him all things hold together. He is also head of the body, the church; and He is the beginning, the first-born from the dead; so that He Himself might come to have first place in everything" (Col. 1:17, 18). Again, headship of the body and resurrection ("first-born from the dead") are seen together.

The Church, as Body of Christ, perpetuates the reality of the resurrection. It is the embodiment of the Living Lord; it is the "continuation of the Incarnation." The distinguishing mark of the Church is not a temple or shrine, as in Judaism and the other first-century religions, but the body of the risen Lord. John notes this when he records that incident from the earliest phase of Jesus' ministry wherein the temple managers asked for a sign or token of authority by which Jesus cleansed the Temple environs of its commercialism. Jesus replied: "Destroy this temple and in three days I will raise it again" (John 2:19). Even though Jesus is speaking of his body and his subsequent resurrection from the dead, He is also implying that the Temple will be replaced by a spiritual dwelling place for God. This is implied again in his statements to the Samaritan woman about worship (not here or there, but "in spirit and in truth," John 4:24). This interpretation becomes even clearer in light of those later charges made against Jesus at His trial: "We heard Him say, 'I will destroy this temple that is made with hands and in three days I will build another made without hands'" (Mark 14:58). The Church of Christ is a community raised from the dead with Jesus Christ to become the temple of the Lord and of His Spirit.

Paul uses the metaphor of body in two senses. In those passages noted above, Headship, authority, ownership, and direction are seen. In certain other passages the body signifies "identity." The Church is Christ's body and therefore is one with Him. In the Corinthian correspondence where disunity and factionalism within the Corinthian Church lies behind much that Paul writes (see chapters 1-4, 11, etc.), Paul emphasized that oneness which this symbolic understanding of Church as body implies. "As the body is one and yet has many members, and all the members of the body, though they are many, are one body, so also is Christ" (I Cor. 12:12). He reinforces this by adding: "For by one Spirit we were all baptized into one body, . . . and were all made to drink of one Spirit" (I Cor. 12:13).[7] "Now you are Christ's body and individually members of it" (I Cor. 12:27).

---

7. In the first chapter, Paul had already pointed out the unitive witness of Christian baptism. "Has Christ been divided? Was Paul crucified for you? Were you baptized in the name of Paul?" (I Cor. 1:13).

But all such metaphors and similies are inadequate to set forth fully the Church's relationship to Christ. Body and bride, as meaningful as these symbols are, but approximate that dynamic relationship which Jesus speaks of in both his farewell discourse to the Apostles and His great High-Priestly prayer to the Father on the eve of His crucifixion. "I am the vine, you are the branches; he who abides in Me and I in him, he bears much fruit; for apart from Me you can do nothing" (John 15:5). Such abiding, Jesus affirms, is in His word, through obeying His commands, and, particularly, abiding in His love (John 15:7-11). In His great prayer of intercession he combines this intimate oneness with concern for the unity of all "who will believe through their [the Apostles] word" (John 17:20). He prays "that they may all be one"; but such unity is given a divine standard, "even as Thou, Father, art in Me, and I in Thee, that they also may be in Us" (John 17:21a). Why is this intimate union to be seen in Christ's people? He answers "that the world may believe that Thou didst send me" (John 17:21b).

The Church is the Body of Christ. As aliens respond in faith, they are baptized into Him who is the crucified, risen Lord and Head of the Church. He adds them to His body (Acts 2:41, 47). They become part of an intimate fellowship, permeated by His love. They are united together because they have been brought into a common life in Christ. Unity deepens as deeper fellowship in Him is experienced. He is alive and, through His Spirit, indwells each believer.

This fellowship with the living Lord, finds its focus in worship, and the worship of the Apostolic Church is a tremendous witness to the resurrection of Jesus. It is somewhat uncertain when the early Christians began meeting on the first day of the week for worship. It may have been from

151

the beginning, since the observance of the ordinance of "breaking of bread" is recorded from the beginning (Acts 2:46); but by the time Paul has begun the great Gentile mission it seems to have been restricted to a weekly observance on the first day of the week (Acts 20:7; I Cor. 16:2). Luke seems to indicate that this was the major purpose for meeting on the first day of the week. Paul's exhortation to the Corinthians relative to the offering for the poor in Judea suggests that, since it is customary to meet on the first day for worship centering in the Lord's Supper, this is an opportune time to "lay by in store as the Lord has prospered." The exhortation of the Hebrew writer not to forsake "the assembling of ourselves together as the manner of some is" (Heb. 10:25), reflects what, apparently, was a widespread, if not universal, practice of the early Church to meet for worship on the first day of the week. It is certain that by the beginning of the second century the custom was universal among Christians. John in the Revelation, is undoubtedly, using current semantic coinage when he refers to this day as the "Lord's Day" (Rev. 1:10).

Why was this day set apart? There must have been some compelling reason. The only reason that would cause religious Jews, steeped in Sabbath worship, to do this was because this was the day on which Christ arose. To meet on that day means celebrating weekly His resurrection from the dead. The Lord's Day, then, becomes a constant reminder of God's mighty act that called the Church into being. "As a 'Festival of Life' the Christian day of worship is a further piece of evidence to the historic event by which our Salvation was won."[8]

---

8. *Ibid*, p. 79.

But the celebration of Resurrection, occurring on the first day, commemorating His power over the grave and His first meetings with His disciples,[9] centers in the sacrament of the Lord's Supper or Eucharist. Those who were baptized into Him and were, symbolically and existentially, participating with their risen Lord in "newness of life" (Rom. 6:4), met on the first day of the week "to break bread" (Acts 20:7). Here in this significant ordinance the reality of God's saving acts—the death and resurrection of Jesus—are embodied and proclaimed. Cross and Resurrection stand together. "This is my body. . . . This is my blood," Jesus said (Matt. 26:28). "Do this in remembrance of me," he commands. Paul writes to the Church at Corinth a scathing criticism of their abuse of what Christ had intended. "When you meet, presumably to eat the Lord's Supper, you are actually eating to your damnation, not to His glory and your spiritual strength," he says (I Cor. 11:17-22). What is important is not the common meal[10] which was being abused but what Paul received from the Lord. What he had received and delivered was that "the Lord Jesus . . . took bread; and when He had given thanks, He broke it, and said, 'This is My body which is given for you; do this in remembrance of Me.' In the same manner He took the cup also, after supper, saying, 'This cup is the new covenant in My blood; do this, as often as you drink it; in remembrance of Me! For as often as you eat this bread and drink the cup, you proclaim the Lord's death until He comes" (I Cor. 11:23-26).

---

9. John seems to go out of his way to point out that the meetings with the Apostles in Jerusalem occurred eight days apart, hence, were "first day" meetings (John 20:26).

10. In the early church corporate worship seems to have centered in a common meal, a "love feast," at which remembrance of Christ through those instituted memorial emblems—bread and wine—and other elements of worship were experienced (See Acts 20:7ff., I Cor. 11:17-22).

153

Fellowship and worship within the Body of the Risen Lord centers in the Table. His Church is a family (the "household of God," I Tim. 3:15); and it focuses its celebration of life around a Table. This table is His, who is living Lord. It is His body symbolized by bread, His shed blood, symbolized in the cup. "We who are many are one loaf, one body, for we all partake of that one loaf" (I Cor. 10:17). The unity of the Church is made possible by the divine action of the Crucified One raised from the dead by God's power. It is entered by baptism, a spiritual symbol of man's participation in that historic death and resurrection; and it is continued by the celebration of Him around a common Table. This memorial act is indeed a "visible word" of God's redemptive action in Jesus' crucifixion; but it is more in that it is to be proclaimed "until He comes." It is an act of anticipation as well. The view backward to resurrection power is to remind the Church that it has a future. That future is focused upon Him who is Lord of His people, Head of the body, and returning Bridegroom receiving His bride. He will indeed drink this cup "new in the kingdom of God" (Luke 22:18). His church experiences that communion with Him in spirit as they worship now; it will experience more intimate communion when He returns for His own.

Resurrection and Life in the Spirit: Dynamic for Christian Living

Those baptized into Christ, thus becoming integral members of His Body, are promised the indwelling Spirit. On that first Pentecost Peter not only explains that strange phenomenon which was occurring as the outpouring of the Spirit of God "upon all flesh," as had been prophesied in

154

Joel (Joel 2:26-28), but he assures those penitents who are baptized in the name of Jesus that they will receive the gift, which is God's Holy Spirit (Acts 2:38). Paul reinforces this truth in writing to the Church at Corinth about the nature of the Church as Body. "For by one Spirit we were all baptized into one body, whether Jews or Greeks, whether slaves or free, and we were all made to drink of one Spirit" (I Cor. 12:13). At baptism, the newborn Christian enters the spiritual family, and receives "breath," the Spirit, which maintains that new life.

Baptism into the fellowship of the Spirit, brings one into Christ. The baptized participate in His death and resurrection, but they also participate in His continuing life. He is the living Lord and Head of His Church. His promised Spirit, this "other" Paraclete (Counselor), (John 14:16), brings recognition and experience of His presence. In that great prayer recorded in Ephesians, Paul equates the Presence of Jesus and the Power of the Holy Spirit. "For this reason, I bow my knees before the Father . . . that He would grant you according to the riches of His glory, to be *strengthened with power through His Spirit* in the inner man; so that *Christ may dwell in your hearts through Faith*; and that you, being rooted and grounded in love, may be able to comprehend with all the saints what is the breadth and length and height and depth, and to know the love of Christ which surpasses knowledge, that you may be filled up to all the fulness of God" (Eph. 3:14, 16-19).

Lesslie Newbigin, outstanding missionary theologian, states this truth so well: "The New Testament begins by describing how the Holy Spirit descended upon Jesus and abode upon Him and how in the Power of the Spirit He lived and spoke, and how the same Spirit was given to His Church to be the permanent principle of its life. . . . The Holy Spirit is now no more an occasional visitant to a favored individual but the abiding and indwelling principle of life in a fellowship. The supreme gift of the Spirit is not the spectacular power by which an individual may gain pre-eminence, but the humble and self-effacing love by which the body is built up and knit together."[11]

Therefore, the dearest token of the believers' assurance is the Holy Spirit. Introduced by the Spirit (through the adequate testimony that the Spirit inspired), baptized into the risen Lord, the convert comes into the Spirit-led community and is made partaker of the Holy Spirit (I Cor. 12:13). He has tasted the powers of the age to come (Heb. 6:5). He is "sealed with the Holy Spirit of promise, which is a downpayment of our inheritance, unto God's redemption of his possession" (Eph. 1:13, 14). The living Word of God and the Holy Spirit creates new humanity, just as in the beginning the Word of creation and the brooding Spirit were linked in the creative activity of God (Ps. 33:6; Gen. 1:2). As Beasley-Murray notes: "In the first creation the Spirit hovered over the lifeless waters and at the word of God light and life appeared on the earth. Significantly enough, the new creation and the gift of the Spirit are connected with the rite of baptism, as though the Holy Spirit broods over the waters wherein the believer plunges for burial and produces from the watery grave a new creature."[12]

The Christian is not only united with the risen Christ and indwelt by the Holy Spirit at that point in time when he is symbolically raised "to walk in newness of life" (Rom. 6:4), but he is also empowered by that Spirit in the living of this

---

11. *The Household of God* (New York: Friendship Press, 1954), p. 115.
12. *Christ is Alive!*, p. 124.

life. Paul emphasizes this truth in different ways. In the second letter to the Corinthians Paul sees the action of the living Lord through His Spirit in the context of freedom and bondage. The new covenant is a ministry of life because of the Spirit (II Cor. 3:6ff.); it involves not tablets of stone but "living epistles" etched out by the Spirit of the living God (II Cor. 3:2, 3). Therefore, where "the Spirit of the Lord is, there is liberty" (II Cor. 3:17), for the Lord of the new covenant is the Spirit. It is through this living Lord, operating through His Spirit, that the transformation of life takes place. This occurs in direct confrontation with the glory of the Lord, not through some veil as necessitated in the Old Testament (II Cor. 3:13). Paul concludes: "But we all, with unveiled face beholding as in a mirror the glory of the Lord, are being transformed into the same image from glory to glory, just as from the Lord, the Spirit" (II Cor. 3:18).[13] Because of the continuing presence of the Spirit in the believer, he need not like Moses go infrequently in before the presence of God and be "re-charged" with divine glory, but he is in constant relation with the Living Lord whose glory is appropriated. The Christian can be changed, then, from one level of glory to another as his life becomes a holy reflector of Christ.

It is perhaps in that great theological tract, which was written as a letter of recommendation to the church at Rome, that we see the relation of the Holy Spirit and the risen Lord to the believer's life and behavior. Following those chapters

---

13. This is another illustration of that pattern in Paul's writings where in writing of the "present spiritual need of the people of Christ" much that he "says about the ministry of the ascended Christ can be paralleled by what he says about the ministry of the Spirit." F. F. Bruce, *Paul: Apostle of the Heart Set Free* (Grand Rapids: Wm. B. Eerdmans, 1977), p. 120.

which show the universal need for the justifying grace of God (Romans 1, 2, 3), Paul shows that this needed justification comes only through God's action in Jesus Christ. Christ's propitiatory death makes it possible for God to be "just and the justifier of the one who has faith in Jesus" (Rom. 3:25-26). Faith in Christ, then, is the only ground for justification; this was true in the shadowy revelation of the Old Testament, for Abraham was justified, not because he worked, but because he believed and trusted God (Romans 4). The one believing in Jesus Christ has a new standing in grace, not law, and rejoices in the hope of God's glory as it produces patience and virtue (Rom. 5:1-4).

At this point, Paul summarizes. "[Our] Hope does not disappoint, because the love of God has been poured out within our hearts *through the Holy Spirit who was given to us.* For while we were still helpless, at the right time Christ died for the ungodly. . . . God demonstrates His own love toward us, in that while we were yet sinners, Christ died for us. Much more then, having now been justified by His blood, we shall be saved from the wrath of God through Him. For if while we were enemies, we were reconciled to God through the death of His Son, much more, having been reconciled, we shall be saved by *His life*" (Romans 5:5, 6, 8-10).

"Christ's life" and the "Holy Spirit given" are introduced in this summary because they are central concepts in what follows. After Paul has contrasted the first Adam, who disobeyed and brought ruin to all men, and the second Adam, whose obedience brought life (Rom. 5:12-21), he shows that the Christian's initial experience—his baptism—is a clear demonstration that sin should no longer have any place in his life (Rom. 6:1-4). This is true because in baptism

158

one participates in the life of the risen Lord and, as his risen life denotes death to the old body, so the Christian's risen life must reflect that same withdrawal from the old manner of living. Paul says, "Even so consider yourselves to be dead to sin, but alive to God in Christ Jesus. Therefore, do not let sin reign in your mortal body that you should obey its lusts, and do not go on presenting the members of your body to sin as instruments of unrighteousness; but present yourselves to God as those alive from the dead, and your members as instruments of righteousness to God" (Rom. 6:12, 13). After reminding his hearers of these great truths, Paul exults: "But thanks be to God that though you were slaves of sin, you became obedient from the heart to that form of teaching to which you were committed, and having been freed from sin, you became slaves of righteousness" (Rom. 6:17, 18).

As Paul continues he faces the question: But surely the Law that had been given to the Fathers is not altogether worthless, is it? Of course not, Paul answers. The law is not sin (Rom. 7:7). The law is good, but it is unable to justify because of the radical weakness of human flesh (Rom. 8:3). Throughout chapter 7 Paul is showing the ambivalent position of the law-abiding Jew under the Law. Here is only anxiety, spiritual depression, hopelessness, wretchedness. The final doxology shows that Paul is not describing the Christians' position. "Wretched man that I am! Who will set me free from the body of this death? Thanks be to God through Jesus Christ our Lord!" (Rom. 7:24, 25a).

The conflict is ended; the victory is won; "there is therefore now no condemnation for those who are in Christ Jesus" (Rom. 8:1). The one participating in Jesus' resurrection as witnessed in his baptism is now dominated by a new law—"the law of the Spirit of life in Christ Jesus" (Rom. 8:2). As Christians walk "according to the Spirit" and "set their minds on the things of the Spirit" (Rom. 8:4, 5), they experience this continued victory. The power that accomplishes this is "the Spirit of Him who raised Jesus from the dead" (Rom. 8:11). This Spirit indwelling Christians guarantees that the same power that raised Jesus from the dead "will also give life to your mortal bodies" (Rom. 8:11).

This indwelling Spirit is the dynamic for Christian living. By the Spirit the Christian is "to put to death the deeds of the body" (Rom. 8:13) and live as children of God. This Spirit gives assurance that the Christian is a child of God. He alone causes the cry, "Abba, Father"; He alone bears witness "with our Spirits that we are children of God" (Rom. 8:16). And if the Christian serves faithfully, even if this involves suffering (Rom. 8:17), then it is through the Spirit that he shall be "glorified with Christ" as a "joint heir" with Him (Rom. 8:17).

This same Spirit "helps our weakness," even in such intimate relations as the prayer life (Rom. 8:26). Through this Spirit the Christian knows that "God causes all things to work together for good to those who love God, to those who are called according to His purpose" (Rom. 8:28). Through this Spirit the Christian anticipates that final victory, since every Christian is joined in faith and existential participation in baptism with Jesus "who died, yes, rather who was raised, who is at the right hand of God, who also intercedes for us" (Rom. 8:34).

It is through this inner dynamic of the Spirit that Christians understand that the "law of the Spirit of life" is, indeed, the "law of love." This capacity to love is a fruit of the Spirit (Gal. 5:22); it is "poured out" by the Spirit (Rom. 5:5); it

160

is, indeed, the "law of Christ" (Gal. 6:2). It reflects Jesus' own interpretation of the ancient law as seen in love of God and love of neighbor (Matt. 22:40). Paul states clearly: "the whole law is fulfilled in one word: 'You shall love your neighbor as yourself'" (Gal. 5:14). Again: "Love does no wrong to a neighbor; therefore love is the fulfilling of the law" (Romans 13:10). This love is never legalized; it is the spontaneous action of the Spirit-led Christian. Because he is led by and "walks by the Spirit" (Rom. 8:14; Gal. 5:25), he is "walking in love" (Rom. 14:15).

Such an emphasis upon the law of love rather than prudential rules and regulations may be regarded by many as encouraging ethical laxness or moral indifference. As a result, many fall back upon the regulations of the Mosaic law as checks against such indifference. Paul on the other hand insisted, as F. F. Bruce writes, that a "man in Christ had reached his spiritual majority and must no longer be confined to the leading strings of infancy but enjoy the birthright of free born sons of God. Here if anywhere Luther entered into the mind of Paul: 'A Christian man is a most free lord of all, subject to none. A Christian man is a most dutiful servant of all, subject to all.' 'Subject to none' in respect of his liberty; 'subject to all' in respect of his charity. This, for Paul, is the law of Christ because this was the way of Christ. And in this way, for Paul, the divine purpose underlying Moses' law is vindicated and accomplished."[14]

To Know the Power of His Resurrection: The Goal of Christian Living

The life of hope, born in that union of the believer with the risen Christ and perpetuated through the Spirit of Him

---

14. *Paul*, p. 202.

who raised Jesus from the dead, is itself a divine "break-through" into human affairs. Just as the ministry of Jesus, and His redemptive accomplishment was a "mystery" revealed only through His resurrection and subsequent preaching (see I Tim. 3:16; Eph. 3:9ff.; Rom. 16:25-27), so His in-dwelling is similarly "mystery." Paul writes: "God was pleased to make known what is the riches of the glory of this *mystery* among the Gentiles, which is Christ in you, the hope of glory" (Col. 1:27).

This hope, based upon Christ's resurrection, and becoming reality in His presence through the Holy Spirit, is the means of power. As Paul languishes in a Roman prison he speaks of knowing contentment even in the midst of difficult circumstances. The secret of that contentment is the living Christ. "I have strength for anything through Him who gives me power" (Phil. 4:13). The sense of lostness, inadequacy, and loneliness are overcome by the power of the Presence of the living Lord.

It is in this same situation that Paul speaks of desiring to "know the power of the resurrection" (Phil. 3:10). Paul is awaiting trial. He has waited for at least two years, guarded constantly by members of the Praetorium Guard. He has endured shipwreck, illness and other hardships for the sake of Christ. Though cautiously optimistic about the outcome of his hearing before Nero, he does not know what his future holds. In spite of this, he writes to the Church at Philippi in joyous terms and urges them to rejoice even in his circum-stances (Phil. 1:6ff.; 3:1f.; etc.). He is aware that men of Judaizing tendencies have been among them and he warns them about these (Phil. 3:2, 3).

This leads him to speak autobiographically. "I certainly would have every reason to boast about my human pedigree and attainments" he says, "I was circumcised the eighth day, of the nation of Israel, of the tribe of Benjamin, a Hebrew of Hebrews; as to the righteousness which is in the Law, found blameless" (Phil. 3:4-6). But all these things, Paul sees as of little value; in fact they are "garbage" in contrast to a vital relationship with Christ. All he desires is to know Christ Jesus as Lord; to be "found in Him"; to depend upon a righteousness "which is through faith in Christ" (Phil. 3:8, 9).

As Paul sets out these goals of authentic life, he relates this knowledge of Christ to both "conformity to death" and "the power of the resurrection" (Phil. 3:10). Paul had experienced, in his baptism, that initial entrance into the "fellowship of His sufferings"; he had experienced a death to self and past ambition; he had experienced participation with the risen Lord; yet he still sees the knowledge of Christ and the power of His resurrection yet to be attained. "Not that I have already obtained it, or have already become perfect, but I press on in order that I may lay hold of that for which also I was laid hold of by Christ Jesus. Brethren, I do not regard myself as having laid hold of it yet; but one thing I do: forgetting what lies behind and reaching forward to what lies ahead, I press on toward the goal for the prize of the upward call of God in Christ Jesus" (Phil. 3:12-14).

This constant effort to "press on," to "reach forward," has as its ultimate goal the "resurrection from the dead" (Phil. 3:11). The "power of His resurrection" energizing Paul's life and motivating Paul's service, would issue in actual participation in Paul's own bodily resurrection. Until that reality occurs the Christian, like Paul, must allow resurrection power to be both actualizer and anticipation. Anticipating the "glory to be revealed to us" (Rom. 8:17), "we ourselves, having the first fruits of the Spirit, even we ourselves groan within ourselves, waiting eagerly for our adoption as sons, the redemption of our body" (Rom. 8:23). But as the Christian waits, the Spirit of Jesus, through resurrection power (Eph. 1:18-20), brings him to a maturity of life that will be rewarded with endless life.

FOR FURTHER READING

F. F. Bruce. *Paul: Apostle of the Heart Set Free.* Grand Rapids: Wm. B. Eerdmans, 1977.

James S. Stewart. *A Man in Christ.* New York: Harper and Row, n.d.

Michael Green. *Man Alive!* Chicago: InterVarsity Press, 1967.

G. R. Beasley-Murray. *Christ is Alive!* London: Lutterworth Press, 1947.

QUESTIONS FOR DISCUSSION

1. Why is the nature of the Church important in our understanding of Christian duty? Discuss.
2. Discuss these images of the Church—body and bride—from the standpoint of their implications for the Christian.
3. Why is worship an important function of the Church? Link resurrection and worship.
4. Relate the resurrection to the indwelling of the Holy Spirit. Why is this so significant for Christian living?
5. Read carefully and discuss Paul's treatment of the Holy Spirit in the life of the Christian in Romans 8.
6. Point out some of the implications of the phrase "to know Him and the power of His resurrection."

Chapter Ten

CHRIST'S RESURRECTION AND THE RESURRECTION OF HIS OWN

"Christ the first fruits after that those who are Christ's at His coming" (I Cor. 15:23).

The early church grew out of Judaism where the belief in a general resurrection for all men was an item of faith. "I know he shall be raised in the resurrection of the last day," sobbed Martha, as she spoke of her dead brother (John 11:24). Jesus appears and claims to be the "resurrection and life" (John 11:25), proving that claim by raising the dead (John 11:43, 44; Mark 5:41, 42; Luke 7:12). He also taught that He would raise the dead on the last day. "For just as the Father raises the dead and gives them life, even so the Son also gives life to whom He wishes. . . . Truly, truly, I say to you, an hour is coming and now is, when the dead shall hear the voice of the Son of God; and those who hear shall live. . . . Do not marvel at this; for an hour is coming, in which all who are in the tombs shall hear His voice, and shall come forth . . ." (John 5:21, 25, 28). On another occasion, He said: "For this is the will of my Father, that every one who beholds the Son, and believes in Him, may have eternal life; and I Myself will raise him up on the last day" (John 6:40).

This resurrection Gospel, centering in Jesus, is proven to be valid, since Jesus "was declared the Son of God with power by the resurrection from the dead" (Rom. 1:4). That Gospel was heralded throughout the Roman world, beginning at Jerusalem. To the Jew, Paul and others could say: "Why should it be thought impossible that God should raise the dead?" (Acts 26:8). After all, the God of Israel was a God of power, Creator of all things. But, to the Gentile, either Greek intellectual or superstitious barbarian, such an

165

item of faith became more of a stumbling-block, so the Athenians could laugh and sneer at Paul's presentation of a man raised from the dead (Acts 17:32).

Some of these Gentiles apparently could believe that God could raise Jesus from the dead, for He is uniquely God's Son and man's Savior. Upon such faith, they had been baptized and become Christian (Acts 18:8), but apparently there were some (perhaps many) who failed to believe the corollary that "He who raised the Lord Jesus will raise us also with Jesus" (II Cor. 4:4).

This is the reality that Paul faces as he writes to the church at Corinth. Some of the members of the Church denied that all would be raised from the dead, compelling the Apostle to develop a systematic exposition of this vital Christian doctrine. Paul answers the denial, says F. F. Bruce, "in some detail, first reminding them of the gospel which they had heard and believed at the beginning of their Christian career, in order to impress upon them that resurrection is integral to the way of salvation."[1]

Resurrection and the Ancient Gospel

In Paul's extended argument, he begins by showing how integral resurrection is to the Gospel. If these who denied the resurrection saw clearly the implications of this denial, they would see that their position contravened the verity and saving worth of the Gospel. Such skepticism would nullify "the faith and hope of the Church as effectually as the party-divisions destroyed its love."[2]

---

1. F. F. Bruce, *1 and 2 Corinthians* New Century Bible (London: Marshall, Morgan and Scott, 1971), p. 137.

2. G. C. Findlay, "St. Paul's First Epistle to the Corinthians," In W. Robertson Nicoll, ed., *The Expositors Greek Testament*, v. 2 (Grand Rapids: Wm. B. Eerdmans, 1979), p. 917.

Paul emphasizes that he "made known" this resurrection gospel to them; he was the one who preached this Gospel in their city (I Cor. 15:1a). They had "received" it and they were "grounded in it; that is, they had their standing (*estēkate*) in this self-same gospel (I Cor. 15:1b). It was this gospel which was the instrument of their salvation, presuming that they were holding fast to that which Paul had originally preached to them (I Cor. 15:2). Of course, Paul notes, they could have "believed in vain," or exercised a "random" or "superficial" faith. This latter would be true if the denial of the resurrection is carried to its logical conclusion, for the gospel then would be worthless, and faith would be fruitless.

Following this introductory statement emphasizing the essentiality of the gospel for salvation and life, Paul shows that the resurrection of Christ is the heart of the saving gospel and that Jesus' resurrection has been splendidly verified. "For I delivered to you as of first importance what I also received, that Christ died for our sins in accordance with the scriptures, that he was buried, that he was raised on the third day in accordance with the scriptures, and that he appeared to Cephas, then to the twelve. Then he appeared to more than five hundred brethren at one time, most of whom are still alive though some have fallen asleep. Then he appeared to James, then to all the apostles. Last of all, as to one abnormally born[3] he appeared also to me" (I Cor. 15:3-8).

---

3. Literally, "as if an abortion." The NEB translates this "as one monstrously born." Paul is not emphasizing a premature birth, but one abnormal, perhaps even "monstrous" in light of his former persecution of the church. He may also be emphasizing abnormality in that his apostleship was different, since he had not "accompanied" Jesus from John's baptism unto the day He ascended (Acts 1:21, 22).

Paul's use of the terms "delivered" (*paradidomi*) and "received" (*paralambano*) shows that he is using the usual idiom for transmitting oral tradition. He is affirming that the gospel message did not originate from him but that he received its full outline and meaning from others. This is not a genuine contradiction of Gal. 1:11f., where he speaks of his gospel in a unique sense, as having come from the Lord and not from man. As Bruce says: "The contradiction is apparent, not real: both senses were equally true to his experience . . . the essence of the gospel, 'Jesus is the risen Lord,' was communicated to him from heaven on the Damascus road: it was no human testimony that moved him to accept it. . . . But the historical details of the teaching of Jesus, the events of Holy Week, the resurrection appearances and so forth were related to him by those who had first-hand experience of them."[4]

The elements of the gospel that are "of first importance" are (1) Christ died for our sins; (2) He was buried; (3) He was raised, and (4) He appeared after his resurrection to many. Whatever variety may be seen in primitive proclamation these elements are fundamental. As Paul says: "Whether then it was I or they [the Apostles] so we preach, and so you believed" (I Cor. 15:11). The death and resurrection of Christ are also linked with Old Testament prophecy, showing that Paul (and others) now see the Old Testament in light of Christ. Newer, deeper meanings are now found in the sacred scriptures, interpreted even as the risen Jesus had given the model (Luke 24:26-27).

One might wonder why the burial of Jesus is raised to such a fundamental position in primitive faith. Undoubtedly,

---

4. *Corinthians*, p. 138.

burial emphasizes the finality of death, calls attention to an empty tomb, and emphasizes the reality of the resurrection. He was buried by men, but God raised Him from the dead, reversing the act of man and giving special significance to this divine act that brought Jesus forth bodily from Joseph's tomb.

This reality is bolstered by a listing of appearances— Groups—"the Twelve, all the apostles"; individuals—Cephas, James, even Paul; and a host of people—"five hundred brethren at one time most of whom still live, but some have died." Here is cumulative historical data that is difficult to explain away.[5] Paul knew these appearances to be facts for he had opportunity to have heard testimony from all of them (see Gal. 1:19; Acts 9:26ff.).

Paul insists that this basic material, enshrined in the gospel which he had preached to the Corinthians (and which they had believed and obeyed), was common to all who were involved in gospel preaching. The resurrection was not a doctrine preached only by Paul; it was a universal tenet of faith. There is no salvation apart from belief in these fundamental truths. Therefore, the resurrection of Christ is the essential foundation of human redemption.

No Resurrection, No Salvation, No Hope

What, then, are the implications? Paul is explicit: "Now if Christ is preached that He has been raised from the dead, how do some among you say that there is no resurrection of the dead? But if there is no resurrection of the dead, not even Chirst has been raised and if Christ has not been raised,

---

5. See Appendix for a treatment of the various theories propounded to explain the resurrection appearances.

then our preaching is vain, your faith also is vain. Moreover we are even found to be false witnesses of God, because we witnessed against God that He raised Christ, whom He did not raise, if in fact the dead are not raised. For if the dead are not raised, not even Christ has been raised; and if Christ has not been raised your faith is worthless; you are still in your sins. Then those also who have fallen asleep [died] in Christ have perished. If we have only hoped in Christ in this life, we are of all men most to be pitied" (I Cor. 15:12-19).

Apparently, the "some" *(tines)* who denied the general resurrection had no quarrel with Paul about Jesus' unique resurrection. They may have seen this as a symbolic occurrence, guaranteeing his saving work on the Cross, but having no relationship at all to believers. In light of the clear antinomian tendencies at Corinth (I Cor. 5-6, 8, etc.) and recognizing that Greek thought was opposed to the resurrection of the body generally (see Acts 17:30f.), these Corinthians may have viewed redemption as wholly spiritual, having nothing to do with their fleshly bodies.[6]

Paul's argument, based upon his recital of the certain fact of Jesus' resurrection, is now launched against these detractors. If there is no resurrection, then Jesus could not have been raised and that would mean the following:

1) Paul, and all the Apostles', preaching is vain. It has all been a sham, a hoax. After all, if the fact is untrue, then the *testimony* to that fact is untrue. All who have given witness are liars!

2) The Corinthians' faith is also vain! They had believed the testimony. But, the testimony is not true; their faith falls to the ground; it is empty. Are these skeptics willing to affirm

---

6. Paul's emphasis in I Cor. 6 on the individual's body as the "temple of the Holy Spirit" may be understood in light of this background.

that both Paul's preaching and the resultant faith and hope of their fellow Christians are illusory? Logic would demand it.

3) Even more drastic, Paul (and others) have been false witnesses. They have been *misrepresenting God* (literally, witnessing against God), for they have proclaimed that God raised Jesus from the dead (Acts 17:3; 17:31; 18:5; etc.). This would be the worst sort of blasphemy.

4) And, if the dead are not raised, Christ is not raised and your faith in Him is futile and worthless. It follows, then, that the Corinthians (and all men) are still in their sins. Only in Christ's resurrection is there assurance of forgiveness and hope of eternal life.

5) Those who have died, firmly believing in Christ, have perished irretrievably. They are eternally cut off from God. Neither they or those alive have hope beyond the grave.

6) Finally, if all the hope a Christian has is in this physical life, all who claim relationship to Christ are men most to be pitied. Why? Because the Christian has given up this life for the vain promise of another. He has let his hold on earth go, in grasping for some fanciful afterlife. Paul himself had "suffered the loss of all things" for the sake of Christ (Phil. 3:8). What fools, if Christ was still in Joseph's tomb! Paul's "regulating his life and work by the prospect of the Lord's assessment at the parousia (4:4f.), his striving to win an imperishable wreath (9:25), would be but hollow mockery."[7]

Such implications are not to be entertained even for a moment. Christ has been raised. It is preposterous to deny it in face of the evidence cited. It is, therefore, preposterous to deny that all believers will also be raised even as He.

---

7. Bruce, *Corinthians*, p. 145.

The Order of Resurrection

Whatever may have been the Corinthians' objections to the general resurrection of all men (they may have thought that with the gift of the Spirit they had received all that anyone could hope for), Paul has shown by clear logic that resurrection has occurred. But such resurrection is not just a singular and unique event in which Jesus was raised from that tomb in Jerusalem. Jesus' resurrection and the resurrection of his followers are inseparable. "But, in fact, Christ has been raised from the dead, the first fruits of those who have fallen asleep [died]" (I Cor. 15:20). First fruits guarantee a continuing harvest: Jesus' resurrection guarantees the resurrection of all who know Him and have been united with Him. As Bruce says: "Basic to his [Paul's] thinking throughout is the conviction that Christ and his people are so vitally and permanently united that his triumph over death must be shared with them, not only in sacramental anticipation but in bodily resurrection."[8]

Certainly, resurrection has occurred; but to hold that "the resurrection is past already," as did Hymenaeus and Philetus, is "to swerve from the truth" (II Tim. 2:17). Paul uses an analogy to undergird his argument. There are two uniquely representative men: Adam and Christ. Unlike his analogy in Romans 5, where Adam and Christ are seen as the two counterparts of disobedience and obedience, here Paul sees the two in relation to death and life. "As in Adam all die, so also in Christ shall all be made alive" (I Cor. 15:22). If, by man, came death into the world (and that as a result of disobedience—Romans 5:12f.), by man also comes life (and that through obedience—Romans 5:15f.). This "free gift of life" is vouchsafed by resurrection (I Cor. 15:21).

---

8. Bruce, *Paul*, p. 309.

But there is a proper order (rank): Christ has been raised. His resurrection and subsequent glory is the first-fruits.[9] The harvest of "those who belong to Christ" will come later. Christ never stands alone. He has a Body with many members. These "members" of His Body are members of Christ" (I Cor. 6:15). What is done in their physical and earthly existence reflect on Him. So Paul had argued earlier that "foods were meant only for the stomach and the stomach only for food" (I Cor. 6:13). God would ultimately destroy both food and stomach; but "by His power" He will raise Christians up even as He "raised the Lord" (I Cor. 6:14). Union with Christ, both now and forever, is stressed. *Now,* such union requires the shunning of immorality and the glorifying of God in the body (I Cor. 6:18-20). *Then,* shall we know that greater union, when the Spirit who dwells in Christians *now* will be experienced as that Spirit of Him who raised the dead (Rom. 8:11).

When all this has been completed—and the beginning has already been seen in Jesus' resurrection—*then* "comes the end" (I Cor. 15:24). That end is envisioned as the conquering Son handing over His dominion to the Father. There may be an indeterminate period between the resurrection of those "who are Christ's at his coming" and this final end; for Paul has already referred to Christ's people as sharing Jesus' kingship (I Cor. 4:8) and judging the world (I Cor. 6:2). But, whatever that period of time between Christ's Parousia and His Presentation of the Kingdom to the Father, may be, all "rule, authority and power" will be His (I Cor. 15:24). These enemies that will cower under the Messiah's

---

9. This analogy of "first-fruits" and "harvest" may have come more readily to mind if it is posited that Paul is writing the Corinthians sometime between Passover (see I Cor. 5:7f.) and Pentecost (see I Cor. 16:1f.), the Feast of First Fruits.

feet (see Ps. 110:1) are those hostile powers and evil forces that oppose God's purposes in this world (Eph. 6:12). Elsewhere these forces, including death itself (II Tim. 1:10), are presented as already disarmed and defeated (Col. 2:15). This is because Christ's death and resurrection constituted the decisive battle. The war will end in the final victory exhibited in the resurrection of Christ's people. Therefore, "the last enemy" (at least in point of time, and perhaps most formidable of all viewed from the human perspective) "to be destroyed is death" (I Cor. 15:26).

Such a future view of victory is tied to the mediatorial ministry of the risen Lord who, in his present rule, brings "the whole estranged creation back into harmony with God."[10] Then His Kingdom and ministry comes to an end and merges into the eternal Kingdom of God. There is no failure in the prophetic promise that Messiah's kingdom will know no end (Isa. 9:7; Luke 1:33). His promise to those who overcome is genuine: "He who conquers, I will grant to sit with me on my throne, as I myself conquered and sat down with my Father on his throne" (Rev. 3:21).

At this point Paul returns to some practical arguments. If there is no future resurrection in which all Christians participate, Paul asks, "what do people mean by being baptized on behalf of the dead?" (I Cor. 15:29). That is, why have some of you become Christians in order to be united with those Christian loved ones already dead?[11] Such motivation for baptism is pointless if the dead are not raised.

---

10. Bruce, *Corinthians*, p. 148.

11. This is not a prooftext for some kind of proxy baptism as held by present-day Mormons and other earlier cultic groups.

Paul's own example is itself a practical argument for resurrection (I Cor. 15:30-32). Why should Paul endure hardships? Why should he "die daily," in order to have as his "pride" such converts as the Corinthians? In fact, if there is no resurrection, then an epicurean antinomianism is in order: "Let us eat and drink, for tomorrow we die" (I Cor. 15:32b).[12] But, the dead are raised; and such immorality is deceptive and to be shunned (I Cor. 15:33-34).

The Nature of the Resurrection Body

But, some will ask, "How are the dead raised? With what kind of body do they go forth?" (I Cor. 15:35). Apparently such questions were being raised by those who denied the resurrection to show that their denial was justifiable. After all, these detractors knew what happened to the physical body after death. If resurrection is the reanimation of that same material, then such resurrection appeared impossible.[13]

To those questions, Paul replies, sharply, "You foolish man!" (I Cor. 15:36a). He proceeds to show that personal identity does not require such material reconstitution. Nature itself witnesses to this in seed sown, dying, and producing, identical fruit (I Cor. 15:36b-38). Each kind of seed produces an identical body; this is God's design seen throughout the natural world. What is true in botany is true biologically. All flesh (life) is not the same. There is human life, animal life, bird life, fish life. Astronomy, too, witnesses to this truth: Celestial bodies and terrestrial bodies are different and their glory is different. The sun has a peculiar and unique

---

12. A quotation from Isa. 22:13, but reflecting the thought of the Preacher in Ecclesiastes 2:24.
13. Jesus' resurrection, of course, was different since his body did not have time to decay.

175

function different from the moon; even the stars are different in their brightness (I Cor. 15:40-41). The infinite variety of God's provision in the world which He created ought to make one cautious about suppositions relative to His provision for His own after death.

But Paul is not solely emphasizing caution for the doubter; he speaks about the positive reality of the resurrection body. The resurrection body is like the analogies to which he has referred. Continuing to use the metaphor of sowing, he says: "What is sown is perishable, what is raised is imperishable. It is sown in dishonor, it is raised in glory. It is sown in weakness, it is raised in power. It is sown a physical body, it is raised a spiritual body" (I Cor. 15:42-44). Paul is underscoring, through this analogic way of speaking, the "somatical identity" of the resurrection body.[14] The resurrection will not be materially identical with the present body of perishable flesh, weakness and dishonor, but the personalistic identity survives in some substantial or somatic form. As Dahl rightly notes, "body" in Paul's usage here "means the whole personality, and resurrection means the restoration—the final salvation—of that unified personality." It is proper, therefore, to talk about, and "insist on the word *identity* as describing this relationship."[15] What Paul is saying has no meaning unless it is the *same person* existing now that is to be raised. The resurrection is a bodily resurrection guaranteeing this personal and somatic identity.

These declarations are strengthened by two other arguments. (1) The argument drawn from the previous recognition of two Adams. The first Adam (man) was a living being,

---

14. See M. E. Dahl, *The Resurrection of the Body* (London: SCM Press, 1962), p. 10.

15. *Ibid.*, p. 94.

but has his origin in the earth. The second Adam (man) is from heaven. All men partake of this earthly existence (in a physical body) because of relationship to that first Adam; but all may also partake of a future heavenly existence (in a spiritual body) because of that second Adam (I Cor. 15:47-49). (2) It is quite apparent that "flesh and blood cannot inherit the kingdom of God nor does what is perishable inherit the imperishable" (I Cor. 15:50). So, if there is any reality in a future kingdom which is imperishable, it must be experienced through a different medium, "the image of the man of heaven"; hence, a spiritual body of power and glory.

In this attempt to answer the question raised about the nature of the resurrection body, Paul sets out four characteristics of this new body. First, it is *incorruptible*. The present body of flesh may be a marvel of design but it is also a deteriorating body. It is subject to decay, disease, destruction. Eventually it will disintegrate and go back to the dust from whence it came (Ecclesiastes 12:7). Whatever God may have designed originally for man, since sin has entered the human sphere, death and destruction has followed. This body which man experiences is a body of sin (Rom. 6:6), a body of death (Rom. 7:24), a body to be kept under discipline (I Cor. 9:27). But the resurrection body is incorruptible, imperishable.

Secondly, this resurrection body, in contradistinction to the natural or physical body, is a body of *glory*. The natural body is a body of dishonor (*atimia*); that is, a body absent of glory or honor, not disgraceful. The resurrection body is a body, full of honor and glory. As Paul notes in the Philippian letter, the natural, lowly (KJV-vile) body *will be changed* like unto Christ's "glorious body" at His Coming (Phil. 3:21). The resurrection body is freed from those limiting factors

177

that cause the present body to die, decay, moulder to dust. It will not only continue eternally, imperishably, but by the power of God it will be filled with glory, radiant with the eternal light and life of God.

A third characteristic is *power*. The natural body of this existence is weak and impotent. Even compared to other creatures of God's creation man is a puny weakling. Comparatively his strength, his sight, his hearing, his swiftness are all surprisingly small. He is susceptible to all kinds of disease and injury. Truly, the human body "is sown in weakness." But, the resurrection body will possess power. If Jesus' existence following his resurrection is any kind of model then space and time are overcome, and a kind of power is displayed not seen in his pre-resurrection state. Jesus was "declared to be the Son of God *in power* . . . by his resurrection from the dead" (Rom. 1:4), and in the resurrection of His followers this power will also be manifest in them. The power now experienced in the Holy Spirit (Rom. 15:13; Eph. 3:17f.) bringing Christians knowledge of the presence of the resurrected Lord (Phil. 3:10) is but a small foretaste of that intrinsic power that will be known in resurrected glory.

Finally, Paul sees the resurrection body as a *spiritual* body, "The present body is animated by 'soul' and is therefore mortal; the resurrection body is animated entirely by immortal and *life giving spirit,* and is therefore called *a spiritual body.*"[16] This terminology may appear at first glance to be contradictory. How can something be both body and spirit? Such contradiction comes only from that frame of mind that sees body only as material. What is set out is a paradox, a

---

16. Bruce, *Corinthians*, p. 152.

seeming contradiction, necessary to express two apparently conflicting truths. The Christian will be raised bodily, but the resurrection body is not natural or material but spiritual. "The resurrection body will be a new instrument and dwelling for the redeemed spirit."[17] The full meaning of the term "spiritual body" lies beyond human comprehension, but Paul is certainly revealing that the new existence is in some substantial way a continued identity, not materially but somatically, of the Christian's present life in Christ.

No wonder Paul can speak of "the glory that is to be revealed to us" (Rom. 8:18). He links this glory with that in which the whole of creation will participate. "For the creation waits with eager longing for the revealing of the sons of God; for the creation was subjected to futility, not of its own will but by the will of him who subjected it in hope; because the creation itself will be set free from its bondage to decay and obtain the glorious liberty of the children of God. We know that the whole creation has been groaning in travail together until now; and not only the creation, but we ourselves, who have the first fruits of the Spirit, groan inwardly as we wait for adoption as sons, the redemption of our bodies" (Rom. 8:19f.). This passage speaks of this glorious resurrection; it shall be accompanied by a "redemption of creation," a "new heaven and new earth" (Rev. 21:1f.).

Paul closes his arguments about the resurrection, by declaring that this is a "mystery" (I Cor. 15:51f.). It is a sacred secret, not revealed before, but now made known. It is to be accepted as special revelation. The dead will be raised. They will come forth with spiritual bodies of power and glory. But, those who are alive at that time—"at the last trumpet"

---

17. Tenney, *The Reality of the Resurrection*, p. 170.

(I Cor. 15:52)—will also "be changed" into imperishable, glorious, powerful spiritual bodies (I Cor. 15:52-54; Phil. 3:20-21). This is the ultimate victory that was foreshadowed in Isaiah 25:8 where the prophet spoke of him who will swallow up death for ever. Paul then asks those ringing questions found in Hosea 13:14: "O death, where is thy Victory? O death, where is thy sting?" Death may do its worst; for its victory is hollow and shortlived. The "sting of death is sin" (I Cor. 15:56), but Jesus "died for our sins" (I Cor. 15:3); "the power of sin is the law" (I Cor. 15:56), but the law has been "canceled" and "set aside" by "nailing it to the cross" (Col. 2:14). All principalities, and enemies, all powers against Christ's people have been "disarmed" and are made a "public example" as He "triumphs over them" in His resurrection (Col. 2:15; cf. Col. 2:12f.).

What is the Christian's attitude in light of this revealed mystery? It is gratitude! "Thanks be to God who gives us the victory through our Lord Jesus Christ" (I Cor. 15:57). But that attitude must eventuate in action. "Therefore, my beloved brethren, be steadfast, immovable, *always abounding in the work of* the Lord, knowing that in the Lord your labor is not in vain" (I Cor. 15:58).

FOR FURTHER STUDY

Bruce, F. F. *Paul, Apostle of the Heart Set Free.* Grand Rapids, Michigan: Wm. B. Eerdmans Publishing Co., 1977.

Dahl, M. E. *The Resurrection of the Body.* Studies in Biblical Theology. London: SCM Press, 1962. Particularly consult his appendix: "A Word List for I Corinthians 15."

Tenney, Merrill C. *The Reality of the Resurrection.* New York: Harper and Row, 1963.

QUESTIONS FOR DISCUSSION

1. Why is Christ's resurrection essential to the Gospel? Can you give instances of persons claiming to "preach the Gospel" apart from belief in the resurrection?
2. Compare the evidence for the resurrection to evidence presented in courts, historical writings, etc. Are other evidences more extensive than what Paul presents for the resurrection?
3. Analyze Paul's arguments leading to utter hopelessness if there is no resurrection. Can you detect any fallacy in Paul's reasoning?
4. What is meant by the term "somatic identity"? Why is this important?
5. Compare Paul's conception of the resurrection to what we know about our own physical existence.
6. How is Paul using the idea of the "two Adams"? Compare this use here in I Corinthians 15 to that in Romans 5.

Chapter Eleven

THE RESURRECTION AS SEEN IN THE GENERAL EPISTLES AND HEBREWS

"[We have been] born anew to a living hope through the resurrection of Jesus Christ from the dead" (*I Peter 1:3*).

In Paul's extended argument for resurrection reality which he presented so forcefully to the Corinthians he claims that the apostolic testimony is unanimous on this vital issue. "Whether . . . it was I or they [the other Apostles] so we preach and so you believed" (I Cor. 15:11). There is not the slightest variation in the authoritative, apostolic witness. Peter, James, and Paul are in perfect accord; they saw, believed, and preached that Jesus arose from the dead.

Those whom Paul recognized as apostles before him, particularly Peter, James, and John, to whom he refers as "pillars in the church" (Gal. 2:6-9), not only give united testimony to the reality of the resurrection of Jesus, but also are led by the Spirit (as was Paul) to reveal the implications of Jesus' resurrection for the faith and life of the Christian. This is seen in the epistle of James in the exalted titles he uses for referring to Jesus. He is the "Lord" (James 1:12; 4:10, 15); the "Lord Jesus Christ" (James 1:1); the "Lord of Glory" (James 2:1). Though the epistle is very practical and is often referred to as an example of New Testament wisdom literature, it still emphasizes certain doctrinal issues. One of these—the sure coming of the Lord (James 5:8, 9)—is based solidly upon resurrection truth. Jesus has been raised and is Lord. This Lord of glory shall return demanding patience (James 5:8) and righteous living, for He will judge (James 5:9).

What is intimated and implied in the epistle of James is brought out in greater detail in other general epistles[1] and in that great Christological message known as the epistle to the Hebrews. A careful study of these documents augments what has been discovered about the resurrection in other segments of Scripture.

Peter's Letters: New Birth and New Hope

Peter had learned his lesson well! In Luke's gospel is that record of the risen Lord suddenly appearing to the Twelve, proving that He was alive. "See My hands and My feet . . . touch Me and see, for a spirit does not have flesh and bones as you see that I have," (Luke 24:39), Jesus says. After they are convinced that he is truly alive, Jesus says to them, "These are my words which I spoke to you while I was still with you, that all things which are written about Me in the Law of Moses and the Prophets and the Psalms must be fulfilled" (Luke 24:44). He added, "Thus it is written that the Christ should suffer and rise again from the dead on the third day" (Luke 24:46). Luke shows that through such statements Jesus was able to "open the minds" of the disciples "to understand the Scriptures" (Luke 24:45).

Peter understood, and in writing to those Christians scattered throughout Asia Minor he emphasizes this truth which had been so indelibly stamped upon his mind. Our salvation, Peter is saying, was predicted by the prophets. These prophets, though making "careful search and inquiry, seeking to know what person or what time" (I Pet. 1:10) the Spirit within them was indicating, could not know the

---

1. This term is used to designate other apostolic writings than those written by Paul.

reality that they predicted as they spoke of the "sufferings of Christ and the glories to follow." This could be known only by those to whom it is now revealed through the proclamation of the gospel (I Pet. 1:12). These gospel facts— centering in the death ("sufferings") and resurrection ("glories to follow")—are so glorious and wonderful that they are "things into which angels long to look" (I Pet. 1:12c).

But the gospel is not only a recital of glorious facts, it is good news of a graceful present. Upon obedience to this gospel, with the consequent "sprinkling with His blood" (I Pet. 1:2), the "sanctifying work of the Spirit" (I Pet. 1:2) begins. The Christian is "born again into a living hope through the resurrection of Jesus Christ from the dead" (I Pet. 1:3). Because of the power of this resurrection, the Christian can endure "various trials" and his faith can be proven as it is thus "tested by fire" (I Pet. 1:5, 6). The end is an "imperishable and undefiled" inheritance "reserved in heaven" (I Pet. 1:4). Loving Him whom one has not seen, yet one does believe Him to be the living Lord and looks forward to that day when he can experience the "revelation of Jesus Christ" and his tested faith be found to result in "praise and glory and honor" (I Pet. 1:7, 8).

In this manner, Peter links *the prophetic past* and its fulfillment, *the graceful present* and its loving commitment and *the glorious future* with its unfading inheritance with the resurrection of Jesus Christ from the dead. It is because of this resurrection that one knows he is "redeemed by precious blood, the blood of Christ, as of a lamb umblemished and spotless" (I Pet. 1:18-20). This divine work was foreknown "before the foundation of the world" but occurred in time for believers (I Pet. 1:20-21). By raising this redeeming One from the dead and giving Him glory, God has made possible "faith and hope" (I Pet. 1:21). This good news is the basis of *the new birth* (I Pet. 1:23-25), *the new life* as holy and "obedient children" (I Pet. 1:13-15; 22; 2:1-3), *the new relationship* as a "holy and royal priesthood" (I Pet. 2:5, 9), "a chosen race . . . a holy nation, a people for God's own possession" (I Pet. 2:9a), and *the new responsibilities* involving offering acceptable "spiritual sacrifices" (I Pet. 2:5) and proclaiming "the excellencies of Him who has called you out of darkness into His marvelous light" (I Pet. 2:9b).

This Jesus who has been raised is the Christian's model. His deportment and demeanor even as He faced the Cross, bearing "our sins in His own body" on that tree (I Pet. 2:24), is to serve as an example (I Pet. 2:21ff.). Hence, Christians ought not to see their suffering for doing right as anything strange, since Christ also suffered even unto death. His death was not deserved but was "for sins, once for all, the just for the unjust, in order that He might bring us to God, having been put to death in the flesh, but made alive in the spirit" (I Pet. 3:18). His resurrection, then, gives meaning to the sinner's baptism. Such baptism "saves," not because of the water, but because it is an "appeal to God for a good conscience—through the resurrection of Jesus Christ" (I Pet. 3:21).

Since this resurrected Lord is "at the right hand of God, having gone into heaven" (I Pet. 3:22), Christians look to him as authority, empowering presence and coming deliverer (I Pet. 4:1-7). If the "end of all things is at hand" (I Pet. 4:7), believers must be "of sound judgment and sober spirit," "fervent in love," "hospitable," employing their "special gifts" as "good stewards of the manifold grace of God" (I Pet. 4:7-10). All Christian activity grows out of resurrection

185

power and is designed "so that in all things God may be glorified through Jesus Christ, to whom belongs the glory and dominion forever and ever" (I Pet. 4:11). After all, suffering for the name of Christ, or "as a Christian" brings glory to God (I Pet. 4:14-16), and one can rejoice ("exult") at the time of the "revelation of His glory" (I Pet. 4:13).

But, Peter cautions his readers about the danger they may face if they suffer as "evildoers" or "troublesome meddlers" (I Pet. 4:15). Hear his stern warning: "For it is time for judgment to begin with the household of God; and if it begins with us first, what will be the outcome for those who do not obey the gospel of God? And if it is with difficulty that the righteous is saved, what will become of the Godless man and the sinner?" (I Pet. 4:17-18). There is no Bonhofferian "cheap grace" in Peter's thinking! It is because God's grace is so costly—witnessed in the suffering death of the risen Christ—that Peter sets out this stern warning.

Even the work of the spiritual leaders ("elders") of the congregation to whom Peter writes is to be carried out in terms of the resurrection. Peter, a "fellow elder," refers to himself as a "witness of the sufferings of Christ, and a partaker also of the glory that is to be revealed" (I Cor. 5:1). From this firm ground he exhorts elders to "exercise oversight," voluntarily and eagerly, and to shepherd the flock, not "lording it" over them, but "proving to be examples" for them (I Pet. 5:2, 3).[2] Upon successful completion of their duties as leaders, the great "Shepherd and Guardian" of all believers (I Pet. 2:25) will appear as the "Chief

---

2. In this passage Peter has combined the three functions of these spiritual leaders. *Elders* are the men who are sharing with their people their wisdom drawn from experience; *Shepherds* (Pastors) are leaders who, like the Good Shepherd, feed and guard; *Bishops* (overseers) are those who are in authority, superintending and guiding by example and persuasion.

Shepherd" and these faithful "undershepherds" will receive the unfading crown of glory" (I Pet. 5:4).

Peter's second letter continues to emphasize this great hope that Christians have because of Christ's death and resurrection. Jesus is referred to in the salutation as "God and Savior" (II Pet. 1:1). As Lord, "His divine power has granted to us everything pertaining to life and godliness, through the true knowledge of Him who called us by His own glory and excellence. For by these He has granted to us everything pertaining to life and godliness, through the true knowledge of Him who called us by His own glory and excellence. For by these He has granted to us His precious and magnificient promises, in order that by them you might become partakers of the divine nature" (II Pet. 1:3, 4). Because of this divine action, which brings "new birth" or participation in the divine nature, Christians must "add to" or "supply with" their faith, moral excellence (virtue), knowledge, self-control, perseverance, godliness, brotherly kindness and agape love (II Pet. 1:5-7). In doing this, the Christian is fruitful and useful; makes his "calling and election (choosing)" certain; is sensitive to the fact that he has been purified "from his former sins"; and will be given a joyous welcome and an "abundant entrance" into the "eternal kingdom of our Lord and Savior Jesus Christ" (II Pet. 1:8-11).

Peter is adamant relative to the foundation of this eternal hope. What he and others have preached are not "cleverly devised tales" (II Pet. 1:16), but come from what they saw and heard (see Acts 4:20). They were "eyewitnesses of His majesty" (II Pet. 1:16). Peter chooses one significant event from Jesus' life to illustrate this. We saw the "honor and glory" given to Jesus in His transfiguration on the "holy mountain." We heard the voice of the Father, "utterance made to Him (Jesus) by the Majestic Glory"—"This is my beloved Son with whom I am well pleased" (II Pet. 1:17-18). Because of experiences like this one, Peter and these other apostolic witnesses were certain about "the prophetic word," which did not come privately or as humanly devised or interpreted but came from God, as "men were moved by the Holy Spirit" to speak God's prophetic word (II Pet. 1:19-21).

This "sure word" about God's prophetic truth, the fulfillment of His Messianic promises in Jesus, His Son, the saving grace that comes to all who are "partakers of the divine nature" through Jesus, must be constantly proclaimed and taught. Why? Because of false teachers who, like those "false prophets" of old, "secretly introduce destructive heresies, even denying the Master who bought them" (II Pet. 2:1). Such false teachers will be destroyed, even as God brought destruction upon unbelief in the past (II Pet. 2:3ff.). Believers are to beware of these who are like "springs without water, mists driven by the storm," lest they too be judged and destroyed (II Pet. 2:17f.).

One particular truth that these "arrogant," "greedy," "sensual" opponents of God will assail is that corollary of Jesus' resurrection, His return. "Where is the promise of His coming?" they will ask derisively. "After all, from long ages past everything has been as it was from creation" (see II Pet. 3:4). But Peter reminds them that there had been the destruction of the ancient world by the flood—"the world at that time was destroyed being flooded with water" (II Pet. 3:6). Their uniformitarian thinking was faulty and limited, and what God has in store for this present universe is beyond their apprehension (II Pet. 3:7). But, more importantly, God's timetable is not subject to man's puny logic. "Do not let this fact escape your notice," Peter says. "With the Lord one day is as a thousand years, and a thousand years as one day" (II Pet. 3:8).

On the positive side, Peter clearly affirms the risen Lord's return, accompanied by Judgment, the end of this present age and the dissolution of the present universe to be recreated a "new heavens and a new earth, in which righteousness dwells" (II Pet. 3:13). These promises are sure and they should create the most joyous anticipation among Christians. If there is any question about delay, this too is positive; since "the Lord is not slow about His promise, as some count slowness, but is patient toward you, not wishing for any to perish, but for all to come to repentance" (II Pet. 3:9). His patience should be regarded as salvation (II Pet. 3:15); for during the day of patience Christians have opportunity to "grow in the grace and knowledge of our Lord Jesus Christ" (II Pet. 3:18), "to be found by Him in peace, spotless and blameless (II Pet. 3:14), and to proclaim this good news of salvation through the crucified, risen *and* returning Lord of glory.

The Letters of John and Jude: Abiding in the Son

There is no question that the first epistle of John was written by the "beloved disciple" who penned the fourth gospel. There are common themes and emphases throughout the two documents. One of those common ideas is that which Jesus introduced in that farewell discourse given to His disciples on the night of His betrayal. In speaking of His departure, He assures them that He will "come again" and will take them to be with Him in that prepared place which He terms "my Father's house" (John 14:1-3). In the interim, they will be aided by the Helper (*Paraclete*) whom He will send to them (John 14:16f.). This Helper, "the Spirit of truth" will not only guide them into all truth (John 14:26; 15:26, 27; 16:13-15), but will "abide in them" (John 14:17). Through the Spirit and the Word, Father and Son will come into the believer and make their "abode with him" (John 14:23).

Such promises are understandable only in terms of Jesus' resurrection. He can abide within His disciples only through the Spirit given by Him. As "branches," believers can "abide in the vine" only if that "vine" continues to live (John 15:1-6). Hence, one significant proof of resurrection and ascension is the presence of the Spirit and the reality of Jesus' abiding presence through that Spirit (John 14:16, 26; 15:26; 16:7).

In John's first epistle, this reality seen under the term abide, is clearly enunciated. Here, it is not predicted but fulfilled; not a probability but an actuality. John speaks about those who say they "abide in Him," but do not show it by their life (I John 2:6). He urges his hearers to "let that abide in" them which they "heard from the beginning. If what you heard from the beginning abides in you, you also will abide in the Son and in the Father" (I John 2:24).

Such "abiding" is related both to the past promise of Jesus concerning His Spirit—"you have an anointing from the Holy One" (I John 2:20); we know by this that He abides in us, by the Spirit whom He has given (I John 3:24)—and the future coming of the risen Lord: "abide in Him, so that when He appears we may have confidence and not shrink away from Him in shame at His coming" (I John 2:28).

There is no question in John's mind as to the identity of the Coming One. He is the *Paraclete*, the Helper or Advocate, now at God's right hand, who will forgive the sins of

His own, since He is the "propitiation" for sins, having died for the sins "of the whole world" (I John 2:1, 2). This is the same One whom John and those other eyewitnesses knew so well—"we have seen with our eyes, what we beheld and our hands handled" (I John 1:1)—and had proclaimed. It is in Him that "fellowship" with the Father is realized. It is through "walking in the light as He Himself is in the light" (I John 1:7) that this fellowship is extended and known. Joined together in fellowship with Him, demonstrated by loving action, Christians continue to experience the efficacy of His cleansing blood (I John 1:7) and to know that they have passed from death to life (I John 3:14). Eternal life (as defined by Jesus himself in John 17:3) is equated with this "abiding," this continuous "fellowship" with the risen Lord (I John 5:11ff.).

While Christians live and walk in loving fellowship with the risen Jesus, who, in "the days of His flesh," demonstrated that God is love (I John 4:7-11), they are called (and *are*) "sons of God" (I John 3:1). That fact denotes God's "great love" and demands loving obedience (I John 2:3-11; 3:16-18; 4:8ff.). At the close of a life of loving obedience to God is the expected "hope" that motivates to "purity" (I John 3:3). That hope centers in the risen Lord's coming ("when He appears") and the Christian's transformation to "be like Him" (I John 3:2). John, himself, expresses ignorance as to what this means in terms of future likeness; he is altogether satisfied that "when He appears, we shall be like Him, because we shall see Him just as He is" (I John 3:2).

The short epistle of Jude, the brother of James, deals mainly with the dangers posed by those "who have crept in unnoticed . . . ungodly persons who turn the grace of our God into licentiousness and deny our only Master and Lord,

Jesus Christ" (vs. 4). Hence, it is important that those who are "kept for Jesus Christ" (note the futuristic note) to "contend earnestly for the faith which was once for all delivered to the saints" (vs. 3). This faith has been sullied by these apostates whose terrible pedigree Jude sets out vividly (vss. 8-16). These were the ones predicted by the "apostles of our Lord Jesus Christ" (vs. 17f.).[3]

Over against such descriptions of these evildoers and godless apostates, Jude encourages his readers to abide in Christ by "building yourselves up on your most holy faith" and by keeping "yourselves in the love of God waiting anxiously for the mercy of our Lord Jesus Christ to eternal life" (vss. 20-21). Here, the risen Lord who is the coming One is seen as the center of faith, the motivator of love and the object of hope.

Hebrews: The Risen Lord as Faithful High Priest

Resurrection and Ascension are frequently viewed as a simple composite in the New Testament witness. In Philippians Paul speaks of the eternal Son, humbling himself as a servant and becoming obedient unto death on the Cross, as being highly exalted by God. This exaltation is such that at His most excellent name "every knee shall bow . . . and every tongue shall confess that Jesus Christ is Lord, to the glory of God the Father" (Phil. 2:8-11). Such exaltation involves both resurrection from the dead and ascension to God's right hand. Or, as reflected in Ephesians, God not only raised Jesus from the dead but "seated Him at His right hand in the heavenly places, far above all rule and

---

3. There is a close corollary between Jude and II Peter. It seems good sense to see Peter as predicting and Jude as pointing to fulfillment.

authority and power and dominion, and every name that is named, not only in this age but also in the one to come" (Eph. 1:20, 21).

Though the two events are not separated as historical events (just as death and resurrection are inseparably linked under such terminology as "Christ crucified"—I Cor. 2:2), they are to be distinguished as theological truths. *Resurrection* demonstrates that Jesus of Nazareth could not be held fast by death, that He is indeed the Son of God (Rom. 1:4), and that the last enemy, death, has been conquered in Him (I Cor. 15:26). *Ascension* emphasizes that the work of Jesus on earth is finished, He has been seated at God's right hand, entering into His heavenly Lordship (Ps. 16), sharing in the omnipresence and omnipotence of God as formerly, and has begun his intercessory work for His people as High Priest, and will return as Redeemer-Judge.

The implications of the Ascension are clearly in view in the letter to the Hebrews. The first three verses serve both as introduction to and a cameo of the inspired author's argument. The continuity of divine revelation is affirmed. God has spoken partially and temporarily to "the fathers in the prophets" but now He speaks fully and finally "in His Son." This Son, who is the final "word of God" (Heb. 4:12), is superior to all former agents—angels (Heb. 1:5-14), Moses (Heb. 3:1-6), Joshua (Heb. 7:4-13), the priests of the Aaronic order (Heb. 4:14—5:10)—and His ministry is superior to all former institutions—tabernacle (Heb. 9:1ff.), temple, sacrificial system (Heb. 9:1-28), feasts and covenants (Heb. 8:1—10:18). Why? Because God has appointed Him "heir of all things" and, through Him, "made the world." The Son is the "radiance of His glory and the exact representation of His nature." He, alone, "upholds all

193

things by the word of His power." To cap off this marvelous description of cosmic and creative power, the inspired writer speaks to the issue of human need. "When He had made purification of sins, He sat down at the right hand of the Majesty on high" (Heb. 1:1-3).

Nowhere in specific terms is the Resurrection of Christ set forth.[4] His exaltation is clearly stated, from which both resurrection and ascension must be inferred. This is seen from the beginning of the argument showing Christ's superiority. He is "much better" than the angels, because He is both *higher* and *lower* than they. To which of the angels did God say "Thou art my Son" (Heb. 1:5, reflecting Ps. 2:7)? To what angel did God say, "Sit at my right hand until I make thine enemies a footstool for thy feet" (Heb. 1:13 reflecting Ps. 110:1)? It is not of angels, but of the Son that it is written "Thy throne, O God, is forever and ever, and the righteous scepter is the scepter of His Kingdom" (Heb. 1:8 reflecting Ps. 45:6). The son is sovereign; angels are but "ministering spirits, sent out to render service for the sake of those who will inherit salvation" (Heb. 1:14).

But this eternal Son, this Sovereign Lord, is also *lower* than the angels (Heb. 2:5f.). He becomes man; and as the Psalmist points out man has been made a "little lower than the angels" (Ps. 8:5). But, man's glory is that he is the ruler of the universe—"thou has put all things under his feet" (Ps. 8:6). The Psalmist is describing man's place in this universe; the inspired writer of Hebrews sees more in this Psalm than that. Jesus is Representative Man. What is said about man applies to Him. "But we do see Him who was made for a little while lower than the angels, namely Jesus,

---

4. The term "resurrection of the dead" is used in Hebrews 6:2, evidently referring to the general resurrection.

194

because of the sufferings of death crowned with glory and honor, that by the grace of God He might taste death for everyone" (Heb. 2:9). It is through "suffering" that this obedient Son, who has become Man, is made perfect. "Although He was a Son, He learned obedience from the things which He suffered" (Heb. 5:8). But, this obedient suffering has two consequences. For Jesus, it issues into "glory"; for humanity, it brings salvation, "bringing many sons to glory" (Heb. 2:10). The suffering Son, as Representative Man, is "made perfect" and "became to all those who obey Him, the source of eternal salvation" (Heb. 5:9).

Through life and death, Jesus shares fully in humanity's nature. But, His death is unique; since it is not only a participation in human existence, but also a saving act of substitutionary atonement (He "tastes death for everyone"—Heb. 2:9b). But, even more, through that unique act, He renders "powerless him who had the power of death, that is, the devil" and delivers "those who through fear of death were subject to slavery all their lives" (Heb. 2:14, 15). This power over the devil and the devil's strategems ("death" and "the fear of death") can be understood only in terms of Resurrection (see II Tim. 1:10; I Cor. 15:26; I John 3:8f.). The "glory and honor" with which the obedient Son and Representative Man is crowned is to be seen in terms of His finished atoning work and God's mighty display of power in raising Him from the dead and seating Him on His Sovereign throne.

"Consider Jesus," the inspired author entreats. He is "Apostle and High Priest" (Heb. 3:1). Apostle, because He was "sent" on a divine mission and accomplished it fully, adequately, perfectly (see Heb. 5:8, 9). Because of that faithfulness (Heb. 3:2) he has been "designated by God as a high priest according to the order of Melchizedek" (Heb.

5:10). This "final word" (Heb. 1:2) is "living and active" (Heb. 4:12)[5] and there is no "creature hidden from His sight, but all things are open and laid bare to the eyes of Him with whom we have to do" (Heb. 4:13). As "a great high priest" he "has passed through the heavens, Jesus the Son of God" (Heb. 4:14). There is no doubt as to identity. It is Jesus who is Apostle and High Priest; Jesus, the Son of God, who lived and died, who can "sympathize with our weaknesses," who has "been tempted in all things as we are, yet without sin" (Heb. 4:15). He has been raised by God, declared High Priest, seated at God's right hand. All who come to Him, can "draw near with confidence to the throne of grace," "receive mercy," and "find grace to help in time of need" (Heb. 4:16).

But, Jesus' High Priesthood is unique. He was not from Aaron's loins nor of the tribe of Levi. He did not take this "honor to himself" but was called to this position by God (Heb. 5:4, 5). This is the meaning of that strange passage in Psalms 110:4: "Thou art a priest forever according to the order of Melchizedek." Just as we know little about Melchizedek—his lineage ("without father and mother"), his origin and destiny ("having neither beginning of days nor end of life")—so Jesus' priesthood is a radical break with that hereditary priesthood connected with the Old Covenant (Heb. 7:1ff.). Since He "abides forever"—and His resurrection and ascension is proof of this—He "holds His priesthood permanently" (Heb. 7:24). Therefore, He is "able to save forever (KJV "to the uttermost") those who draw near

---

5. There are some who would limit the "word" of Heb. 4:12 to Scripture or the "oral word" of proclamation and teaching, but the context suggests that the "living word" revealed in Jesus seems to be a better interpretation.

to God through Him, since He always lives to make intercession for them" (Heb. 7:25).[6] He can do this because He lived a "holy, innocent, undefiled, separated" life (Heb. 7:26) and He "offered up Himself" for the sins of the people (Heb. 7:27). Consequently, He has been "exalted above the heavens" (Heb. 7:26) and "has taken His seat at the right hand of the throne of the Majesty in the heavens" (Heb. 8:1).

Such exaltation, proving His unique High Priesthood, guarantees "a better covenant" (Heb. 7:22). This covenant's ministry takes place not in "an earthly tent," conducted by a continuum of priests (Heb. 9:1f.), centering in the "blood of calves and goats" (Heb. 9:19-22), but in the "true tabernacle, which the Lord pitched, not man" (Heb. 8:2). This "sanctuary," in contradistinction to that "holy place" in the earthly tent, is "heaven itself." Christ, as High Priest and Minister of a new and better covenant, "did not enter a holy place made with hands, a mere copy of the true one, but into heaven itself, now to appear in the presence of God" for His new covenant people (Heb. 9:24). But, He does not enter empty-handed. Like the priests of old, He comes with a blood offering ("without the shedding of blood there is no forgiveness"—Heb. 9:22), His own body and blood offered once and for all (Heb. 9:25; 10:10-18). He has inaugurated "a new and living way" through the "veil" (Heb. 10:20). This is accomplished by His sacrificial blood (Heb. 10:19), and the efficacy of that atoning work finished at Calvary, is applied to all who "draw near with a sincere heart in full assurance of faith, having our hearts sprinkled

---

6. In classic theology, the "intercessory ministry of Christ" is based upon passages such as this.

clean from an evil conscience and our bodies washed with pure water" (Heb. 10:22).[7]

As members of a new covenant, with a better sacrifice, a superior priesthood, Christians have a better hope. This hope is based solidly upon the unchangeableness of God guaranteed by an oath (Heb. 6:17). That eternal God has worked out His purpose, through Abraham, Moses, His covenant people, and finally through Jesus the fulfillment of all past promises. Jesus is the "forerunner," having entered "within the veil" through His blood. He has set "hope" as "an anchor of the soul both sure and steadfast" (Heb. 6:19) upon the mighty rock of God's unchanging grace. He does this as crucified, risen, ascended Lord; promising salvation now and judgment at his coming (Heb. 9:27, 28).

In light of the superiority of Christ and His ministry over all former agents and institutions of religion, the call is to faithfulness. One cannot "shrink back" for that leads to "destruction." Only faithful commitment to Christ leads "to the preserving of the soul" (Heb. 10:39). The heroes of faith illustrate this (Heb. 11:1f.). Abel, Enoch, Noah, Abraham, Moses, Joshua, Rahab, and many other Old Testament people demonstrated such faithfulness even though they did not receive the promises (Heb. 11:13). But such faithfulness did produce mighty wonders.

By faith these heroes of the past "conquered kingdoms, performed acts of righteousness, obtained promises, shut the mouths of lions, quenched the power of fire, escaped the edge of the sword, from weakness were made strong,

---

7. Here is a clear reference to the full meaning of the baptismal act. Upon baptism, which is a response of the sincere believer, the promise of inner cleansing is given.

became mighty in war, put foreign armies to flight. Women received back their dead by resurrection; and others were tortured, not accepting their release, in order that they might obtain a better resurrection" (Heb. 11:33-35).

That "better resurrection" was not theirs to experience. Only in "the fulness of time" did Jesus come to become the "author" or "pioneer" (see Heb. 12:2; also Heb. 2:10; 6:20) of faith, opening up that "new and living way" (Heb. 10:20). But He is also the "perfecter of faith" (Heb. 12:2), bringing to completion all that had been promised in the past. So, apart from those who have come to faith in this crucified, risen Lord, this great High Priest for and Representative of His New Covenant people, those saints of the past could "not be made perfect" (Heb. 11:40), nor enter into that "city which has foundations" (Heb. 11:10) or that "better country, that is a heavenly one" (Heb. 11:15).

Jesus is the key to the fulfillment of all hopes and desires. No wonder, Luke records that when Jesus was transfigured on the mountain, He and Moses and Elijah were "speaking of His departure which He was about to accomplish at Jerusalem" (Luke 9:31). This departure—including sacrificial death, glorious resurrection and heavenly ascension—makes possible the salvation of all, past, present and future. Christians must fix their eyes upon Jesus, "who for the joy set before Him, endured the cross, despising the shame, and has sat down at the right hand of the throne of God" (Heb. 12:2). Like disciplined athletes, they must run patiently "the race that is set before" them (Heb. 12:1), knowing that "Jesus Christ is the same yesterday and today, yes and forever" (Heb. 13:8).

After pointing out the practical demands of the Christian's

life "within the general assembly and church of the first-born[8] who are enrolled in heaven" (Heb. 12:22) in the closing sections of the letter, the inspired author closes with that great benediction which focuses upon resurrection power. "Now the God of peace, who brought up from the dead the great Shepherd of the sheep through the blood of the eternal covenant, even Jesus our Lord, equip you in every good thing to do His will, working in us that which is pleasing in His sight, through Jesus Christ, to whom be glory forever and ever. Amen." (Heb. 13:20, 21).

One can only bow in silent gratitude, "offer up a sacrifice of praise to God," give "thanks to His name" (Heb. 13:15), and repeat the "Amen" loudly and fervently.

FOR FURTHER STUDY

Bruce, F. F. *The Epistle to the Hebrews, New International Commentary on the New Testament.* Grand Rapids: Wm. B. Eerdmans, 1964.

Fudge, Edward. *Our Man in Heaven.* Grand Rapids: Baker Book House, 1979.

Hughes, Philip E. *A Commentary on the Epistle to the Hebrews.* Grand Rapids: Wm. B. Eerdmans, 1977.

Thompson, James. *The Letter to Hebrews.* Austin, TX: R. B. Sweet Co., 1971.

QUESTIONS FOR DISCUSSION

1. Discuss the linking, in Peter's writings, of the prophetic past, the graceful present, and the glorious future as it relates to Christians.

---

8. The concept "first-born" refers to Jesus' "first-born" from the dead. It is the assembly of the Risen One, the Church of Christ.

2. How ought Christians view their suffering for living the Christian life?
3. Discuss the role of spiritual leaders today in light of Christ's resurrection.
4. Why is Christ's second coming so vital a truth to Christians? In light of the resurrection, why is Christ's return necessary?
5. Relate the indwelling Holy Spirit to Christ's resurrection and His return.
6. How is Christ's resurrection seen in the Epistle to the Hebrews?
7. Compare and contrast the intercessory work of the risen Christ with that of the Old Testament High Priest.

Chapter Twelve

RESURRECTION AND THE SECOND ADVENT
OF CHRIST

*"The dead in Christ shall be raised first . . . to meet
the Lord in the air" (I Thess. 4:16, 17).*

Not only are Resurrection and Ascension inseparably
linked, another event must also be seen interlocking with
these two. *Parousia,* or the Second Advent of Jesus, is set
out in the New Testament documents as integrally related
with these other great themes of Christian faith. Luke's
record of that early activity clustering around the creation
of the Church on Pentecost, A.D. 30, spells this out so
clearly. If apostolic preaching could announce that "this
same Jesus" crucified is raised and exalted to be both "Lord
and Christ" (Acts 2:36), apostolic witness could also report
that angelic message that occurred following Jesus' ascension:
"Men of Galilee, why do you stand looking into the sky? *This
same Jesus,* who has been taken up from you into heaven,
will come in just *the same way* as you have watched Him
go into heaven" (Acts 1:11).[1]

One of the basic emphases of the ancient kerygma (apostolic preaching) was Jesus' glorious return. God's servant
Jesus has been delivered up, disowned before Pilate, put
to death on a cross, and raised from the dead (Acts 3:13-
15). Sins can now be blotted out completely, times of renewal
and refreshing may come from the presence of the Lord,
if only sinful man will respond in obedient faith and repent
(Acts 3:19). Then, the risen, exalted Lord—*this same Jesus*
—will be sent to "restore and renew all things" (Acts 3:20,

---

1. G. C. Berkouwer emphatically sees this as "a meaningful connection between" the two appearances. *The Return of Christ* (Grand Rapids: Wm. B.
Eerdmans, 1972), p. 141.

21). Until that time, however, "heaven will be his home" (Acts 3:21 in *Twentieth Century New Testament* translation).

The divine message proclaimed to all men has its roots in established fact—the death and resurrection of Christ— but it has its ultimate hope in a future event which is proclaimed as fervently and is seen as the same kind of divine reality as the highly attested resurrection. The past—"Christ *died* and *rose*"—the present—"He *lives* as Lord of all life"; and the future—"He will come to restore all things to proper order"—are all combined in apostolic preaching. The offer of the Gospel is both "good news" to those who accept (Acts 3:19, 20), but warning of certain judgment to those who reject (Acts 17:30, 31).

The Truth of the Second Advent

The term "second coming" or "second advent" is not found in the New Testament. It is used quite early in the history of Christendom to refer to what is clearly spelled out in the New Testament—Jesus' return for His own. As early as 150 A.D., Justin Martyr speaks of "two advents— the second, when according to prophecy, He shall come from heaven with glory, accompanied by his angelic hosts, when also He shall raise the bodies of all men who have lived, and shall clothe those of the worthy with immortality and shall send those of the wicked, endued with eternal sensibility into everlasting fire with the wicked devils."[2]

Various terms are used in the New Testament to refer to this coming event. The verbs for "return," "reveal," and "come," are used to speak of Jesus' second advent (I Pet.

---

2. "The First Apology" *The Ante-Nicene Fathers* (Grand Rapids: Wm. B. Eerdmans, 1958), Vol. I, p. 180.

1:5; 4:13; II Thess. 1:7). The noun, "revelation" (I Pet. 1:13)[3] is also used. However, the word most often used to refer to this divine reality is *parousia,* coming. Jesus uses this term to refer to this future event; Paul, Peter, James and John all use it in similar fashion. It is used by the early Church fathers often coupled with the adjective "second" (*hē deutera parousia*). There is no question but that the New Testament uniformly refers to the second advent of Jesus and sees it in inseparable relation to that activity centering in the cross and the open tomb.

It is interesting to observe the declaration of this coming event by Jesus Himself. His prophetic utterances relative to this future reality are even more significant in light of the contexts in which they are found. Near Caesarea-Philippi, He is confessed by Peter (Matt. 16:16) and He foretells the coming of the Church. Immediately, Jesus begins to speak of his imminent death to which Peter vigorously objects. Jesus rebukes Peter and declares that not only did He, as Messiah, have a cross, but all who follow Him must accept crosses themselves. It is within this context of Confession, Church and Cross, that Jesus speaks of His future Coming. His words are quite clear: "If anyone wishes to come after Me, let him deny himself, and take up his cross, and follow Me. For whoever wishes to save his life shall lose it; but whoever loses his life for My sake shall find it. For what will a man be profited, if he gains the whole world, and forfeits his soul? Or what will a man give in exchange for his soul? For the Son of Man is going to come in the glory of His Father with His angels; and will then recompense every man according to his deeds" (Matt. 16:24-27).

---

3. This same noun, *apokalypsis,* is translated "coming" in I Cor. 1:7.

On another occasion Jesus declared His return at a time that false pride was being expressed by the disciples. The Twelve had accompanied Jesus into the Temple during that last fateful week of His ministry. As they left, some of the disciples were admiring this magnificent structure: "Teacher, behold what wonderful stones and what wonderful buildings!" Jesus replied: "Do you see these great buildings? Not one stone shall be left upon another which will not be torn down" (Mark 13:12; Luke 21:5f.). It was not until they had ascended to the Mt. of Olives and were resting, that the disciples, now recovered from the shock of His reply, ask Him to explain and tell them when this would happen. They, of course, assume that it would occur at "His coming" and that this would be the "end of the age" (Matt. 24:3). In His rather enigmatic reply, Jesus clearly affirms His Coming and warns them to "be on the alert" for they would not know "which day their Lord might come" (Matt. 24:29-31, 42-44). Dr. Robert Fife says: "It is noteworthy that at such a time, when disciples showed pride in the work of men's hands—pride in human achievement—Jesus declared His return. In effect they said, 'Master, these magnificent stones will be here forever,' implying by these words that human achievement was an adequate ground of human hope. By his radical reply Jesus called to their attention that hope is not to be founded in human achievement, but in divine power—the power of God revealed in the Second Advent."[4]

The third significant context is found in the Gospel accounts of Jesus' trial before the High Priest. It is coupled with Jesus' own affirmation of His Deity. In questioning

---

4. Robert O. Fife, *Christ, Our Hope*, p. 40.

him the High Priest asked, "Are you the Christ, the Son of the Blessed One?" To this Jesus replied: "I am, and you shall see the Son of Man sitting at the right hand of power, and coming with the clouds of heaven" (Mark 14:61, 62). This was interpreted by those who tried Him blasphemy; it is significant, however, that Jesus, even while facing death, "declared to those who presumed to judge Him that He would someday appear to judge them."[5]

In light of these significant revelations of Jesus Himself and, particularly, His promises given to the Apostles (John 14:1ff.), it is not strange to see both Resurrection and Return proclaimed. The apostolic writings are filled with references to and the implications of Christ's Second Advent. This coming event is demanded for the completion of God's saving, redeeming work. So proclaims Peter (Acts 3:19-21) and so teaches Paul (Romans 8:18-24). It is that "blessed hope" the "appearing of the glory of our great God and Savior, Christ Jesus" (Tit. 2:13) which Christians are to await eagerly. That hope consummates the salvation resulting from God's grace (Tit. 2:11). That hope provides motive power so that the Christian can "deny ungodliness and worldly desires and to live sensible, righteously and godly in the present age" (Tit. 2:12).

But it is also an event demanded by the presence of evil and lawlessness in God's "good" earth. Sinful, autonomous man, inspired by the Evil One has sullied and distorted God's creation. The "grandeur of man" as created in God's image gives man as sinner present opportunities unparalled in past ages. The cosmic struggle between good and evil, light and darkness, God and Satan is sharpened with every new advance in human knowledge and technology.

---

5. *Ibid.*, p. 40.

This "mystery of iniquity" which is "already at work" will reach its climax in that "lawless one" who will be conquered by the "appearance of His coming" (II Thess. 2:7, 8). Christ appears "a second time" not only for "salvation" to "those who eagerly await Him" but for judgment of those who have rejected Him (Heb. 9:27, 28). So Paul could speak of Jesus being "revealed from heaven with His mighty angels in flaming fire, dealing out retribution to those who do not know God and to those who do not obey the gospel of our Lord Jesus" (II Thess. 1:7, 8).

This same truth is seen in that symbolic picture found in the Revelation given to John. There, the Coming One, the "King of Kings and Lord of Lords" is seen on a white horse, judging and "waging war." From his mouth comes a "sharp two-edged sword." He leads his armies to victory over the "beast and the kings of the earth and their armies" who have opposed Him. The Beast, the false prophet, and all who had received the Beast's mark and worshiped him were "thrown alive into the lake of fire" (Rev. 19:11-20).

Christ's Coming is also demanded to complete and perfect the "communion of the saints." In the Thessalonian correspondence Jesus' Coming not only issues in judgment and "eternal destruction away from the presence of the Lord" (II Thess. 1:9), but brings to completion His saints. He comes "to be glorified" in them, "to be marveled at among all who have believed" (II Thess. 1:10). Elsewhere Paul sees the "perfecting" of the saints as a present process which will be completed at His Coming (Col. 1:28; 4:12; Eph. 4:12). In that great analogy where Paul compares the relation of husband and wife to that between Christ and the Church, Jesus is seen as giving Himself for the Church and sanctifying her and cleansing her through His word. This has been done so that "He might present to Himself the Church in all her glory" (Eph. 5:25-27). The strong inference suggested is that this occurs when that divine Bridegroom returns for His waiting Bride.

The present "communion of the saints" centers in a table spread with a loaf and cup. But this is only "until He comes" (I Cor. 11:26). He has promised that He would be the unseen guest at this table; but that same promise encompasses a more real fellowship at His Coming in His Kingdom (Luke 22:16-18; Mark 14:25; Matt. 26:29). John also saw this day in a prophetic and apocalyptic vision. A voice like that of a great multitude, or like a swelling ocean, or like mighty peals of thunder, was heard by John, demanding praise for the Omnipotent God, saying: "Let us rejoice and be glad and give the glory to Him, for the marriage of the Lamb has come and His bride has made herself ready" (Rev. 19:7). Blessed, indeed, are those "who are invited to the marriage supper of the Lamb!"

The New Testament writings are quite clear as to the fact of Christ's coming. They also explicate the "Why" of the Coming. They are not as lucid as to the manner of Christ's coming. It is quite evident that He comes *personally*. It is the *same Jesus* who shall come (Acts 1:11). It can be inferred that He shall come *visibly*. "In like manner as you have seen Him go" testified those messengers (Acts 1:11). Every eye shall see Him (Luke 21:27), Jesus affirms. "The Lord, *Himself* will descend," Paul says (I Thess. 4:16). He will come *gloriously*. He comes "in the glory of His Father" (Matt. 16:27); with "power and great glory" (Matt. 24:30); in his own glory (Matt. 25:31). Departed saints will appear "with Him in glory" (Col. 3:4) and present saints shall receive a "crown of glory" (I Pet. 5:4). At His Coming His glory "shall be revealed" (I Pet. 4:13). He comes not as the lowly man of Galilee but as that glorious King of Kings and Lord of Lords. At that time, His prayer in the upper room will be answered: "Father, I desire that they also, whom Thou hast given Me, be with Me where I am, in order that they may behold My glory, which Thou hast given me; for Thou didst love Me before the foundation of the world" (John 17:24).

The Second Advent and Resurrection

If the Second Advent is indeed the "blessed hope," the fulfillment of the Christian's expectations, the Resurrection of Jesus is the ground of that hope. Resurrection and Return belong together; the Return of Christ is the realization of that which the Resurrection reveals. The belief in Resurrection is expressed in the sincere confession of heart-felt faith. "If you confess with your mouth Jesus as Lord and believe in your heart that God raised Him from the dead, you shall be saved" (Rom. 10:9). Spiritual participation in that Resurrection faith is expressed in baptism (Rom. 6:3, 4). But, belief in that one great fact, and submission to that one great symbolizing act, only come to final fulfillment in that future event so inseparably tied to Jesus' resurrection.

As has been indicated, the Return of Christ not only brings blessings to those who are His, but it also promises judgment to the unbeliever and evildoer (II Thess. 1:9, 10). Paul is certainly explicit about this latter point in his address at Athens. Judgment is certain because God Himself has appointed a Day of Judgment in which "He will judge the world in righteousness." The agent of that Judgment is a "Man whom He has appointed"; a Man who has every right to make such judgment because of His perfect obedience, His righteous life. What is proof of this? God has raised this Man "from the dead" (Acts 17:31). Paul is reflecting what Jesus had taught. To those Pharisees in Jerusalem Jesus said that the Father had "given all judgment to the Son" (John 5:22). Those who hear the voice of the Son of God and believe His word will not come into judgment. Because they do "good deeds" they will experience a "resurrection of life." All others will experience "a resurrection of judgment" (John 5:28, 29).

It is in the Thessalonian correspondence where Paul sets out most clearly the blessings that come to those who await the Lord's Coming. In spelling this out he carefully links the resurrection of the saints to this coming event. The first letter to Thessalonica begins with an expression of gratitude and thanksgiving for the faithfulness of the church in that place (I Thess. 1:2-8). Even though Paul had not been able to stay with them for any length of time, he rejoiced in that fact that their "work of faith and labor of love and steadfastness of hope" in Christ had become "an example to all the believers in Macedonia and in Achaia" (I Thess. 1:3, 7). The evidence was overwhelming. They had turned from their idols to "serve a living and true God, and to wait for His Son from heaven, whom He raised from dead, that is Jesus, who delivers us from the wrath to come" (I Thess. 1:9, 10).

Apparently, Paul felt he had not had time to instruct them fully relative to this end-time hope centering in Jesus' return. In this letter he concludes each of the first three major paragraph sections with a strong emphasis upon the Coming of Jesus and its results. In chapter 1:10 (as quoted above), Paul admonishes his hearers to wait expectantly for God's

210

Son who is coming to deliver His people from the wrath to come. This Coming One is Jesus whom God raised from the dead. Resurrection not only proves Sonship (Rom. 1:4), but is the foundation for belief in His sure coming. In chapter 2:19, Paul terms his converts in Thessalonica as his hope, joy, and crown. Such joy will be made full when Paul beholds thems, and they be "in the presence of our Lord Jesus at His Coming." In chapter 3, Paul tells them how gratified he was of the news that Timothy had brought concerning their fidelity and continued love. He prays that he might be able to visit them soon and that the Lord might continue to help them to "abound in love for one another" (I Thess. 3:6, 11, 12). What is the end of all this? "So that He may establish your hearts unblamable in holiness before our God and Father at the coming of our Lord Jesus with all His saints" (I Thess. 3:13).

Such an emphasis upon Christ's coming and what it means for His people prepares the way for Paul's explicit teaching directed to specific Thessalonian need. In a sense, the Thessalonians were concerned about the destiny of those Christians who had died. Apparently, Christ's Coming had been understood in such imminent terms that they assumed that only those alive would participate in the glory of His coming. In correcting this mistaken notion Paul links resurrection and return and gives a comforting word to those who had lost loved ones in death. He desires that their grief over the departed dead be hopeful sorrow, not the deep, unrestrained, and uncontrollable sorrow of the heathen (I Thess. 4:13).

Paul's affirmations of future hope for the "dead in Christ" are built solidly upon resurrection reality. "If we believe that Jesus died and rose again" (I Thess. 4:14a), then it follows that God will not let any of his redeemed perish ultimately. Jesus died to put away sin and He was raised, proving His atoning work satisfactory. It follows then that He will come, and when He does He will come "with His saints" (I Thess. 3:13). So, God "will bring with Him [Jesus] those who have fallen asleep in Jesus" (I Thess. 4:14b).

Paul's affirmation is more than the result of logical reasoning; it is grounded in "the word of the Lord." Paul is speaking by revelation when he states that Christians who are alive ("we" is to be understood in this sense) at the time of the Lord's Coming, "shall *not* (an emphatic negative in the original) precede" or forestall[6] "those who have fallen asleep" (I Thess. 4:15). On the contrary, when that notable event occurs with all its marvelous accompaniments—"the Lord Himself descending with a shout, accompanied by the voice of the archangel and the trumpet of God" (I Thess. 4:16)—it will be those who are "dead in Christ" who will precede the then living. "The dead in Christ shall rise first, then we who are alive and remain shall be caught up together with them in the clouds to meet the Lord in the air, and thus we [both risen dead and changed living[7]] shall always be with the Lord" (I Thess. 4:16c, 17).

---

6. One could translate, or paraphrase, this in this manner: we "will have no advantage over those who have fallen asleep." Ray Summers, *The Life Beyond*, p. 58.

7. It is elsewhere that Paul explains the transformation of the last generation of Christians remaining until the Lord's return. In Phil. 3:20-21, Paul speaks of the "transformation of the body of humility" into the likeness of His glorious body. In I Cor. 15:51-52, Paul sees this transformation, whether of the raised dead or the changed living, as a "sacred secret" now revealed. This change will occur in "a moment, in the twinkling of an eye, at the last trumpet; for the trumpet will sound and the dead will be raised imperishable and we shall be changed."

Paul is not only providing comfort for those who grieve he is also showing how the Christian, in life or death, is involved with the Risen Lord. The Christian lives recognizing Christ's saving power and presence, eagerly awaiting His personal return. He dies fully aware that death is not the end for he, too, shall be raised and will be among those who first encounter the living Lord who comes for His own. This resurrection and rapture ("catching up") is that "first resurrection" of Revelation 20:5, in which the whole Church participates. Blessed indeed are those who have "a part in the first resurrection; over these the second death has no power, but they will be priests of God and of Christ and will reign with Him" (Rev. 20:6). The controversy over the "thousand years" (or millennium) mentioned in this passage does not really detract from this great truth. The Church reigns with Christ by virtue of His Resurrection power now, and, in a special way, subsequent to His Coming.

The Dead and the Second Advent

The "dead in Christ" shall be raised first; but this does not speak to the question of the state of the dead now prior to Jesus' Second Coming. In both the Thessalonian correspondence and Paul's first letter to the Corinthians the dead are promised Resurrection. F. F. Bruce points out that there appears to be no distinction "drawn between those who have died and those who will still be alive, for Paul is emphasizing that the body comes within the scope of God's redemptive purpose and that present bodily actions have therefore a serious relevance for the future state of Christians."[8] This is

8. *Paul: Apostle of the Heart Set Free*, p. 310.

213

particularly stressed in I Corinthians 6:14 where Paul emphasizes both God's resurrection of Jesus and the resurrection
of His followers within the context of exhortations to moral
living.

But in Paul's second letter to Corinth there is a new perspective presented. It may be this new perspective grown
out of Paul's awareness—of his own death. At least he writes
to that effect, "We are afflicted in every way, but not crushed;
perplexed, but not despairing; persecuted, but not forsaken;
struck down, but not destroyed; always carrying about in
the body the dying of Jesus, that the life of Jesus also may
be manifested in our mortal flesh. So death works in us,
but life in you" (II Cor. 4:8-12). Then comes that great
affirmation of faith in which Paul sees himself among the
dead not those alive at Jesus' Coming. "I know," cries out
Paul, "that He who raised the Lord Jesus will raise us also
with Jesus and will present us with you" (II Cor. 4:14).

But if it is more probable that Paul will be among the "us"
of the dead in Christ rather than the "we who are alive"
(I Thess. 4:17), what does this mean about his state of
existence following death? Even here Paul does not think
of existence as a "disembodied soul." If the "earthly tent
which is his house is torn down," Paul knows that he has
"a building from God, a house not made with hands, eternal
in the heavens" (II Cor. 5:1). If this present body is "decay-
ing," the inner man is being "renewed day by day" (II Cor.
4:16). The expectation of the Christian following death is
"an eternal weight of glory far beyond all comparison"
(II Cor. 4:17). The Christian can look to "the things which
are not seen," which are eternal not temporal (II Cor. 4:18).
So Christians may "groan" in this earthly tent, not "desiring
to be unclothed but to be clothed" (II Cor. 5:4), longing

214

for that "clothing" of immortality. But as long as they are clothed with mortality ("at home in the body"), they are "absent from the Lord" (II Cor. 5:6). Paul would rather be "absent from the body" and "at home with the Lord" (which is "better by far" as he puts it in Phil. 1:23); but whether present or absent, his greatest ambition is to please his Lord (II Cor. 5:8, 9).

In this passage, as elsewhere, Paul "evidently could not contemplate immortality apart from resurrection; for him a body of some kind was essential to personality."[9] At death, the Christian is not some disembodied spirit but has a building or garment, is not naked. A new, immortal body is implied. It is as if Paul is saying: "We do not want to have the old body stripped off, leaving a naked soul. No! Our desire is to have a new body put on over it, so that our mortal part may be absorbed into life immortal. God, Himself, has shaped us for this very end; and as a pledge He has given us His Spirit" (II Cor. 5:4ff.).[10]

Paul could not see death as destroying that union with Christ that Christians have now by virtue of His resurrection power. They will continue to share with Him following death, prior to His Parousia Glory. They are with the Lord, "at home," without any waiting interval. "The coming consummation is in no way diminished" says Dr. Bruce; "but those eschatological features which are realized in life on earth at present do not cease to be realized in the interval between death and the final consummation; they continued indeed to be more intensely realized than is possible during life on earth."[11]

---

9. Bruce, *ibid.*, p. 311.
10. See Bruce, *ibid.*, p. 312.
11. *Ibid.*, p. 313.

215

But what about the wicked dead? Apparently, they too shall be raised at the consummation of all things. They are the "second resurrection" of Revelation 20. The nature of this "resurrection of judgment" (John 5:29) is not described in detail but Scripture "supplies hints which imply that it will be the negative counterpart of the resurrection of the righteous."[12] Apparently, both believers and unbelievers participate in a mode of existence following resurrection in which they "will realize the full consequences of their deeds in the present life."[13]

But all this is at His Coming! "Every tongue shall confess; every knee shall bow" says Paul in Philippians 2. Some however will confess and bow with rapturous joy; others in shame and fear.

FOR FURTHER STUDY

Berkouwer, G. C. *The Return of Christ*. Grand Rapids: Wm. B. Eerdmans, 1972.

Hoekema, Anthony A. *The Bible and the Future*. Grand Rapids: Wm. B. Eerdmans, 1979.

Johnson, Ashley S. *Resurrection and the Future Life*. Knoxville Lithographing Co., 1913.

Kunneth, Walter. *The Theology of the Resurrection*. St. Louis: Concordia Publishing House, 1965.

Summers, Ray. *The Life Beyond*. Nashville: Broadman Press, 1959.

---

12. Tenney, p. 175.
13. *Ibid.*, p. 175.

QUESTIONS FOR DISCUSSION

1. Sketch out the Biblical evidence for the Second Coming of Christ. Discuss some of these passages in detail.
2. Why are the historical circumstances in which Jesus speaks of His return so important?
3. What are some of the reasons demanding the Second Coming of Jesus?
4. Show how Jesus' Resurrection and His Return are inseparable.
5. Discuss the state of the dead of both believer and unbeliever prior to and following the Coming of Jesus (look up this topic—the state of the dead—in a Topical Bible for additional help).

Chapter Thirteen

THE RESURRECTION AND THE FUTURE LIFE

"I am the living One; I died and behold I am alive forever more, and I have the keys of Death and Hades" (Rev. 1:18).

There is a general resurrection! All shall be raised! But, some participate in a resurrection of life; some in a resurrection of judgment (John 5:29). Resurrection and Judgment are the two correlated acts of the final consummation of all things. As Geerhardus Vos points out, Resurrection and Judgment are like "twin-woes in the travail by which the age to come is brought to birth."[1] Resurrection *is* judgment to the believer in the sense of vindication. So Jesus could say that he "who hears My Word and believes Him who sent Me, has eternal life, and does not come into judgment, but has passed out of death into life" (John 5:24). Judgment comes to the believer only in terms of Vindication and Reward. Eternity, The Age to Come, is already being experienced by the believer (John 17:3; Heb. 6:5), because he has been "raised with Christ" (Rom. 6:3, 4; Col. 2:12; Eph. 2:5, 6). If the "judgment seat of Christ" is yet future it relates only to reward (II Cor. 5:10; Rom. 14:10).

But the resurrection of the wicked to appear before the final tribunal of God is a more serious event. Of this the New Testament Scriptures are full. It is true that Judgment has occurred because the wicked have not come to faith in Christ who alone can save and shelter from coming doom (John 3:17-20; 5:24, 29). But such Judgment is destined to be made public at that final Day (Heb. 9:27; 10:27; II Pet. 2:4, 3:7; Jude 6; etc.). John depicts this symbolically:

---

1. *The Pauline Eschatology* (Grand Rapids: Wm. B. Eerdmans, 1961), p. 261.

And I saw a great white throne and Him who sat upon it, from whose presence earth and heaven fled away, and no place was found for them. And I saw the dead, the great and the small, standing before the throne, and books were opened; and another book was opened which is the book of life; and the dead were judged from the things which were written in the books, according to their deeds. And the sea gave up the dead which were in it, and death and Hades gave up the dead which were in them; and they were judged, every one of them according to their deeds. And death and Hades were thrown into the lake of fire. This is the second death, the lake of fire. And if anyone's name was not found written in the book of life, he was thrown into the lake of fire" (Rev. 20:11-15).

Judgment not only follows resurrection but presupposes separation and an eternal state following. That eternal state is a fixed state for both the saved and lost, the saint and the wicked one. Resurrection precedes and prepares the sons of Adam—both the disobedient and the obedient—for a future life.

The Future Life Revealed in the Gospels

Jesus is somewhat reticent about spelling out the nature of the Future Life that follows resurrection and judgment. He does refer to "rewards" as coming in the future (Matt. 10:41). The reward of the one who does good to the one unable to repay will be "repaid at the resurrection of the righteous" (Luke 14:14). The Twelve will be rewarded in a special way, since they have renounced all to follow Jesus. In this connection Jesus is more expansive, if not necessarily specific, about the nature of these rewards. He says,

You who have followed Me, in the regeneration when the Son of Man will sit on His glorious throne, you also shall

219

sit upon twelve thrones, judging the twelve tribes of Israel.
And everyone who has left houses or brothers or sisters, or
father or mother or children or farms for My name's sake,
shall receive many times as much, and shall inherit eternal
life" (Matt. 19:28, 29).

The life of the righteous in the eternal state is different
than life in this present age, even though Jesus may have
to speak of it in terms analogous of present existence.
Negatively, as he answers the Sadducees concerning the
Resurrection, such life does not include typical human
relations—"they neither marry or are given in marriage"
—but is more like the life of the "angels in heaven" (Mark
12:25). On the other hand, Jesus sees the future life of the
saved as likened to a feast (Mark 14:25), more particularly
a wedding feast (Matt. 25:1-13; Matt. 22:1-14, Luke 13:29;
14:16-24). In Luke 22:29, 30, Jesus combines this banquet
imagery with the reward promised the Twelve. "Just as
my Father has granted me a Kingdom," Jesus says, "I grant
you that you may eat and drink at My Table in My kingdom,
and you will sit on thrones judging the twelve tribes of
Israel." This figurative language is also seen in first century
Jewish literature relating to the future and doubtless suggests
that abundant joy and satisfaction will be granted those
who are raised in the "resurrection of life."

There are other passages which seem to indicate that
the future life "will be a sphere of enlarged responsibilities
and opportunities."[2] In those somewhat parallel parables
of "pounds" and "talents," proven responsibility leads not
only to "authority over cities" (Luke 19:12-27), to be "put
in charge of many things," but also to entrance into "the

---

2. T. W. Manson, *The Teachings of Jesus* (Cambridge: Cambridge University Press, 1963), p. 277.

joy of the master" (Matt. 25:14-30). That faithful steward-servant found faithful at the Master's coming (*parousia*) is blessed, for the Master "will put him in charge of all his possessions" (Luke 12:43-44).

The fact of eternal blessedness for the possessors of the Kingdom is quite clear from Jesus' words. "Come you who are blessed of my Father, inherit the kingdom prepared for you from the foundation of the world" (Matt. 25:34), the Son of Man will say to all gathered before Him. They have proven themselves worthy in their works ("inasmuch as you have done these to the least of these my brethren"—Matt. 25:40), and like sheep separated from goats, they are judged righteous and enter "into eternal life" (Matt. 25:46). But, Jesus does no more than show something of the quality of the life in this consummated Kingdom. As Dr. Manson summarizes, "It is spiritual; it is full of joy but not merely passive enjoyment; for it is also a more intense activity than is possible in the present world."[3]

But Jesus speaks of the future life of those "raised unto a resurrection of Judgment" (John 5:29), that is, the evil-doers. In that graphic picture of judgment that Matthew records Jesus painting in bold strokes in the closing days of His ministry, the "goats" who have not done those acts of kindness and mercy are sent "away unto eternal punishment" (Matt. 25:46). Since this is correlated to the "eternal life" of the righteous, it is safe to assume that this future is eternal as well. This punishment is referred to by Jesus as "hell," [*gehenna*] (Matt. 10:28; 23:33; Luke 12:5).

This word "*gehenna*" traces far back into history. It was a definite place. In the Old Testament it was that place where

---

3. *Ibid.*, p. 277.

wicked kings burnt incense and even offered their children as burning sacrifices to Moloch (I Kings 11:7; II Chron. 28:1-3). In Jeremiah's day, in this valley of Hinnom, high places had been built to the gods (Jer. 7:31). In the New Testament, due to this past history it came to be the garbage pit of Jerusalem. Here "criminals and the bodies of dead animals were burned . . . fire was perpetual and resistless, . . . the smoke rose continually and the fire did not go out."[4] No wonder Jesus used this term to symbolize eternal separation from God, eternal punishment. The fate of the wicked is "unquenchable fire" (Mark 9:43), gehenna, "where their worm does not die, and the fire is not quenched" (Mark 9:48). No more terrible revolting picture could be given to characterize the eternal punishment of the wicked.

This gehenna is also described by Jesus as a place of "outer darkness" (where there is "weeping and wailing and gnashing of teeth"). On two different occasions it is the result of judgment upon unprofitable servants (Matt. 25:30), or an unprepared wedding guest (Matt. 22:13). In the third passage Jesus marvels at the faith of the Centurion of Capernaum, saying, "Truly I say to you, I have not found such great faith with anyone in Israel" (Matt. 8:10). This lead him to speak futuristically:

> And I say to you, that many shall come from east and west, and recline at the table with Abraham, and Isaac, and Jacob, in the kingdom of heaven; but the sons of the kingdom [the unbelieving Jews] shall be cast out into the outer darkness; in that place there shall be weeping and gnashing of teeth (Matt. 8:11, 12).[5]

---

4. A. S. Johnson, Resurrection and the Future Life, p. 388.
5. There is a similar passage in Luke 13:28, 29.

The most vivid description of the fate of the wicked is that presented by Jesus in that story of the rich man and Lazarus (Luke 16:19-31). Some have argued that this is not a parable since Jesus uses the expressions "a certain rich man" and "a certain poor man," even naming the latter. But, whether actual event or parabolic illustration, that which Jesus is emphasizing is the same. At death separation occurs. A judgment has already taken place with alternate destinies. Lazarus is carried away by angels to "Abraham's bosom," a picture of glorious Paradise; the rich man lifts up his eyes "in torment" in Hades, the place of the dead. There is a great gulf fixed between the two alternative areas of dead ones. There is also consciousness, at least of the wicked dead. A consciousness of what might have been. There is memory, now lacerated and punishing ("Son, Remember" says Abraham). There is also a concern for others, though no hope of doing anything about implementing this concern. Such a picture, whether real or figurative, is a rather bleak depiction of hopelessness and despair. If this is what occurs during that intermediate state between death and the final resurrection, how much more terrible it is to contemplate an eternity of such existence.

The Future Life Set Out in Acts and Epistles

In the book of Acts there is little specific information about the future life of either the righteous or wicked. The general theme of making and confirming disciples seems to preclude any concerted attention given to these more doctrinal matters. This subject was undoubtedly one of the themes of the "apostles' teaching" (Acts 2:42), but Luke does not elaborate at all. Judgment of all men and the eternal destruction of the unbeliever (Acts 24:25) is certainly set out (Acts 3:23; 10:42; 13:40, 41; 17:30, 31). The resurrection of Jesus Christ is proof of this (Acts 17:30, 31), for Paul sees as corollary to Jesus' resurrection "a resurrection of both the righteous and the wicked" (Acts 24:15).

The future blessedness of the believers in Christ is also assumed. In speaking to the Ephesian elders Paul promises that they will receive an inheritance if they faithfully discharge their leadership responsibilities (Acts 20:32). Such a future inheritance is promised to all the sanctified in another connection (Acts 26:18). The nature of this inheritance is not disclosed. One could infer from Stephen's vision of "the Son of Man standing at the right hand of God" (Acts 7:56) that such an inheritance will be related closely to the resurrected and reigning Jesus.

The message Peter delivered in Solomon's porch following the healing of the lame man at the Temple gate, links Jesus' resurrection to His return. At Jesus' return there will be "times for the restoring of all things" (Acts 3:19-21). Such a "renewing" had been foretold by the prophets (Isa. 34:4; 50:6; 65:17). It had become the hope of the Jews, often interpreted in nationalistic terms.[6] Peter is showing that this "restoration" is closely connected to the risen Lord's return and involves repentance and commitment as prerequisite for participation. This emphasis may well be another way of expressing "new heavens and a new earth, in which righteousness dwells" (II Pet. 3:13).

The book of Acts is not really concerned with setting out what may be in the future. "This is what happened" Luke is saying. "Now what has happened in the redemptive

---

6. See Alfred Edersheim, *Jesus the Messiah*, Vol. II, p. 343.

action of Jesus, the Son of God, may have tremendous implications for the future state of believer and unbeliever alike; but I want my readers to know the certainty of what Jesus continues now to do through Spirit-led Apostles in fulfilling His divine purpose." It is not in *kerygma* (gospel preaching) but in *didache* (the teaching of disciples "all things commanded"—Matt. 28:20) that these future issues are set forth.

The teachings of the Apostles provide additional insights into the future state. Fourteen times in Paul's letters the future age is described as eternal (Rom. 2:7; 5:21; 6:22, 23; II Cor. 4:17, 18; 5:1; Gal. 6:8; II Thess. 1:9; 2:16; II Tim. 2:10; Tit. 1:2; 3:7; Philemon 15). These passages are not just emphasizing quantity but quality as well. Eternity has a certain character about it; it is not just endless time.

This is true of hell as well as heaven. In the second letter to the church at Thessalonica, Pauls speaks of that future event when "the risen Lord Jesus" shall be revealed from heaven with His mighty angels in flaming fire, dealing out retribution to those who do not know God and to those who do not obey the gospel of our Lord Jesus. And these will pay the penalty of eternal destruction (*olethron aiōnion*), away from the presence of the Lord and from the glory of His power" (II Thess. 1:7-9). Destruction, ruin, perdition is the lot of the wicked. If it is eternal, then "never-ending punishment" is implied. God's "day of wrath" (Rom. 2:5, 8, 9) brings tribulation and distress to the wicked. Salvation from such wrath comes only through faith in Christ's sacrifice (Rom. 5:9).

The dreadful consequence of those who spurn the Son of God is set out vividly in Hebrews 10. "Anyone who has set aside the Law of Moses dies without mercy on the testimony of two or three witnesses. How much severer punishment do you think he will deserve who has trampled under

225

foot the Son of God, and has regarded as unclean the blood of the covenant by which he was sanctified, and has insulted the Spirit of grace? . . . It is a terrible thing to fall into the hands of the living God" (Heb. 10:28, 29, 31). Though the endlessness of God's wrath is not specifically mentioned, it is implied as a necessary consequence of the crimes committed against Him.

In those somewhat parallel passages in II Peter and Jude one sees further amplification of this state of eternal punishment of the lost. The "nether gloom of darkness has been reserved" for those "godless men" who are predicted as coming (II Pet. 2:17). Jude (v. 13) sees these apostates as already present, describing them in similar terms as "wild waves of the sea, casting up their own shame like foam; wandering stars." But, Jude adds, "for whom the black darkness has been reserved forever."

But it is a token of God's graciousness that the positive aspects of the eternal state are emphasized more than the negative. Judgment is sure; separation is necessary; eternal destruction is inevitable. This tragic note that is the dark side of the good news of the Gospel should add deep seriousness to preaching and teaching. The eternal destiny of the unbeliever *should* be preached and taught, for it is a part of God's revelatory Word. But it should be preached with grief, perhaps even tears; even as Jesus sets the example of his lament over Jerusalem (Matt. 23:37; Luke 13:34). The terrible consequences of unbelief give powerful motivation and urgent zeal to the great missionary enterprise awaiting the Church.

The Christian, on the other hand, is promised eternal life. This life begins now as God's free gift of salvation through Jesus Christ (Rom. 6:23). But it is extended beyond death and beyond the general resurrection as an eternal state, marked by glory, honor and immortality (Rom. 2:7; II Tim. 2:10). There is an "eternal house," not made with hands, replacing this earthly structure, which is the Christian's at death (II Cor. 4:17—5:1). In his resurrection body, the Christian will enter fully into this eternal state (I Cor. 15:20-26, 50-57). This is the "hope of eternal life" that brightens life for the Christian (Tit. 3:7).

This eternal state of blessedness is referred to in the "apostles' teaching" as an inheritance (I Cor. 6:10; 15:50; Heb. 6:12; 9:1b; Eph. 5:5; I Pet. 1:4). It is not only promised to those who are children of God and "joint heirs with Christ" (Rom. 8:17) but guaranteed by that Spirit of Him "who raised Jesus from the dead" (Rom. 8:11) and now dwells in the obedient believer. It is through this indwelling Spirit that the Christian is "sealed" and this Spirit is "a pledge (down payment) of our inheritance with a view to the redemption of God's own possession" (Eph. 1:13, 14). This final redemption will be a redemption of the "body," the ultimate adoption ceremony (Rom. 8:23). When it occurs, the whole of creation will participate in the glory "that shall burst upon us" (Rom. 8:18—Moffatt). Then, the curse will be lifted (Gen. 3:17-19; Rev. 22:3) and "new heavens and new earth" will stand forth (II Pet. 3:13). The gates of the "eternal kingdom" will be opened and an "abundant entrance" supplied for the righteous (II Pet. 1:5-11).

But the apostles say little about the nature of this eternal abode of the righteous. They are more concerned about its reality and the preparation to be made to enjoy that reality. It may be that Paul's statement about his own out-of-the-body experience is applicable to the understanding of eternity's nature. Caught up to the "third heaven" or "Paradise,"

227

Paul heard "inexpressible words" (and, undoubtedly, saw inexpressible sights) which he could not possibly communicate (II Cor. 12:1-4). This is a mystery "not made known," for it concerns "things which eye has not seen and ear has not heard, and which have not entered the heart of man, all that God has prepared for those who love Him" (I Cor. 2:8, 9).

The Future Life as Depicted in the Apocalypse of John

That enigmatic book that closes the New Testament is filled with strange symbols. Yet these symbols reflect genuine reality. Judgment and eternal destiny are clearly seen. The wicked dead are judged and "cast into the lake of fire" (Rev. 20:14). This is a symbol of that "second death," that is, a spiritual rather than a physical death. Prior to this judgment scene, there is a reference to those who worship the Beast and his image, receiving the Beast's mark upon forehead or hand (Rev. 14:9). These shall "drink of the wine of the wrath of God . . . and will be tormented with fire and brimstone . . . and the smoke of their torment goes up forever and ever; and they have no rest day and night" (Rev. 14:10, 11). Underneath these symbols, there is a clear message. The wicked will be punished. This punishment is eternal. In light of this dreadful fate, it is no surprise to see unbelievers trying to hide in the "caves and among the rocks of the mountains" saying to these mountains, "Fall on us and hide us from the presence of Him who sits on the throne, and from the wrath of the Lamb" (Rev. 6:15, 16).

The future state of the righteous is also seen in symbolic language in this apocalyptic revelation given to the aged John while exiled on Patmos. This blessed state is inaugurated in a meal—the marriage supper of the Lamb (Rev.

19:7). The Bride is prepared—the "fine linen is the righteous acts of the saints" (Rev. 19:8). The Bride is raised—"this is the first resurrection" (Rev. 20:5). The Bride enters into all the inheritance, all the privilege of her Groom—she "reigned with Christ" (Rev. 20:4). Here, intimate fellowship and personal presence are revealed in these figurative expressions.

But there is also a Millennium. The saints reign with Christ "for a thousand years" (Rev. 20:4). Many scholars see this as an essential stage in God's redemption and transformation.

> The transformation began in the resurrection of the Lord and is completed in the era introduced by the second coming. The Old Testament prophets connect this consummation with the advent of the messianic kingdom but the developed eschatology of the book of Revelation appears to interpose the millennial kingdom between the second coming and the end of the historical process. The prophet would show us that the triumph of Christ is to take effect in this earth scene which once He hallowed by His presence, where He was rejected of men but wrought their redemption. In that case the kingdom of God marks its advance by three great interventions of God in Christ: it was inaugurated in the resurrection of Christ and its powers experienced through the subsequent gift of the Holy Spirit; it is carried to victory by the second coming of Christ, when all earth acknowledges His sway; it is brought to final consummation after the Last Judgment in the new heavens and earth, when all nature is united in praise to God.[7]

If the Millennium is a brief intermediate stage vindicating God's goodness by lifting the "curse" and allowing God's

---

7. G. R. Beasley-Murray, *Christ is Alive*, p. 177.

"good creation" to become what it once was (Rom. 8:20ff.), the "new heavens and new earth" are the permanent eternal state of the saints. All those things associated with the older existence are done away. There are no longer tears, or "death . . . mourning, nor crying, or pain; the final things have passed away" (Rev. 21:4). The God who makes "all things new" (Rev. 21:5) is among His saints. He wipes the final tears away. He will not allow this blessed newness to be penetrated by evil. Therefore, the "cowardly, and unbelieving and abominable and murderers and immoral persons and sorcerers and idolators and all liars" are not to be found. Their place is in the "lake of fire . . . the second death" (Rev. 21:8). In this new heaven and new earth only "righteousness dwells" (II Pet. 3:13).

The saints dwell in a new City. It is "the holy city, Jerusalem coming down out of heaven from God, having the glory of God" (Rev. 21:10, 11). They had known an earthly city set on Mt. Zion; they had come to a spiritual city in faith and obedience, that "Jerusalem above," the mother of all those freed in Christ (Gal. 4:26). They had indeed come to "Mount Zion and to the city of the living God, the heavenly Jerusalem, and to myriads of angels, to the general assembly and church of the first-born who are enrolled in heaven, and to God, the Judge of all, and to the spirits of righteous men made perfect, and to Jesus, the mediator of a new covenant, and to sprinkled blood, which speaks better than the blood of Abel" (Heb. 12:22-24). But, now that spiritual faith is crowned by sight; that hoped for has become reality. The heavenly Jerusalem has come down to righteous men to be their abode for all eternity.

But this city is not like Babel of old, or Babylon, the great harlot (Rev. 17, 18). This city is perfectly designed to accommodate the saints of all the ages. The symbolic pictures

—the symbols within the symbol—reflect this (Rev. 20:11ff.). There are high protective walls the foundations of which are of precious stones. The city is of pure transparent gold and jasper. The twelve gates, symbolic of the city's access and openness, are twelve large pearls. This city needs no Temple, for God and His Son are there. It has no need of that artificial light seen in sun and moon, for God's glory and Jesus, the Lamb and Light of God provide all needed illumination. Through the city winds the river of life clear as crystal, coming from God's throne. The tree of life grows along its bank, yielding twelve different monthly fruits. The leaves of this tree are for the healing of the nations (Rev. 22:1-3). Paradise has been regained! The garden lost became a city restored and given. The tree of life available in a garden then is available again in a garden.

But, most glorious of all, God is present again, walking and talking with His creatures. They see His face! They serve Him forever! This glorious, intimate fellowship is not marred by sin, for all uncleanness has been left behind and the perfected saints, "without spot or wrinkle or any such thing" (Eph. 5:27), are in the presence of the holy God; but not just as servants, but as children (Rev. 21:7). "All that was lost to man in his first home, lost because of sin, because of disobedience, is restored to him in this final home, restored through righteousness and obedience—not his own righteousness and obedience, but the righteousness and obedience of the Lamb who is the Christ."[8]

The Resurrection and the Future Life

Future destiny and resurrection are inseparable. They focus in Christ and His redemptive work, the reality of which

---

8. Ray Summers, *The Life Beyond* (Nashville: Broadman Press, 1959), p. 207.

is guaranteed by His resurrection from that borrowed tomb so long ago. Because He was raised, His followers will be raised to life everlasting; but it is equally true that His resurrection is the "first fruits" of the resurrection of all men. "All who die in the tombs shall hear the voice of the Son of Man and come forth" says Jesus (John 5:28, 29); some to a resurrection of eternal life and the rest to a resurrection of judgment and eternal death.

The distinction is made as a result of how persons treat the "lamb of God that takes away the sin of the world" (John 1:29). Those that honor this Lamb, accepting Him as their Passover "sacrificed for them" (I Cor. 5:7) will experience the "first resurrection" (Rev. 20:4). As they prepare for that glorious hope, they "proclaim His death" at a new covenant paschal table "till He come" (I Cor. 11:26). They have experienced death with Him and have been raised in His likeness (Rom. 6:3, 4; Gal. 2:20). They look forward to that greater resurrection day when the Lamb standing now at God's throne, bearing the marks of His slaughter, will come (Rev. 5:6-12; 19:7-10). Then, the banqueting table will not be an occasional reminder of the absent Lamb but a Table spread continuously for the Bride of the Lamb and the Lamb Himself as they enjoy intimate and eternal fellowship (Rev. 21:9—22:3). No wonder the cry of the early Christians was "Maranatha" (I Cor. 16:22). No wonder the Apocalypse closes with an invitation to "Come to this water of life" and a cry "Come, Lord Jesus" (Rev. 22:17, 20).

But that same Lamb sets into motion that judgment that eventuates in the Resurrection and Judgment of the wicked (Rev. 20:11f.). It is this Lamb which appears "as one slain" who is able to open the scroll depicting intense judgment held in the hand of the Holy One seated on the throne (Rev.

232

5:5ff.). It is the "Lamb" who "overcomes" the Beast and all his unholy hordes, because He is "Lord of lords and King of kings" (Rev. 17:7-14). It is that same Lamb who comes to "judge and make war" against His enemies (Rev. 19:11ff.). The "rest of the dead" rise in a second resurrection to be sentenced at that great final tribunal ("the great white throne") to an eternity of hopelessness, the second death (Rev. 20:11-15). It is "the lamb's book of life" (Rev. 21:27) that becomes the final arbiter of this eternal judgment and destiny.

But, whereas the resurrection destiny of the righteous is spelled out in such beautiful, symbolic terms, the resurrection destiny of the wicked is shrouded by a curtain of silence. As Dr. Tenney suggests:

> One can only speculate by contrast with the destiny of the righteous what the fate of the unbelieving will be. The main thrust of revelation is concerned with salvation, not with damnation, for it was not God's prime choice that we should be condemned, but rather that they should enjoy Him and His provisions for them eternally. If they persistently reject His love, they can expect no other alternative than to continue existence apart from Him in a progressive alienation from His goodness and fellowship. The resurrection would be for them the point of fixation of their final doom, as it will be the ultimate reward for the righteous.[9]

There is a final destiny. There is a future lying beyond death. Men who have no hope in Christ may fear that which is beyond. Like Epicurus of ancient days, what they fear

---

9. *The Reality of the Resurrection*, p. 177. It has been suggested that Hell is God's last "act of kindness and love" toward the unbeliever. For those who have wanted nothing to do with Him, His Son, His love, God has set aside an eternal place where every thought, vestige, and influence of Him will be banned. This indeed would be Hell!

"is not that death is annihiliation, *but that it is not!*" and modern man's dread is pictured so clearly by T. S. Eliot in those lines in *Murder in the Cathedral*:

> . . . behind the face of Death the Judgment
> And behind the Judgment, the Voice, more horrid than
>   active shapes of hell;
> Emptiness, absence, separation from God;
> The horror of the effortless journey to the empty land
> Which is no land, only emptiness, absence, the Void,
> Where those who were men can no longer turn the mind
> To distraction, delusion, escape into dreams, pretense . . .

But the Christian faces this "last enemy" with confidence for he believes that victory over death is possible through Resurrection. One came back from Death to proclaim that victory! So the Christian can sing triumphantly of an eternal Home, and with G. K. Chesterton, exult:

> To an open house in the evening
> Home shall men come,
> To an older place than Eden
> And a taller town than Rome;
> To the end of the way of the wandering star,
> To the things that cannot be and that are,
> To the place where God was homeless
> And all men are at home.[10]

FOR FURTHER STUDY

Green, Michael. *Man Alive!* London: InterVarsity Press, 1967.

---

10. *The House of Christmas*, quoted by James Stewart, *A Faith to Proclaim* (New York: Charles Scribner's Sons, 1963), p. 11

Johnson, Ashley S. *Resurrection and the Future Life*. Knoxville: Knoxville Lithographing Co., 1913.
Summers, Ray, *The Life Beyond*. Nashville: Broadman Press, 1959.

QUESTIONS FOR DISCUSSION

1. Show that both righteous and wicked will participate in judgment and a future destiny.
2. What does Jesus mean when he says to the Twelve: "You shall judge the twelve tribes of Israel"? Is this a promise to the Twelve only?
3. Discuss the concept of hell or *gehenna* as seen in the Scriptures.
4. Is the story of the rich man and Lazarus actual or figurative (a parable)? Would this make any difference to its meaning?
5. What is the main concern in the book of Acts relative to the future?
6. Do the New Testament epistles teach that the wicked shall suffer eternally? Support your answer.
7. React to the idea of a Millennium as presented here.
8. Discuss the features of the eternal state of the righteous as set out in the book of Revelation.

Appendix I

A CLASSIFICATION OF PASSAGES IN THE NEW TESTAMENT RELATING TO THE RESURRECTION OF CHRIST AND THE DOCTRINE OF THE RESURRECTION

I. CHRIST'S PREDICTIONS OF HIS RESURRECTION

   A. In the early Judean ministry

      1. "Destroy this temple and in three days I will raise it up," John 2:19-22. This bold statement, misunderstood, formed one of the charges against Jesus, nearly three years later—Matthew 27:40, 63, 64; Mark 15:29.

   B. In His Galilean ministry

      1. "As Jonah—so shall the Son of Man be three days and three nights in the heart of the earth," Matthew 12:40. Though this verse does not actually contain words indicating resurrection, all agree that it is of such that Jesus is speaking.

      2. "The third day be raised up," Matthew 16:21; Luke 9:22. "After three days rise again," Mark 8:31.

      3. After Transfiguration. "Tell . . . no man, until the Son of Man be risen from the dead," Matthew 17:9; Mark 9:9.

      4. Shortly thereafter, Matthew 17:23; Mark 9:31.

   C. During the Perean ministry

      1. "After three days He shall rise again," Matthew 20:19; Mark 10:34; Luke 18:33.

   D. On Thursday of Passion Week

      1. "After I am raised up, I will go before you into Galilee," Matthew 26:32; Mark 14:28. They

would see Him again, John 16:16, 17, 19, 22.

It is in regard to such statements as these that the angel said to the women at the tomb—"He is not here, but is risen: remember how He spake unto you when He was yet in Galilee, saying," etc. Luke 24:6, 7; Matthew 28:6.

II. THE TEN POST-RESURRECTION APPEARANCES OF CHRIST

A. On Easter Sunday
  1. To Mary Magdalene, John 20:11-18; Mark 16:9-11.
  2. To a group of women at the tomb, Matthew 28:9, 10.
  3. To Simon Peter, Luke 24:34; I Corinthians 15:5, 7.
  4. To two disciples on the road to Emmaus, Mark 16:12, 13; Luke 24:13-35.
  5. To the Ten in an upper room, Mark 16:14; Luke 24:36-43; John 20:19-25; I Corinthians 15:5.

B. One week later
  1. To the Eleven, John 20:26-29.

C. Three subsequent appearances
  1. To James, I Corinthians 15:7.
  2. To seven disciples at the Sea of Galilee, John 21:1-24.
  3. To eleven disciples on a mountain in Galilee, Matthew 28:16-20; Mark 16:15-18.

III. CHRIST'S TEACHING ABOUT RESURRECTION

A. During the Galilean ministry
  1. In the astonishing statement recorded in John 5:25-29, Christ speaks of the time when

237

       a. "the dead shall hear the voice of the Son of God";

       b. "all that are in the tombs shall hear His voice and come forth";

       c. there will be "the resurrection of life," and, "the resurrecton of judgment." With this compare the resurrection of the just and the unjust" in Acts 24:15.

Note:—Many interpret this passage as referring to a spiritual resurrection, i.e., to new birth.

    2. That Christ would raise up all whom the Father had given Him, "at the last day," John 6:39, 40, 44.

B. During the Perean ministry

    1. Of Lazarus—"thy brother shall rise again," John 11:23.

C. On Tuesday of Passion Week

    1. In replying to the insincere question of the Sadducees, Matthew 22:23-33; Mark 12:18-27; Luke 20:27-38, our Lord affirms that

       a. in the life to come there will be no marriage relationship;

       b. they will then be "sons of the resurrection," Luke 20:37.

IV. TITLES OF CHRIST IN RELATION TO RESURRECTION

A. Given by Christ

    1. "I am the Resurrection and the Life," John 11:25.

B. Given by the Apostles

    1. "Firstborn from the dead," Colossians 1:18.

    2. "The First Begotten of the dead," Revelation 1:5.

V. SUBSEQUENT TESTIMONY TO THE GREAT FACT OF CHRIST'S RESURRECTION

A. The testimony of the angels on Easter morning
Matthew 28:6, 7; Mark 16:6; Luke 24:6, 7.

B. The testimony of John the Apostle
"after He was risen from the dead," John 21:14.

C. The testimony of the Apostle Peter
1. In discussing the choice of a successor to Judas, Acts 1:22.
2. In his preaching, Acts 2:24, 31, 32; 3:15; 4:10; 5:30; 10:40; regarding which the priests and Sadducees were "grieved," 4:2.
3. In his First Epistle
   a. by His Resurrection we are begotten again unto a living hope, 1:3, 21;
   b. concerning which baptism is a type, 3:21.

D. All the Twelve were to be witnesses to the fact of Christ's resurrection.
Acts 1:22; 2:32; 3:15; 10:41.

E. The testimony of the Apostle Paul
1. In his preaching
   a. at Antioch in Pisidia, Acts 13:29-34. Note that while Paul does not specifically state that the tomb in which the body of Jesus was placed was empty on Easter morning, v. 29 certainly implies such;
   b. in Thessalonica, Acts 17:3;
   c. in Athens, Acts 17:18, 31.
2. In his various defenses
   It is significant that in the numerous references to this truth, the text states Paul's assertions

239

concerned the doctrine of resurrection, rather than the Resurrection of Christ, 23:6; 24:15, 21; 26:6-8; but that actually he did also refer to Christ's Resurrection is clearly implied in the words of Festus to Agrippa in 25:19.

3. In his Epistles

Here I would list only those passages in which simply the fact of Christ's Resurrection is stated. I have thought Paul's doctrine of Resurrection warranted a separate division in this outline study.

F. The testimony of the writer of the Epistle to the Hebrews

Hebrews 13:20.

G. The testimony of the Risen Lord

Revelation 1:18. While the actual nomenclature of resurrection is not here, the fact is clearly implied. I believe this is the only reference to the Resurrection of Christ in the Apocalypse.

VI. THE TEACHING OF ST. PAUL REGARDING THE RESURRECTION

A. It is God who raiseth the dead

II Corinthians 1:9.

B. The fact of Christ's Resurrection

Romans 4:24; 6:4, 9; 7:4; 8:34; 10:9; I Corinthians 6:14; 15:20; II Corinthians 4:14; 5:15; Galatians 1:1; Ephesians 1:20; Colossians 2:12; I Thessalonians 1:10; II Timothy 2:8.

C. Some consequences of Christ's Resurrection

1. He was thus declared to be the Son of God, Romans 1:4.

2. He is thus Lord both of the dead and of the living, Romans 14:9. In this passage only do we have a verb (anazao) meaning to revive, used in reference to Christ's resurrection. It is the verb used in Revelation 20:5.

3. He makes our justification possible, Romans 4:25.

4. Because He was raised from the dead, we will be also, Romans 6:5; I Corinthians 6:14; 15:21; II Corinthians 4:14.

D. The appalling consequences if Christ has not risen from the dead

I Corinthians 15:14-19.

E. The resurrection of believers

1. Time—at the coming of Christ, I Thessalonians 4:16.

2. The nature of the resurrection body, I Corinthians 15:42-48, 52; II Corinthians 5:1-5 (in this passage the actual term for resurrection is not used); Philippians 3:21.

3. In the factors that urged Paul on in his service for God, Philippians 3:11.

F. There will be a resurrection "both of the just and the unjust"

Acts 24:15.

G. The present experience of "resurrection" as newness of life

Romans 6:13; Ephesians 2:6, Philippians 3:10; Colossians 1:12. It is generally held that Romans 8:11 is to be so interpreted, but some affirm this refers to actual bodily resurrection. (See also Ephesians 5:14).

VII. THE TESTIMONY OF THE NEW TESTAMENT TO THE FACT THAT RESURRECTION WAS TAUGHT IN THE OLD TESTAMENT

A. In general

   1. "That the dead are raised up even Moses showed," Luke 20:37.

   2. Abraham believed God would, if Isaac were sacrificed, raise up Isaac from the dead, Hebrews 11:19.

   3. Paul frequently refers to the belief of Israel that God would raise the dead, Acts 23:6; 24:15, 21; 26:8, 23.

   4. "Women received their dead raised to life again," Hebrews 11:35.

   5. Our Lord drew from the revelation that God is not the God of the dead but of the living the truth that there must therefore be a resurrection, Matthew 22:31, 32; Mark 12:26, 27; Luke 20:37, 38. See Exodus 3:6, 15, 16; etc.

B. Specifically—in relation to the resurrection of Christ

   1. His Resurrection was "according to the Scriptures," Luke 24:46; I Corinthians 15:4; Acts 17:3.

   2. The Psalms are declared to contain prophecies of Christ's Resurrection.

     a. Psalm 2:7 — Acts 13:33.

     b. Psalm 16:8-11 — Acts 2:25-31; 13:34-37.

242

VIII. PASSAGES IMPLYING RESURRECTION BUT NOT USING SUCH WORDS

A. Of Jesus, when stating He would lay down His life, added, "I take it again," John 10:17, 18.

B. "He shewed Himself alive," Acts 1:3.

With which compare the assertion that Paul "affirmed (Jesus) to be alive," Acts 25:19.

C. Two passages in the epistle to the Romans
  1. That God will "quicken our mortal bodies," 8:11.
  2. All Christians are waiting for "the redemption of the body," 8:23.

D. Three additional passages
  1. The intricate declaration regarding our having "a building of God," II Corinthians 5:1.
  2. "Who shall change our bodies of corruption," etc., Philippians 3:21.
  3. Christ was "put to death in the flesh, but quickened by the Spirit," I Peter 3:18.

E. Words of the Risen Lord
  "I was dead . . . I am alive," Revelation 1:18, 2:8.

IX. RESURRECTION IN THE NEW TESTAMENT APART FROM THAT OF CHRIST

A. In general
  "The dead are raised up," Matthew 11:5; Luke 7:22; compare the commission of Jesus to the Twelve, Matthew 10:8.

B. Certain individuals during the ministry of Jesus
  1. The son of the widow of Nain, Luke 7:11-17.

2. The daughter of Jairus, Matthew 9:18, 19, 23-26; Mark 5:22-24, 35-43; Luke 8:41, 42, 49-56.

3. Lazarus, John 11; 12:1, 9, 17.

C. An unidentified group, after Christ's Resurrection Matthew 27:52, 53.

D. Dorcas
Acts 9:36-42.

E. A future individual resurrection will be that of the two witnesses of Revelation 11:11.

X. SOME MISCELLANEOUS STATEMENTS

A. The Samaritans believed in a resurrection, John 11:24.

B. The doctrine of the resurrection should be a foundation truth for believers.
Hebrews 6:2.

C. Once in the New Testament we have the phrase "the first resurrection"
Revelation 20:5, 6.

XI. ERRONEOUS OPINIONS CONCERNING RESURRECTION

A. The Sadducees — "Who say that there is no resurrection," Matthew 22:23; Mark 12:18; Luke 20:27; Acts 23:8; I Corinthians 15:12.

B. That John the Baptist was risen from the dead
Mark 6:14, 16; Luke 9:7.

C. That the resurrection is past,
II Timothy 2:18.

244

D. In Athens, when they heard Paul preaching the resurrection "some mocked," Acts 17:32.

In the above classification, I have sometimes used a passage in relation to two different aspects of this subject, and in four cases, I have used a passage three times—Acts 24:15; I Corinthians 3:21; and Colossians 2:12. In estimating the totals which I am about to give, I have reckoned, for example, the three Gospel accounts of the raising of the daughter of Jairus as three different passages. I feel one is justified in speaking of separate passages on the Resurrection in identifying six of them in the 15th chapter of I Corinthians. In the enumeration that follows, it will be discovered that in the Four Gospels, there are fifty-seven different references to the Resurrection and the Resurrection of Christ, embracing 172 verses. In Acts, there are 21 separate passages, totaling 43 verses. In the Epistles of St. Paul, there are 36 references, totaling 54 verses, and in the remaining books of the New Testament, there are 12 passages, totaling 13 verses. Thus, we find there are 126 different passages in the New Testament referring to the subject of the Resurrection and the Resurrection of Christ, totaling 282 verses.

LIST OF PASSAGES REFERRED TO IN THE ABOVE OUTLINE

| Matthew | 9:18, 19, 23-26; 10:8; 11:5; 12:40; 16:21; 17:9, 23; 22:23-33; 26:32; 27:40, 52, 53, 63, 64; 28:6, 7, 1-8, 9, 10, 16-20 |

Mark	5:22-24, 35-43; 6:14, 16; 8:31; 9:9, 31; 10:19, 20; 12:18-27; 14:28; 15:29; 16:1-8, 6, 9-11, 12, 13, 14, 15-18
Luke	7:11-18, 22; 8:41, 42, 49-56; 9:7, 21; 18:33; 20:27-38, 37; 24:1-12, 6, 7, 13-35, 34, 36-43, 44-53, 46
John	2:19-22; 5:26-29; 6:39, 40, 44; 10:17, 18; 11:1-57, 23, 24, 25; 20:1-10, 11-18, 19-25, 26-29; 21:1-24, 14
Acts	1:1-9, 3, 22; 2:24-31, 31, 32; 3:15; 4:10; 5:30; 9:36-42; 10:40, 41; 13:29-34, 33, 35-37; 17:3, 18, 31, 32; 23:6, 8; 24:15, 21; 25:19; 26:6-8, 23
Romans	1:4; 4:24, 25; 6:4, 5, 9, 13; 7:4; 8:11, 23, 34; 10:9; 14:9
I Corinthians	6:14; 15:4, 6, 7, 12, 14-19, 20, 21, 42-48, 52
II Corinthians	1:9; 4:14; 5:1-5, 1, 15
Galatians	1:1
Ephesians	1:20; 2:6
Philippians	3:10, 11, 21
Colossians	1:18; 2:12
I Thessalonians	1:10; 4:16
II Timothy	2:8, 18
Hebrews	6:2; 11:19, 35; 13:20
I Peter	1:3, 21; 3:18
Revelation	1:15, 18; 2:8; 11:11; 20:5, 6

Wilbur M. Smith, *Great Sermons on the Resurrection of Christ* (Natick, MS: W. A. Wilde Co., 1964), pp. 269-278.

Appendix II

THE RELIABILITY OF NEW TESTAMENT SOURCES

Throughout this work it has been assumed that the New Testament documents are historically reliable. What the Gospel writers attribute to Jesus in both deed and word has been taken at face value. Some current New Testament criticism would look upon these assumptions as suspect.

This is an important question since New Testament Christianity is clearly tied to the historical order. It centers in an *historical person* who comes into the *stream of history* at a given point in *historical time*. As such, Christianity is distinguishable from other religious and philosophical systems which are not specifically related to any particular historical time or series of historical events. Therefore, if the documents which provide understanding of the Christian system are historically unreliable, then Christianity itself becomes genuinely suspect. After all, if the bodily resurrection of Jesus Christ did not occur three days following His death as claimed in these documents, then Christianity is a false religion and those who foisted it upon the citizens of the Roman Empire were deceivers.

The first five books of the New Testament collection are the focus of attention. These are set out in narrative form; they speak of historical persons and relate historical events. They speak of the very foundation of Christian faith for they spell out what "Jesus began to do and teach" (Acts 1:1) and what He continued to do and teach through His apostolic witnesses (Acts 1:8). The former is evidenced by four volumes referred to as "gospels"; the latter by that continuing volume of one of these gospels, known as "the Acts of the Apostles."

According to the principles of logic all one would need to do is show that those attacks made upon the historicity of these volumes have proven groundless. After all, according to the laws of evidence, the burden of proof is upon those who deny the historical reliability of the documents. Such denials go back into the early stages of the nineteenth century, and in all instances have proven to be without foundation. Archaeological research and careful historical analysis of ancient texts have, as William Foxwell Albright says, "dealt the *coup de grace* to such extreme critical views of the New Testament as the speculations of the Tuebingen School, founded by F. C. Baur, and the Dutch School headed by Van Manen."[1]

The close proximity of the writing of these narratives to the events they depict is itself attestation of their genuineness. The ministry of Jesus concluded in His crucifixion (and resurrection) about A.D. 30. These four documents were written within the next 60 to 70 years. In fact Adolph Harnack, a very liberal scholar, dates the book of Acts and the Synoptic Gospels (Matthew, Mark, and Luke) as early as A.D. 60-65. Even if later dates (65-85) are assigned to the Synoptic Gospels it must be remembered that there would still be many alive who could remember the things Jesus said and did. It is hardly likely that unauthentic gospels could be written, circulated widely, and accepted universally by the mid-second century (as these were!). The evidence of the general acceptance of these as historically valid and authoritative is greater for these documents than for "any other ancient writings of comparable date."[2] Sir Frederick Kenyon,

---

1. W. F. Albright, *The Archaeology of Palestine* (Baltimore: Penguin, 1949), p. 240.

2. F. F. Bruce, *The New Testament Documents: Are The Reliable?* Fifth Edition. (Downers Grove, IL: InterVarsity Press, 1960), p. 15. This little volume gives a conclusively positive answer to the question posed in the title.

an outstanding Biblical scholar, gives this summary verdict: "The interval then between the dates of original composition and the earliest extant evidence becomes so small as to be in fact negligible, and the last foundation for any doubt that the Scriptures have come down to us substantially as they were written has now been removed. Both the *authenticity* and the *general integrity* of the books of the New Testament may be regarded as finally established."[3]

Perhaps the writings of Luke are more crucial than any other under consideration. Author of both the third Gospel and the Acts of the Apostles (a two-volume work on the origins and early development of Christianity), Luke sets out both the events of Jesus' life and the history of the early Church deliberately within the context of Roman imperial history. He refers to Roman emperors: Augustus, Tiberius and Claudius; to Roman governors: Quirinius, Pilate, Sergius Paulus, Gallio, Felix, Festus; to Herod the Great and several of his descendants: Antipas, Agrippa I and II, Berenice and Drusilla; to leading members of the priestly party of Jerusalem: Annas, Caiaphas, Ananias; and to Gamaliel, the greatest contemporary Rabbi and Pharisaic leader. As Dr. Bruce says: "A writer who thus relates his story to the wider context of world history is courting trouble if he is not careful; he affords his critical readers so many opportunities for testing his accuracy."[4]

Luke stands the test admirably. In fact, not only does he prove to be accurate in all these references, he is also accurate in his use of political terms, Roman provincial boundaries, unique geographical and topographical locations, and even "local color and atmosphere."[5] The weight

---

3. *The Bible and Archaeology* (London: Harrap, 1940), pp. 288, 289.
4. *Op. cit.*, p. 82.
5. *Ibid.*, p. 88.

of scholarship today acknowledges the historical trustworthiness of Luke-Acts.

If Luke-Acts is trustworthy and reliable, then, it follows that similar events described in the other Gospels are reliable as well. It also follows that the rise of Christianity as pictured here and substantiated in other Apostolic writings, such as Paul's letters, is authentic and factual. Therefore, the main outline of the origins of Christianity in the resurrection power of Jesus, presented for us in these documents, is factually true and to be trusted implicity.

Appendix III

TRADITIONAL EXPLANATIONS OF THE RESURRECTION SUGGESTED BY CRITICS

Through the centuries "critics" have denied the actuality of the resurrection of Jesus and have attempted to explain the cluster of events centering around this presumed fact in numerous ways. The most ancient explanation is that which the soldiers guarding the tomb were instructed to make: "His disciples came by night and stole him away while we were asleep" (Matt. 28:13). This explanation has surfaced at various times in history. Celsus, the early third-century heretic, used this argument in his debate with Origen. H. Reimaurus, a German scholar, revived this view in a work entitled, *The Goal of Jesus and His Disciples*, published in 1778.

Origen's answer to Celsus still stands. Frightened men do not risk their lives and suffer martyrdom to perpetuate a lie. If the Gospel records are reliable these disciples are trembling behind locked doors, afraid to venture out, unwilling even to believe the stories of the women about an empty tomb. Can anyone genuinely believe these men had enough courage to steal away the body and carry off this deception?

What is known as the "swoon theory" was suggested by Paulus, another German scholar. In his life of Jesus, published in 1828, he explains the "resurrection" in this fashion: Jesus' death, which was amazingly swift, was only a "death-like" trance. The spear thrust was only a flesh wound. The cool grave and pungent spices revived him and the storm and earthquake opened the tomb and he went out, put on a gardener's outfit, and appeared to Mary (John 20:15).

A recent version of this "swoon theory" is defended in Hugh Schonfield's *The Passover Plot* (New York: Bernard

251

Geis, 1965). According to Schonfield, Jesus felt himself called to preach repentance, but this mission is unsuccessful. He decides that, since the Old Testament depicts a suffering Servant, he would deliberately "plot" to bring this about but to stop short of death. He provokes Judas to betray him; he utters blasphemy against Caesar not God (see Mark 14:64); and is handed over to the Romans for crucifixion. He "plotted" with Joseph of Arimathea to arrange for his death and resurrection by prearranging the "I thirst" signal so that he could receive a powerful drug from the sponge which would put him in a death-like trance. Joseph was to seek the body from Pilate and place it in the tomb from whence Jesus would then appear as risen. But, the unexpected happens. The soldier's spear thrust had not been anticipated. Jesus died, but not before sending word to his disciples that he would meet them in Galilee. He is taken from Joseph's tomb and laid in some unknown tomb. The tomb being empty, with the grave clothes lying in it, led Mary, Peter, and John to suppose that he had risen.

This is, of course, a fanciful piece of fiction and runs counter to those events recorded in the Gospel accounts. Then, too, it is not only the "empty tomb" that gives rise to faith; his actual appearances are merely supported by such external evidence. If Jesus is a "trickster," as he must be if either version of this "swoon theory" is genuine, then he is not worthy to be followed. But such a view is utterly incredible and cannot be held in light of the evidence that is related in the Gospels.

More recently alternative explanations for the resurrection have centered in visionary phenomena. Since visions, even though subjective, are intensely real to the one experiencing the vision, this may account for "resurrection appearances." Rudolph Bultmann's explanation is typical: "The historian can perhaps to some extent account for that faith [in the resurrection] from the personal intimacy which the disciple had enjoyed with Jesus during his earthly life and so reduce the resurrection appearances to a series of subjective visions."[1] Others have followed this pattern of explanation with some variations.

Dr. William Milligan exploded this subjective vision theory long ago.[2] Such a theory is both inconsistent with the state of mind of the disciples and cannot explain how five hundred could have had a simultaneous subjective vision. Then, too, such visions do not continue over a period of forty days nor cease so abruptly as is evident in the New Testament records. It is also assumed by those who hold such a theory that all Jesus' appearances were to believers in whom the impact of his personality would have created susceptibility. Dr. Ladd says: "This simply is not true on two scores. The disciples were not believers after Jesus' death and burial; and James and Paul never had been disciples; they were both unbelievers when Jesus appeared to them."[3]

All such hypotheses are found wanting when applied to the historical evidence. The only hypothesis that is an adequate explanation of all the facts is that Jesus actually arose from the dead and appeared to His disciples as recorded. To fly into the face of such overwhelming evidence is a clear indication that those who do have closed minds. They do not want to entertain the possibility that Jesus rose bodily from the grave. Whatever their motive, they demonstrate an unwillingness to face Biblical facts and come to the only possible conclusion—Jesus of Nazareth has risen from the dead!

---

1. *Kerygma and Myth,* quoted by G. E. Ladd, *I Believe in the Resurrection of Jesus* (Grand Rapids: Wm. B. Eerdmans, 1975), pp. 136, 137.

2. See his *The Resurrection of Our Lord* (New York: The Macmillan Co., 1917), p. 81f.

3. Ladd, *op. cit.,* p. 138.

Appendix IV

CURRENT THINKING ABOUT THE RESURRECTION

The position taken in this book is not a universally accepted position. The author believes it is the only position that does justice to the Biblical data; but he would be remiss were he not to point out that others have taken different positions relative to resurrection reality. Perhaps a brief survey of current views of the resurrection is in order.

To do justice this survey must be seen against the backdrop of nineteenth century liberalism which Walter Kunneth calls a "secularized theology."[1] This theology has its origin in Schleiermacher and Ritschl who denied the historical reality of Jesus' resurrection and ascension. Those who have followed in this pattern of thought no longer regarded the resurrection of Jesus as a necessary element of the Christian faith. What was essential was the life and attitude of the historical Jesus who was only prophet and teacher. The "quest for the historical Jesus," in terms of various critical attempts to peel off the layers of theological or mythological accretions of the Biblical documents (such as the resurrection and the ascension), paralleled this theological reinterpretation.

It was in the light of such theological liberalism and radical Biblical criticism that some of the more traditional attempts to explain the resurrection were revived and modified (See Appendix Three). For example, a modified vision theory was set forth by Theodor Keim in his mammoth work, *History of Jesus of Nazara* (1867-1872). He saw the resurrection as explained by God-given visions, a kind of "telegraph from heaven." B. H. Streeter picks this idea up and popularizes it among the English-speaking world in his essay in

---

1. *The Theology of the Resurrection* (St. Louis: Concordia Publishing House, 1965), p. 16.

the volume entitled *Foundations,* published in 1910.[2] Others have modified this "objective vision" theory into a kind of "telepathic theory." Raised not bodily but as Spirit, Jesus was implanting "doctrines" in their minds and projecting an "apparitional figure so that they heard the apparition giving them the teaching which Jesus wished them to absorb and reflect upon."[3]

Other New Testament scholars, like Kirsopp Lake, attempted to show difficulties in the primitive traditions recorded in the Gospel accounts. In his work, *The Historical Evidence for the Resurrection of Jesus Christ,* published in 1907, Lake suggests that the women's report to the disciples about an empty tomb may be seen only as a report about the wrong tomb. Presuming that the only historical element is the empty tomb, Lake rejects the historicity of the empty tomb. But even though Lake himself denies the historical evidence (as he understands it) for the resurrection, he does make this rather remarkable observation: "The historical evidence is such that it can be fairly interpreted consistently with either of the two doctrinal positions . . . but it does not support either. The story of the empty tomb must be fought out on doctrinal, not on historical or critical grounds."[4] In other words, if one believes in a God who can and does raise the dead, the historical material is consistent. If one only believes "in the unbroken survival of personal life" (as does Lake), then the historical material can be interpreted differently!

But there came a strong reaction against this liberal approach to theology and to the cavalier way in which Biblical

---

2. See A. M. Ramsey, *The Resurrection of Christ,* pp. 49, 50.

3. Michael, Clark, *The Easter Enigma,* p. 195, quoted by M. C. Tenney, *The Reality of the Resurrection,* p. 190.

4. Quoted in Ramsey, *op. cit.,* pp. 51, 52.

data was being treated. The resurrection of the body came to center stage. It was no longer theological accretion or non-historical myth, a stumbling block to be moved from the progressive optimistic path upward. As Reinhold Niehbuhr confessed in his book, *Beyond Tragedy*: "Some of us have been persuaded to take the stone which we then rejected and to make it the head of the corner. In other words there is no part of the Apostolic Creed which, in our present opinion, expresses the whole genius of the Christian faith more neatly than just that despised phrase, 'I believe in the Resurrection of the Body.' "[5] Karl Barth, whose commentary on Romans began this trek back toward a more Biblically oriented theology (often known as a "theology of the Word" or a Neo-Reformation), became more and more committed to the reality of the resurrection of the *man* Jesus.[6] The appreciation of the significance of the resurrection for the theological task reaches its zenith in Walter Kunneth's significant study, *The Theology of the Resurrection*. First developed in 1933, revised and expanded in 1951, and translated into English in 1965, this work is a masterful treatment of both the Biblical data and theological significance. Listen to Kunneth's conclusion: "Our study has led us to the following summary conclusion: *The raising of the Christ is the* act of God, whose significance is not to be compared with any event before or after. *It is the primal datum of theology, from which there can be no abstracting,* and the normative presupposition for every valid dogmatic judgment and for the meaningful constructing of a Christian theology. Thus

---

5. Quoted by Ramsey, p. 101. Daniel Fuller, in chapter six of his book, *Easter Faith and History* (Grand Rapids: Wm. B. Eerdmans, 1965), entitled "The Resurrection and Historical Reasoning" gives an excellent overview of this movement away from the older liberalism.

6. See his *Church Dogmatics*, Vol. III, part ii (Edinburgh: T. and T. Clark, 1960), pp. 442-448.

the resurrection of Jesus becomes the Archimedean point for theology as such, not derivable from empirical reflection, and established beyond any religious *a priori*. All theological statements are oriented in one way or another towards this focal point. There is no Christian knowledge of God which does not acquire its ultimate fulness and depth from the revelation of God in the Risen One. The constructing of a Christology without an understanding of the Kyrios is inconceivable. Pneumatology, too, has no other content than the reality of the Spirit of the Exalted Christ. The concept of the Church, as well as that of Christian ethics, is essentially determined by the resurrection of Jesus. Important insights into creation and nature, into history and existence, cannot be acquired without the resurrection faith. In it alone is there the possibility of a universal interpretation of the world.

"Christian faith exists only where the resurrection of Jesus is acknowledged to be a reality. Its heart is the living Christ. It is in the Risen One that the whole life of mankind ultimately comes to a decision. The ultimate decision, however, is that between life and death.

"The word of the resurrection of Jesus is the assault of life upon the dying world. It is decisive. Out of this assault there grows the faith that knows: *Extra resurrectionem nulla salus.*"[7]

But, in spite of this more healthy approach to an understanding of the resurrection, all have not come to view resurrection as an historical reality. "Resurrection talk" to some modern scholars is interpreted as merely affirming some great principle (e.g., "love conquers") through symbolic narratives. Resurrection is still being interpreted as the

---

7. Kunneth, *op. cit.*, pp. 294, 295.

"'miraculous' emergence of faith."[8] So Paul vanBuren, Lloyd Geering, and Willi Marxen are so interpreted by O'Collins. Still, the prevailing view is more positive, not critical; and the ripest of Biblical scholars stand firmly upon the apostolic testimony. Dr. Raymond Brown's judgment reflects this: "From a critical study of the biblical evidence I would judge that Christians can and indeed should continue to speak of a *bodily* resurrection of Jesus." He points out that this commitment is of grave importance: "The understanding that the resurrection was bodily in the sense that Jesus' body did not corrupt in a tomb has important theological implications. The resurrection of Jesus was remembered with such emphasis in the Church because it explained what God had done for men. The resurrection was and remains, first of all, what God has done *for Jesus.* It was not an evolution in human consciousness, nor was it the disciples' brilliant insight into the meaning of the crucifixion—it was the sovereign action of God glorifying Jesus of Nazareth. Only because God has done this for His Son are new possibilities opened for His many children who have come to believe in what He has done.

"The fact that these future possibilities for Christians *are* patterned on what God has already done for Jesus lends a special importance to the question of bodily resurrection. In man's anticipation of God's ultimate plan, one of two models is usually followed: the model of eventual destruction and new creation, or the model of transformation. Will the material world be transformed and changed into the city of God? The model that the Christian chooses will have an effect on his attitude toward the world and toward the corporeal.

---

8. Gerald O'Collins, *What Are They Saying about the Resurrection?* (New York: The Paulist Press, 1978), p. 43.

What will be destroyed can have only passing value; what is to be transformed retains its importance. Is the body a shell that one sheds, or is it an intrinsic part of the personality that will forever identify a man? If Jesus' body corrupted in the tomb so that his victory over death did not involve bodily resurrection, then the model of destruction and new creation is indicated. If Jesus rose bodily from the dead, then the Christian model should be one of transformation. The problem of the bodily resurrection is not just an example of Christian curiosity; it is related to a major theme in theology: God's ultimate purpose in creating."[9]

Christians committed to the reliability of the Scriptural text are encouraged by these views, even though they may come from a more radical tradition. Faith, which "comes by hearing the word," (Rom. 10:17) believes that the resurrection of Jesus occurred. History and theology justify that faith!

---

9. Raymond Brown, *The Virginal Conception & Bodily Resurrection of Jesus* (New York: The Paulist Press, 1973), pp. 128, 129.

Appendix V

THE SHROUD OF TURIN: PROOF
OF RESURRECTION?

In recent years, a Roman Catholic relic, known as *Santa Sindone* (in Italian) or Holy Shroud, reposing in the Turin Cathedral of St. John the Baptist, has become the object of the most careful scientific and historical study. This study of the Shroud of Turin (as it is popularly known) has been transdenominational, with Roman Catholic officials themselves serving as effective Devil's Advocates as they have blocked the way for even more carefully-drawn scientific analyses of this phenomena.

The Shroud is kept in the circular, block marble Royal Chapel of the Cathedral at Turin. It reposes in a locked cavity known as the "sepulchre" in a second altar surmounting the altar of the Chapel. It lies rolled around a velvet staff and wrapped in red silk within a four-foot-long wooden casket ornamental in silver with emblems of the Passion. This casket is kept in an iron chest wrapped in asbestos and sealed with three locks. This chest, so wrapped and sealed, is set within a wooden box with a painted cover. It is only this cover which is visible behind two iron grills in the upper altar section of the Chapel.

From medieval times this Shroud has attracted controversy. When it first appeared in the West it was denounced as a fraud "cunningly painted" and "deceitful." Others described it as "a harmless piece of buffoonery." On the other hand some have seen it as the authentic burial shroud of Jesus and have made wild claims as to how it disproves the resurrection, showing that Jesus was not dead but merely revived in the tomb.[1]

---

1. See Ian Wilson, *The Shroud of Turin* (Garden City, NY: Doubleday & Co., Inc., 1978), p. 2ff. Much of the material presented in this appendix is drawn from Wilson's excellent study.

The speculation has been able to flourish due to the Shroud's inaccessibility. Since Napoleonic times the Shroud has been seen publicly on only a few occasions and it has only been in the 1970s that any careful study has been allowed. This became possible when Cardinal Pellegrino agreed, not to a traditional exposition with crowds of tourists and pilgrims filing through the Cathedral, but a showing on television over the Eurovision network beamed into Italy, Spain, France, Portugal, Belgium, and even as far west as Brazil. In addition a special showing would be granted to the press and other interested people the day before the television program.

On Thursday, November 22, 1973, this rather informal press conference occurred. This conference opened up a whole new chapter in attitudes toward the Shroud. It stimulated interest in the Shroud for not only the religious believer or the doubter, but for a whole host of scientific experts—textile experts, forensic scientists, physicists, photographers, criminologists, hematologists, historians, and theologians. All of these would contribute new and intriguing information from their specific fields.

The image on the Shroud is of a bearded figure whose death has appeared to have come in the way that the Gospels describe the events of Jesus' crucifixion. There is the visual evidence of blood from wounds in the forehead, hands (actually wrists), and side. Since the image is of both the back as well as the front of a body lying prone, there is also visual evidence (upon the back, buttocks and legs) of a beating by an instrument similar to (if not exactly like) the kind of whips used by the ancient Romans.

The Shroud was first photographed in 1898 by Secondo Pia. Wilson writes:

According to his own account [Pia's], his first thoughts were of relief when he saw the negative image begin to appear under the developer. Seconds later, they were to turn to astonishment, then to a chilling awe. On the glass negative there slowly appeared before him, not a ghost of the shadowy figure visible on the cloth, as he had expected, but instead an unmistakable photographic likeness.

The double figures of the Shroud had undergone a dramatic change. Now there was natural light and dark shading, giving relief and depth. Bloodstains, showing white, could realistically be seen to flow from the hands and the feet, from the right side and from all around the crown of the head. Instead of having a masklike, almost grotesque appearance, the man of the shroud could be seen to be well-proportioned and of impressive build. Most striking of all was the face, incredibly lifelike against the black background.[2]

Since that time other photographs have revealed the same phenomena, only in a more sophisticated manner as photographic quality has developed since 1898. Giuseppe Enrie, under carefully controlled and guarded conditions, made several photographs of the Shroud in 1931, revealing the same kind of phenomena first discovered by Pia. There can be no question regarding the authenticity of the phenomenon thus reproduced, since every stage of Enrie's work was checked by a specially appointed commission of expert photographers. It was photographed again in 1969 and during the 1973 showing. "The result is always the same; the image is there whenever the Shroud is reversed by the cameras."[3] Wilson adds:

---

2. *Ibid.*, p. 14.
3. *Ibid.*, p. 16.

It is important that we attempt to define what appears on the negative. On the Shroud, although the figures are very pale, against the ivory-colored cloth they appear dark or light. A photographic negative, therefore, shows them light or white on the cloth which now appears dark or black, as one would expect. It can be seen how this reversal has happened in a perfectly straightforward way in the relatively dark bloodstains which show up white on the negative. Also, there is left-to-right reversal, as when looking in a mirror— i.e., the lance wound switches from the left to the right side, etc. But it is in the relief or tonal values that something different has happened.

In the case of a normal portrait photograph, we understand that the face, when reversed on the negative, will appear strange and grotesque because the areas that were in light show up as dark tones. When the negative is exposed in its turn to photographic paper, these light values are reversed to produce once again a life-like picture.

In the case of the image on the Shroud there is one less stage to the process. The face and body *are* not lifelike on the cloth itself; they *become* lifelike when their light values are reversed by a photographic negative.

Not unreasonably, therefore, it has been claimed that the Shroud itself is in a sense a photographic negative—a negative that, as we have seen, can unquestionably be traced at least as far back as the Middle Ages, many centuries before the invention of photography.[4]

Since these earlier photographs, experts from various areas of scientific study have given careful attention to this phenomenon. Medical science was the first to enter the picture. A small team of medical scientists from the Sorbonne, led by Paul Vignon, began to make a special

---

4. *Ibid.*, pp. 16-17.

study of the photographs. One of the group, Yves Delage, professor of anatomy, gave a lecture in 1902 in which he explained that the wounds and other data "were so anatomically flawless that it seemed impossible that they could be the work of any artist. He pointed out how difficult and pointless it would have been for anyone to work in negative, and how there was, in any case, no trace of known pigment on the cloth."[5] Later, in the 1930s (after Enrie's better photographs had been more widely distributed), Dr. Pierre Barbet of St. Joseph's Hospital, Paris, after conducting numerous experiments on cadavers, concluded that the wounds visible on the Shroud are genuinely those of a victim of crucifixion. Others since then have continued to study the Shroud's image and have concluded that blood flow, wounds about face and forehead, and the dumbell shaped marks on back, hips, buttocks, shoulders, arms, and legs all are consistent with the data seen in the Gospels relative to Jesus' torture and crucifixion.[6]

Evidence from New Testament archaeology as to Roman methods of crucifixion, Roman instruments of torture, spears used, etc., also seem to point to the Shroud's authenticity; at least to the conclusion that this was a Jew crucified under the Romans. The inevitable question is, Could it have been Jesus? Does the image on the Shroud correspond to what is recounted in the Gospels? The following table suggests a positive answer to these questions:[7]

---

5. *Ibid.*, p. 19.

6. Dr. Barbet showed his findings to an agnostic colleague, Professor Hovelaque, who is reported to have said, "But then, mon dieux, Jesus Christ really did rise from the dead!" *Ibid.*, p. 31.

7. *Ibid.*, pp. 36-37.

Gospel Evidence	Source	Evidences on the Shroud
1. Jesus was scourged.	Matt. 27:26, Mark 15:15, John 19:1	The body is literally covered with the wounds of a severe scourging.
2. Jesus was struck a blow to the face.	Matt. 27:30, Mark 15:19, Luke 22:63, John 19:3	There appears to be a severe swelling below the right eye and other superficial face wounds.
3. Jesus was crowned with thorns.	Matt. 27:29, Mark 15:17, John 19:2	Bleeding from the scalp indicates that some form of barbed "cap" has been thrust upon the head.
4. Jesus had to carry a heavy cross.	John 19:17	Scourge wounds in the area of the shoulders appear to be blurred, as if by the chafing of some heavy burden.
5. Jesus' cross had to be carried for him, suggesting he repeatedly fell under the burden.	Matt. 27:32, Mark 15:21, Luke 23:26	The knees appear severely damaged, as if from repeated falls.
6. Jesus was crucified by nailing in hands and feet.	John 20:25 (by implication)	There are clear blood flows as from nail wounds in the wrists and at the feet.
7. Jesus' legs were not broken, but a spear was thrust into his side as a check that he was dead.	John 19:31-37	The legs are clearly not broken, and there is an elliptical wound in the right side.

In 1969 another breakthrough came. A small group of people—three priests and five scientists—were allowed to make a detailed visual study of the Shroud itself during a two-day period (June 16-17, 1969). The Shroud was examined with the unaided eye, under the microscope, and viewed with Wood's light and infrared light. This led to a recommendation of a series of tests upon "minimal samples" of the actual material of the Shroud. This recommendation was accepted and implemented in November, 1973. From these samples, textile experts were able to determine the kind of weave of the linen cloth and the approximate age and location from whence the cloth originally came. Their conclusions place this cloth in the Mid-East with a weave that is compatible with what was common in the first century of the Christian era.

Some of the samples were taken from the dorsal image upon which the "bloodstains" appear. Modern forensic and hematological scientists studied these carefully but were unable to find any actual blood or hermatic substance on the Shroud. "Instead, whatever created the image would seem to have no actual substance of its own. It would seem to have been a 'dry' process as from some physical force reacting with the surface fibers on the Shroud threads, the granules thereby being formed, as it were, from the fibers themselves."[8]

It was also noticed by Dr. Max Frei, a noted Swiss criminologist, that the surface of the cloth was covered with minute dust particles. He gained permission to remove some of these particles for analysis. He found that in addition to mineral particles, bacteria spores, and fragments from hairs and fibers, that microscopic pollen grains were also present. As a botanist, Frei knew that these grains could retain their physical characteristics for thousands of years and that they could be classified rather precisely and might suggest the geographical regions in which the Shroud had been. After careful study Frei identified certain of these pollen grains as typical "halophytes, plants common to the desert regions around the Jordan Valley and unique in one respect: They

---

8. *Ibid.*, p. 59.

are specifically adapted to live in a soil with a high content of sodium chloride such as is found almost exclusively around the Dead Sea."[9] This significance is set out in Frei's own statement:

> These plants are of great diagnostic value for our geographical studies as identical desert plants are missing in all the other countries where the Shroud is believed to have been exposed to open air. Consequently, a forgery, produced somewhere in France during the Middle Ages, in a country lacking these typical halophytes, could not contain such characteristic pollen grains from the desert region of Palestine.[10]

But, how could the image have been produced? If it was not a painted forgery (since there is no evidence of paint or pigmentation in the pieces of cloth studied), what did produce this image? Recent studies in the United States have attempted to explore these questions. As early as 1968 two Air Force scientists (both captains), Dr. John Jackson and Dr. Eric Jamper began a research project on the measurement of the actual distances involved in the image formation. They made a "dummy" Shroud upon which was projected a transparency of the Shroud and all its phenomena—burns, patches, shadings relative to facial features, body, stains of apparent blood, etc.—which were carefully transcribed on this "dummy." They found an Air Force officer who was almost a perfect fit as far as the Shroud image was concerned, to serve as a "model." This model was placed within the Shroud, positioned over and under the corresponding part of the Shroud image. He was photographed from the side, first with the Shroud in position and then with it removed. By this means it was possible to measure the perpendicular distance of cloth from body at every point. Following this,

9. *Ibid.*, pp. 62-63.
10. Quoted by *Ibid.*, p. 63.

these scientists ran the image of the Shroud under a micro-densitometer, which measures image intensity, "following exactly the ridge line from which the date of cloth-body distance had been obtained. The resulting graph revealed clearly a varying intensity of the image at each landmark giving in itself a distorted outline of the Shroud 'body.'"[11] Upon making a mathematical correlation between image intensity and cloth-to-body distance, they found (what they had scarcely hoped for), "a perfect curve—demonstrating beyond question that there was a positive and precise relationship between image intensity and the degree to which the cloth was separated from the body at any given point."[12]

Later, Jackson consulted Bill Mottern, an image enhancement specialist at the Sandia Laboratories in New Mexico. An ordinary three-by-five transparency of the Shroud was put into a machine known as an Interpretation Systems VP-8 Image Analyzer (a device which "plots shades of image brightness as adjustable levels of vertical relief"[13]), and the results were astonishing as a three-dimensional relief image was seen perfectly on the television screen linked to the machine. Further experiments in image-enhancement tended to confirm a Jewish burial custom of laying coins or pieces of potsherd over the eyes when laying a corpse out for burial, as bulges consistent with the size of lepton (the "widow's mite" of the New Testament) were discovered. These studies also tended to show that there was no directionality except in the scourge marks, which as would be expected, would be seen as going one way and then the other. This argued powerfully that the image had not been made by an artist.

But if the image was not made by an artist, and if it was not the simple product of blood and sweat working into the

---

11. *Ibid.*, p. 198.
12. *Loc. cit.*
13. *Ibid.*, p. 199.

cloth (as other studies confirmed), then how does one explain the image? One suggestion made was that the process was akin to images made by certain preserved plants.[14] But the time element here is a problem (these images often take seventy or more years to develop) as well as the three-dimensionality shown in the image-enchancement tests (which a pressed plant would not genuinely have).

A more promising suggestion is that the image is something akin to a scorch, which would explain the sepia tone which is like the first stage of the oxidation process. But how could a genuinely dead body produce some kind of burning or radiance "sufficient to scorch cloth, acting in so controlled a manner that it dissolved and fused blood flows onto the cloth, yet created at the same time the perfect impression of a human body?"[15] The idea of some kind of thermonuclear blast similar to what occurred at Hiroshima has been the most reasonable speculation, since there were observable at Hiroshima shadows of a light reddish tint upon concrete and other building materials. John Hersey notes that even "*a few vague human silhouettes were found.*"[16] Of course, there are differences between the Shroud and this thermonuclear phenomenon. The Shroud was seemingly scorched from within rather than from without and with an evenness of intensity that is not witnessed at Hiroshima. But the idea of some such force as in a thermonuclear flash is more than idle speculation. To the believer, the New

---

14. "For centuries it has been normal in the collection of botany specimens to sandwich these between thick sheets of paper. After a long period of time there tends in some cases to 'develop' on the paper, both above and below the plant, strikingly precise images in a sepia color closely akin to that of the Shroud." *Ibid.*, p. 207.

15. *Ibid.*, pp. 208-209.

16. *Ibid.*, p. 209 (Italics are Hersey's).

Testament concept of "resurrection power" would certainly be adequate explanation.[17]

In light of these various scientific studies of the Shroud and its image, Ian Wilson believes that these "significant interim conclusions" can be drawn:

> . . . from the careful analysis of the Shroud's textile fibers by Professor Frei the linen can be said to offer no inconsistency with known weaves of the first century A.D. It also beyond doubt bears traces of cotton that confirm it has come from the Middle East.
>
> The chemical microanalytical work by the 1973 Italian commission scientists, while inconclusive, suggests that of whatever substance the shroud image is composed it is not of any readily identifiable pigment that would have been used by a medieval artist.
>
> The word of Dr. Jackson and Dr. Jamper corroborates this by indicating, from the manner in which the image was formed, that no human agency was involved.
>
> The palynological research of Dr. Max Frei provides evidence that at some stage before its known post-fourteenth-century peregrinations in France and Italy the Shroud was in Palestine and Turkey.
>
> Frei's evidence also corroborates the author's theory that the Shroud and the Mandylion are the same. The theory at this stage cannot be considered conclusively proven; nevertheless it invalidates any argument that the Shroud cannot be genuine because there is no documentary record of it before the fourteenth century.[18]

---

17. Jesus said in John 10, "I have power to lay down my life and I have power to take it up again."

18. Almost one-half of Wilson's book is an historical reconstruction in which he identifies the Shroud with the Mandylion (a portrait of Christ, often referred to in ancient times in areas such as Edessa, Constantinople, etc.), the Mandylion being only the face of the Shroud image with the Shroud folded in such a way as to display only the face. Suggesting this identification, Wilson tries to show how it would finally come to Western Europe (through the Knights Templar). See *Ibid.*, pp. 66-194.

Medical opinion is as firmly emphatic today as in the time of Vignon and Delage that, whatever the substance of the image, it is genuinely the imprint of a Roman corpse which has suffered the agonies of crucifixion.

Lastly, but by no means least, comparison of gospel evidence with the imprint of that corpse strongly suggests that if it is to be identified with anyone in history, that identity must be none other than Jesus Christ.

All these conclusions, provisional, though they are, seem sufficient to rule out the old claim that the Shroud is merely a painting by a fourteenth-century artist.[19]

What can be said in light of all this research and these tentative conclusions? First, the Shroud may be genuine and may indeed be that in which Jesus was buried. The scorched image may well be evidence for some form of radiant energy and this may be secondary evidence for the actual miraculous power that brought forth Jesus from the dead. If so, the Shroud would be no different as secondary evidence of the resurrection of Jesus Christ than the open tomb was in the Gospel record (note the implication of an empty tomb in Peter's reference to David's occupied tomb in Acts 2:29). To conclude that the Shroud is a genuine article and does carry this kind of evidence for the resurrection ought not to be derided as though such proof is unnecessary or that such an idea is unworthy. When Jesus said, "Blessed are those who have not seen and yet believe" (John 20:29), he was speaking to Thomas. Just prior to this he had said to Thomas, "Reach hither thy finger, and behold my hands; and reach hither thy hand and thrust it into my side: and be not faithless, but believing" (John 20:27). Jesus did not see Thomas' request as unworthy;

---

19. *Ibid.*, pp. 205-206.

therefore we ought not to disparage evidence from whatever source it may come, if it is evidence indeed.

It is certain that the faith a Christian has in the resurrection of Jesus, the central fact of Christianity, is based upon the evidence provided in the testimony of eye witnesses. However, other corroborative evidence does not diminish this primary evidence; it enhances it. So, when archaeological discoveries tend to confirm what is witnessed to in the Scriptures, we accept such confirmation without disparagement. If the Shroud is proved to be authentic it would fall in the same category as confirming and corroborating what we accept as true on the evidence of competent eye witnesses.

Appendix VI

IMMORTALITY OF THE SOUL
OR RESURRECTION OF THE DEAD*

The Witness of the New Testament

"The Ingersoll Lecture for 1955" — by Oscar Cullmann

If we were to ask an ordinary Christian today (whether well-read Protestant or Catholic, or not) what he conceives to be the New Testament teaching concerning the fate of man after death, with few exceptions we should get the answer: "The immortality of the soul." Yet this widely accepted idea is one of the greatest misunderstandings of Christianity. There is no point in attempting to hide this fact, or to veil it by reinterpreting the Christian faith. This is something that should be discussed quite candidly. The concept of death and resurrection is anchored in the Christ-event (as will be shown in the following pages), and hence is incompatible with the Greek belief in immortality; because it is based in *Heilsgeschichte*[1] it is offensive to modern thought. Is it not such an integral element of the early Christian proclamation that it can neither be surrendered nor reinterpreted without robbing the New Testament of its substance?[2]

But is it really true that the early Christian resurrection faith is irreconcilable with the Greek concept of the immortality of the soul? Does not the New Testament, and above all the Gospel of John, teach that we already have eternal life? Is it really true that death in the New Testament

---

* Published first in *Harvard Divinity School Bulletin 21* (1955/56), pp. 5-36. Also published as a separate book by Epworth Press, London, in 1958.

1. "Salvation history."

2. See on the following also O. Cullmann, "La foi à la résurrection et l'espérance de la résurrection dans le Nouveau Testament," *Etudes théol. et rel.* (1943), pp. 3ff.; *Christ and Time* (1945), pp. 231ff.; Ph. H. Menoud, *Le sort des trépassés* (1945); R. Mehl, *Der letzte Feind* (1954).

is always conceived as "the last enemy" in a way that is diametrically opposed to Greek thought, which sees in death a friend? Does not Paul write: "O death, where is thy sting?" We shall see at the end that there *is* at least an analogy, but first we must stress the fundamental differences between the two points of view.

The widespread misunderstanding—that the New Testament teaches the immortality of the soul—was actually encouraged by the rocklike *post-Easter* conviction of the first disciples that the bodily resurrection of Christ had robbed death of all its horror[3] and that, from the moment of Easter onward, the Holy Spirit had awakened the souls of believers into the life of the resurrection.

The very fact that the words "*post-Easter*" need to be underlined illustrates the whole abyss which nevertheless separates the early Christian view from that of the Greeks. The whole of early Christian thought is based in *Heilsgeschichte*, and everything that is said about death and eternal life stands or falls with a belief in a real occurrence, in real events which took place in time. This is the radical distinction from Greek thought. The purpose of my book *Christ and Time* was precisely to show that this belongs to the substance, to the essence of early Christian faith, that it is something not to be surrendered, not to be altered in meaning; yet it has often been mistakenly thought that I intended to write an essay on the New Testament attitude toward the problem of time and eternity.

---

3. But hardly in such a way that the original Christian community could speak of "natural" dying. This manner of speaking of Karl Barth's in *Die kirchliche Dogmatik*, III, 2 (1948), pp. 776ff., though found in a section where otherwise the negative valuation of death as the "last enemy" is strongly emphasized, still seems to me not to be grounded in the New Testament. See I Cor. 11:30.

If one recognizes that death and eternal life in the New Testament are always bound up with the Christ-event, then it becomes clear that for the first Christians the soul is not intrinsically immortal, but rather became so only through the resurrection of Jesus Christ, and through faith in him. It also becomes clear that death is not intrinsically the friend, but rather that its "sting," its power, is taken away *only* through the victory of Jesus over it in his death. And lastly, it becomes clear that the resurrection already accomplished is not the state of fulfillment, for that remains in the future until the body is also resurrected, which will not occur until "the last day."

It is a mistake to read into the Fourth Gospel an early trend toward the Greek teaching of immortality, because there also eternal life is bound up with the Christ-event.[4] Within the bounds of the Christ-event, of course, the various New Testament books place the accent in different places, but common to all is the view of *Heilsgeschichte*.[5] Obviously one must reckon with Greek influence upon the origin of Christianity from the very beginning,[6] but so long as the Greek ideas are subordinated to the total view of *Heilsgeschichte*, there can be no talk of "Hellenization" in the proper

---

4. Insofar as John's Gospel is rooted in *Heilsgeschichte*, it is not true, as Rudolf Bultmann wrongly maintains, that a process of demythologizing is already to be discerned in it.

5. As Bo Reicke correctly maintains, "Einheitlichkeit oder verschiedene Lehrbegriffe in der neutestamentlichen Theologie," *Theol. Zeitschr.*, 9 (1953), pp. 401ff.

6. All the more as the Qumran texts show that the Judaism to which embryonic Christianity was so closely connected was already itself influenced by Hellenism. See O. Cullmann, "The Significance of the Qumran Tests for Research into the Beginning of Christianity," *Journ. of Bibl. Lit.*, 74 (1955), pp. 213ff.; also in K. Stendahl (ed.), *The Scrolls and the New Testament* (1957), pp. 18-32. So too Rudolf Bultmann, *Theology of the New Testament* (1955), Vol. II, p. 13 note.

sense.[7] Genuine Hellenization occurs for the first time at a later date.

The Last Enemy: Death

Socrates and Jesus

Nothing shows more clearly than the contrast between the death of Socrates and that of Jesus (a contrast which was often cited, though for other purposes, by early opponents of Christianity) that the biblical view of death from the first is focused in salvation-history and so departs completely from the Greek conception.[8]

In Plato's impressive description of the death of Socrates, in the Phaedo, occurs perhaps the highest and most sublime doctrine ever presented on the immortality of the soul. What gives his argument its unexcelled value is his scientific reserve, his disclaimer of any proof having mathematical validity. We know the arguments he offers for the immortality of the soul: Our body is only an outer garment which, as long as we live, prevents our soul from moving freely and from living in conformity to its proper eternal essence. It imposes upon the soul a law which is not appropriate to it. The soul, confined within the body, belongs to the eternal world. As long as we live, our soul finds itself in a prison, that is, in a body essentially alien to it. Death, in fact, is the great liberator. It looses the chains, since it leads the soul out of the prison of the body and back to its eternal home.

---

7. Rather, it would be more accurate to speak of a Christian "historicization" (in the sense of *Heilsgeschichte*) of the Greek ideas. Only in this sense, not in that employed by Bultmann, are the New Testament "myths" already "demythologized" by the New Testament itself.

8. Material on this contrast in E. Benz, *Der gekreuzigte Gerechte bei Plato, im N.T., und in der alten Kirche* (1950).

Since the body and soul are radically different from one another and belong to different worlds, the destruction of the body cannot mean the destruction of the soul, any more than a musical composition can be destroyed when the instrument is destroyed.

Although the proofs of the immortality of the soul do not have for Socrates himself the same value as the proofs of a mathematical theorem, they nevertheless attain within their own sphere the highest possible degree of validity, and make immortality so probable that it amounts to a "fair chance" for man. And when the great Socrates traced the arguments for immortality in his address to his disciples on the day of his death, he did not merely *teach* this doctrine: at that moment he lived this doctrine. He showed how we serve the freedom of the soul, even in this present life, when we occupy ourselves with the eternal truths of philosophy. For through philosophy we penetrate into that eternal world of ideas to which the soul belongs, and we free the soul from the prison of the body. Death does no more than complete this liberation. Plato shows us how Socrates goes to his death in complete peace and composure. The death of Socrates is a beautiful death. Nothing is seen here of death's terror. Socrates cannot fear death, since indeed it sets us free from the body. Whoever fears death proves that he loves the world of the body, that he is thoroughly entangled in the world of the senses. Death is the soul's great friend. So he teaches; and so, in wonderful harmony with his teaching, he dies—this man who embodied the Greek world in its noblest form.

And now let us hear how Jesus dies. In Gethsemane he knows that death stands before him, just as Socrates expected death on his last day. The synoptic evangelists furnish us,

277

by and large, with a unanimous report. Jesus begins "to tremble and be distressed," writes Mark (14:33). "My soul is troubled, even to death," he says to his disciples.[9] Jesus is so thoroughly human that he shares the natural fear of death.[10] Jesus is afraid, though not as a coward would be of the men who will kill him, still less of the pain and grief which precede death. He is afraid in the face of death itself. Death for him is not something divine: it is something dreadful. Jesus does not want to be alone in this moment. He knows, of course, that the Father stands by to help him. He looks to him in this decisive moment as he has done throughout his life. He turns to God with all his human fear of this great enemy, death. He is afraid of death. It is useless to try to explain away Jesus' fear as reported by the evangelists. The opponents of Christianity who already in the first centuries made the contrast between the death of Socrates and

---

9. Despite the parallel Jonah 4:9 which is cited by E. Klostermann, *Das Markus-Evangelium*, 3rd Edition (1936), ad loc., and E. Lohmeyer, *Das Evangelium des Markus (1937)*, ad loc., I agree with J. Weiss, *Das Markus-Evangelium*, 3rd Edition (1917), ad loc., that the explanation: "I am so sad that I prefer to die" in this situation where Jesus *knows* that he is going to die (the scene is the Last Supper!) is completely unsatisfactory; moreover, Weiss's interpretation: "My affliction is so great that I am sinking under the weight of it" is supported by Mark 15:34. Also Luke 12:50, "How distressed I am until the baptism (= death) takes place," allows of no other explanation.

10. Old and recent commentators (J. Wellhausen, *Das Evangelium Marci*, 2nd Edition (1909), ad loc., J. Schniewind in *Das N.T. Deutsch* (1934), ad loc., E. Lohmeyer, *Das Evangelium des Markus* (1937), ad loc., seek in vain to avoid this conclusion, which is supported by the strong Greek expressions for "tremble and shrink," by giving explanations which do not fit the situation, in which Jesus already knows that he must suffer for the sins of his people (Last Supper). In Luke 12:50 it is completely impossible to explain away the "distress" in the face of death, and also in view of the fact that Jesus is abandoned by God on the cross (Mark 15:34), it is not possible to explain the Gethsemane scene except through this distress at the prospect of being abandoned by God, an abandonment which will be the work of death, God's great enemy.

the death of Jesus saw more clearly here than the exponents of Christianity. He was really afraid. Here is nothing of the composure of Socrates, who met death peacefully as a friend. To be sure, Jesus already knows the task which has been given him: to suffer death; and he has already spoken the words: "I have a baptism with which I must be baptized, and *how distressed* (or *afraid*) I *am* until it is accomplished" (Luke 12:50). Now, when God's enemy stands before him, he cries to God, whose omnipotence he knows: "All things are possible with thee; let this cup pass from me" (Mark 14:36). And when he concludes, "Yet not as I will, but as thou wilt," this does not mean that at the last he, like Socrates, regards death as the friend, the liberator. No, he means only this: If this greatest of all terrors, death, must befall me according to thy will, then I submit to this horror. Jesus knows that in itself, because death is the enemy of God, to die means to be utterly forsaken. Therefore he cries to God; in the face of this enemy of God he does not want to be alone. He wants to remain as closely tied to God as he has been throughout his whole earthly life. For whoever is in the hands of death is no longer in the hands of God, but in the hands of God's enemy. At this moment, Jesus seeks the assistance, not only of God, but even of his disciples. Again and again he interrupts his prayer and goes to his most intimate disciples, who are trying to fight off sleep in order to be awake when the men come to arrest their master. They try; but they do not succeed, and Jesus must wake them again and again. Why does he want them to keep awake? He does not want to be alone. When the terrible enemy, death, approaches, he does not want to be forsaken even by the disciples whose human weakness he knows. "Could you not watch one hour?" (Mark 14:37).

Can there be a greater contrast than that between Socrates and Jesus? Like Jesus, Socrates has his disciples about him on the day of his death; but he discourses serenely with them on immortality. Jesus, a few hours before his death, trembles and begs his disciples not to leave him alone. The author of the epistle to the Hebrews, who, more than any other New Testament author, emphasizes the full deity (1:10) but also the full humanity of Jesus, goes still further than the reports of the three Synoptists in his description of Jesus' fear of death. In 5:7 he writes that Jesus "with loud cries and tears offered up prayers and supplications to him who was able to save him."[11] Thus, according to the epistle to the Hebrews, Jesus wept and cried in the face of death. There is Socrates, calmly and composedly speaking of the immortality of the soul; here Jesus, weeping and crying.

And then the death-scene itself. With sublime calm Socrates drinks the hemlock; but Jesus, thus says the evangelist Mark (15:34)—we dare not gloss it over, cries: "My God, my God, why hast thou forsaken me?" And with another inarticulate cry he dies (Mark 15:37). This is not "death as a friend." This is death in all its frightful horror. This is really "*the last enemy*" of God. This is the name Paul gives it in I Corinthians 15:26, where the whole contrast between Greek thought and Christianity is disclosed.[12] Using different

---

11. The reference to Gethsemane here seems to me unmistakable. J. Héring, *L'Epître aux Hébreux* (1954), ad loc., concurs in this.

12. The problem is presented in entirely false perspective by J. Leipoldt, *Der Tod bei Griechen und Juden* (1942). To be sure, he correctly makes a sharp distinction between the Greek view of death and the Jewish. But Leipoldt's efforts always to equate the Christian with the Greek and oppose it to the Jewish only become comprehensible when one notes the year in which this book was published and the series (*Germanentum, Christentum und Judentum*) of which it is a part.

280

words, the author of the Johannine Apocalypse also regards death as the last enemy, when he describes how at the end death will be cast into the lake of fire (Rev. 20:14). Because it is God's enemy, it separates us from God, who is life and the creator of all life. Jesus, who is so closely tied to God, tied as no other man has ever been, for precisely this reason must experience death much more terribly than any other man. To be in the hands of the great enemy of God means to be forsaken by God. In a way quite different from others, Jesus must suffer this abandonment, this separation from God, the only condition really to be feared. Therefore he cries to God: "Why hast thou forsaken me?" He is now actually in the hands of God's great enemy.

We must be grateful to the evangelists for having glossed over nothing at this point. Later (as early as the beginning of the second century, and probably even earlier) there were people who took offense at this—people of Greek provenance. In early Christian history we call them Gnostics.

I have put the death of Socrates and the death of Jesus side by side. For nothing shows better the radical difference between the Greek doctrine of the immortality of the soul and the Christian doctrine of the resurrection. Because Jesus underwent death in all its horror, not only in his body, but also in his soul ("My God, why hast thou forsaken me"), and as he is regarded by the first Christians as the mediator of salvation, he must indeed be the very one who in his death conquers death itself. He cannot obtain this victory by simply living on as an immortal soul, thus fundamentally *not* dying. He can conquer death only by actually dying, by betaking himself to the sphere of death, the destroyer of life, to the sphere of "nothingness," of abandonment by God. When one wishes to overcome someone else, one

281

must enter his territory. Whoever wants to conquer death must die; he must really cease to live—not simply live on as an immortal soul, but die in body and soul, lose life itself, the most precious good which God has given us. For this reason the evangelists, who nonetheless intended to present Jesus as the Son of God, have not tried to soften the terribleness of his thoroughly human death.

Furthermore, if life is to issue out of so genuine a death as this, a new divine act of creation is necessary. And this act of creation calls back to life not just a part of the man, but the whole man—all that God had created and death had annihilated. For Socrates and Plato no new act of creation is necessary. For the body is indeed bad and should not live on. And that part which is to live on, the soul, does not die at all.

If we want to understand the Christian faith in the resurrection, we must completely disregard the Greek thought that the material, the bodily, the corporeal is bad and *must* be destroyed, so that the death of the body would not be in any sense a destruction of the true life. For Christian (and Jewish) thinking, the death of the body is *also* destruction of God-created life. No distinction is made: even the life of our body is true life; death is the destruction of *all* life created by God. Therefore it is death and not the body which must be conquered by the resurrection.

Only he who apprehends with the first Christians the horror of death, who takes death seriously as death, can comprehend the Easter exultation of the primitive Christian community and understand that the whole thinking of the New Testament is governed by belief in the resurrection. Belief in the immortality of the soul is not belief in a revolutionary event. Immortality, in fact, is only a *negative* assertion: the soul does *not* die, but simply lives on. Resurrection is a *positive* assertion: the whole man, who has really died, is recalled to life by a new act of creation by God. Something has happened—a miracle of creation! For something has also happened previously, something fearful: life formed by God has been destroyed.

Death in itself is not beautiful, not even the death of Jesus. Death before Easter is really the death's head surrounded by the odor of decay. And the death of Jesus is as loathsome as the great painter Grünewald depicted it in the Middle Ages. But precisely for this reason the same painter understood how to paint, along with it, in an incomparable way, the great victory, the resurrection of Christ: Christ in the new body, the resurrection body. Whoever paints a pretty death can paint no resurrection. Whoever has not grasped the horror of death cannot join Paul in the hymn of victory: "Death is swallowed up—in victory! O death, where is thy victory? O death, where is thy sting?" (I Cor. 15:54f.).

The Wages of Sin: Death

Body and Soul—Flesh and Spirit

Yet the contrast between the Greek idea of the immortality of the soul and the Christian belief in the resurrection is still deeper. The belief in the resurrection presupposes the Jewish connection between death and *sin*. Death is not something natural, willed by God, as in the thought of the Greek philosophers; it is rather something unnatural, abnormal, opposed to God.[13] The Genesis narrative teaches

---

13. We shall see that death, in view of its conquest by Christ, has lost all its horror. But I still would not venture as does Karl Barth, *Die kirchliche Dogmatik*, III, 2 (1948), pp. 777ff. (on the basis of the "second death" distinguished in Rev. 21:8), to speak in the name of the New Testament of a "natural death" (see I Cor. 11:30!).

us that it came into the world only by the sin of man. Death is a curse, and the whole creation has become involved in the curse. The sin of man has necessitated the whole series of events which the Bible records and which we call the story of redemption. Death can be conquered only to the extent that sin is removed. For "death is the wages of sin." It is not only the Genesis narrative which speaks thus. Paul says the same thing (Rom. 6:23), and this is the view of death held by the whole of primitive Christianity. Just as sin is something opposed to God, so is its consequence, death. To be sure, God can make use of death (I Cor. 15: 35ff., John 12:24), as he can make use of Satan to man.

Nevertheless, death *as such* is the enemy of God. For God is life and the creator of life. It is not by the will of God that there are withering and decay, dying and sickness, the by-products of death working in our life. All these things, according to Christian and Jewish thinking, come from human sin. Therefore, every healing which Jesus accomplishes is not only a driving back of death, but also an invasion of the province of sin; and therefore on every occasion Jesus says: "Your sins are forgiven." Not as though there were a corresponding sin for every individual sickness; but rather, like the presence of death, the fact that sickness exists at all is a consequence of the sinful condition of the whole of humanity. Every healing is a partial resurrection, a partial victory of life over death. That is the Christian point of view. According to the Greek interpretation, on the contrary, bodily sickness is a corollary of the fact that the body is bad in itself and is ordained to destruction. For the Christian an anticipation of the resurrection can already become visible, even in the earthly body.

That reminds us that the body is in no sense bad in itself, but is, like the soul, a gift of our creator. Therefore, according to Paul, we have duties with regard to our body. God is the *creator* of all things. The Greek doctrine of immortality and the Christian hope in the resurrection differ so radically because Greek thought has such an entirely different interpretation of creation. The Jewish and Christian interpretation of creation excludes the whole Greek dualism of body and soul. For indeed the visible, the corporeal, is just as truly God's creation as the invisible. God is the maker of the body. The body is not the soul's prison, but rather a temple, as Paul says (I Cor. 6:19): the temple of the Holy Spirit! the basic distinction lies here. Body and soul are not opposites. God finds the corporeal "good" after he has created it. The Genesis story makes this emphasis explicit. Conversely, moreover, sin also embraces the whole man, not only the body, but the soul as well; and its consequence, death, extends over all the rest of creation. Death is accordingly something dreadful, because the whole visible creation, including our body, is something wonderful, even if it is corrupted by sin and death. Behind the pessimistic interpretation of death stands the optimistic view of creation. Wherever, as in Platonism, death is thought of in terms of liberation, there the visible world is not recognized directly as God's creation.

Now, it must be granted that in Greek thought there is also a very positive appreciation of the body. But in Plato the good and beautiful in the corporeal are not good and beautiful in virtue of corporeality but rather, so to speak, *in spite* of corporeality: the soul, the eternal and the only substantial reality of being, shines faintly through the material. The corporeal is not the real, the eternal, the divine. It is merely that through which the real appears—and then only in debased form. The corporeal is meant to lead us to contemplate the pure archetype, freed from all corporeality, the invisible idea.

To be sure, the Jewish and Christian points of view also see something else besides corporeality. For the whole creation is corrupted by sin and death. The creation which we see is not as God willed it, as he created it; nor is the body which we wear. Death rules over all; and it is not necessary for annihilation to accomplish its work of destruction before this fact becomes apparent—it is already obvious in the whole outward form of all things. Everything, even the most beautiful, is marked by death. Thus it might seem as if the distinction between Greek and Christian interpretation is not so great after all. And yet it remains radical. Behind the corporeal appearance Plato senses the incorporeal, transcendent, pure idea. Behind the corrupted creation, under sentence of death, the Christian sees the future creation brought into being by the resurrection, just as God willed it. The contrast, for the Christian, is not between the body and the soul, not between outward form and idea, but rather between the creation delivered over to death by sin and new creation; between the corruptible, fleshly body and the incorruptible resurrection body.

This leads us to a further point: the Christian interpretation of man. The anthropology of the New Testament is not Greek, but is connected with Jewish conceptions. For the concepts of body, soul, flesh, and spirit (to name only these), the New Testament does indeed use the same words as the Greek philosopher. But they mean something quite different; and we understand the whole New Testament amiss when we construe these concepts only from the point of view of Greek thought. Many misunderstandings arise thus. I cannot present here a biblical anthropology in detail. There are good monographs on the subject,[14] not to mention the appropriate articles in Kittel's *Theologisches Wörterbuch.* A complete study would have to treat separately the anthropologies of the various New Testament authors, since on this point there exist differences which are by no means unimportant.[15] Of necessity I can deal here only with a few cardinal points which concern our problem, and even this must be done somewhat schematically, without taking into account the nuances which would have to be discussed in a proper anthropology. In so doing, we shall naturally have to rely primarily upon Paul, since only in his writings do we find an anthropology which is definable in detail, even though he too fails to use the different ideas with complete consistency.[16]

The New Testament certainly knows the difference between body and soul, or more precisely, between the inner and the outer man. This distinction does not, however, imply opposition, as if the one were by nature good, the other by nature bad.[17] Both belong together, both are created by God. The inner man without the outer has no proper,

---

14. W. G. Kümmel, *Das Bild des Menschen im Neuen Testament* (1948).

15. Also the various theologies of the New Testament should here be mentioned.

16. W. Gutbrod, *Die paulinische Anthropologie* (1934); W. G. Kümmel, *Römer 7 und die Bekehrung des Paulus* (1929); E. Schweizer, "Röm. 1:3f. und der Gegensatz von Fleisch und Geist vor und bei Paulus," *Evang. Theol.,* 15 (1955), pp. 563ff.; and especially the relevant chapter in R. Bultmann, *Theology of the New Testament* (1955).

17. Also the words of Jesus in Mark 8:36, Matt. 6:25 and 10:28 (*psyche* = life) do not speak of an "infinite value of the immortal soul" and presuppose no higher valuation of the inner man. See also (also re Mark 14:38) Kümmel, *Das Bild des Menschen,* pp. 16ff.

full existence. It requires a body. It can, to be sure, somehow lead a shady existence without the body, like the dead in Sheol according to the Old Testament, but that is not a *genuine life*. The contrast with the Greek soul is clear: it is precisely apart from the body that the Greek soul attains to full development of its life. According to the Christian view, however, it is the inner man's very nature which demands the body.

And what now is the role played by the flesh (*sarx*) and (*pneuma*)? Here it is especially important not to be misled by the secular use of the Greek words, though it is found in various places even in the New Testament and even within individual writers whose use of terminology is never completely uniform. With these reservations, we may say that according to the use which is characteristic, say, for Pauline theology, flesh and spirit in the New Testament are two *transcendent* powers which can enter into man from without; but *neither is given with human existence as such*. On the whole it is true that the Pauline anthropology, contrary to the Greek, is grounded in *Heilsgeschichte*.[18] "Flesh" is the power of sin or the power of death. It seizes the outer and the inner man *together*. *Spirit* (*pneuma*) is its great antagonist: the power of creation. It also seizes the outer and inner man *together*. Flesh and spirit are active powers, and as such they work within us. The flesh, the power of death, entered man with the sin of Adam; indeed it entered the whole man, inner and outer; yet in such a way that it is very closely linked with the body. The inner man finds

---

18. This is what Kümmel means when he states that in the New Testament, including the Johannine theology, man is always conceived as an *historical* being.

itself less closely connected with the flesh;[19] although through guilt this power of death has more and more taken possession even of the inner man. The spirit, on the other hand, is the great power of life, the element of the resurrection; God's power of creation is given to us through the Holy Spirit. In the Old Testament the spirit is at work only from time to time in the prophets. In the end-time in which we live—that is, since Christ has broken the power of death in his own death and has arisen—this power of life is at work in all members of the community (Acts 2:17: "in the last days"). Like the flesh, it too already takes possession of the whole man, inner and outer. But whereas, in this age, the flesh has established itself to a substantial degree in the body, though it does not rule the inner man in the same inescapable way, the quickening power of the Holy Spirit is already taking possession of the inner man so decisively that the inner man is "renewed from day to day," as Paul says (II Cor. 4:16). The whole Johannine Gospel emphasizes the point. We are already in the state of resurrection, that of eternal life—not immortality of soul: the new era is already inaugurated. The body, too, is already in the power of the Holy Spirit.

Wherever the Holy Spirit is at work we have what amounts to a momentary retreat of the power of death, a certain foretaste of the end.[20] This is true even in the body, hence

---

19. The body is, so to speak, its locus, from which point it affects the whole man. This explains why Paul is able to speak of "body" instead of "flesh," or conversely "flesh" instead of "body," contrary to his own basic conception, although this occurs in very few passages. These terminological exceptions do not alter his general view, which is characterized by a sharp distinction between body and flesh.

20. See my article, "La délivrance anticipée du corps humain d'après le Nouveau Testament," *Hommage et Reconnaissance. 60 anniversaire de K. Barth* (1946), pp. 31ff.

the healings of the sick. But here it is a question only of a retreat, not of a final transformation of the body of death into a resurrection body. Even those whom Jesus raised up in his lifetime will die again, for they did not receive a resurrection body, the transformation of the fleshly body into a spiritual body does not take place until the end. Only then will the Holy Spirit's power of resurrection take such complete possession of the body that it transforms it in the way it is already transforming the inner man. It is important to see how different the New Testament anthropology is from that of the Greeks. Body and soul are both originally good insofar as they are created by God; they are both bad insofar as the deadly power of the flesh has hold of them. Both can and must be set free by the quickening power of the Holy Spirit.

Here, therefore, deliverance consists not in a release of soul from body but in a release of both from flesh. We are not released from the body; rather the body itself is set free. This is made especially clear in the Pauline epistles, but it is the interpretation of the whole New Testament. In this connection one does not find the differences which are present among the various books on other points. Even the much-quoted saying of Jesus in Matt. 10:28 in no way presupposes the Greek conception. "Fear not them that kill the body, but cannot kill the soul." It might seem to presuppose the view that the soul has no need of the body, but the context of the passage shows that this is not the case. Jesus does not continue: "Be afraid of him who kills the soul"; rather: "Fear him who can slay both soul *and* body in Gehenna." That is, fear God, who is able to give you over completely to death; to wit, when he does not resurrect you to life. We shall see, it is true, that the soul is the

290

starting-point of the resurrection, since, as we have said, it can already be possessed by the Holy Spirit in a way quite different from the body. The Holy Spirit already lives in our inner man. "By the Holy Spirit who dwells in you (already)," says Paul in Rom. 8:11, "God will also quicken your mortal bodies." Therefore, those who kill only the body are not to be feared. It can be raised from the dead. Moreover, it must be raised. The soul cannot always remain without a body. And on the other side we hear in Jesus' saying in Matt. 10:28 that the soul can be killed. The soul is not immortal. There must be resurrection for both; for since the Fall the whole man is "sown corruptible." For the inner man, thanks to the transformation by the quickening power of the Holy Spirit, the resurrection can take place already in this present life: through the "renewal from day to day." The flesh, however, still maintains its seat in our body. The transformation of the body does not take place until the end, when the whole creation will be made new by the Holy Spirit, when there will be no death and no corruption.

The resurrection of the body, whose substance[21] will no longer be that of the flesh, but that of the Holy Spirit, is only a part of the *whole new creation*. "We wait for a new heaven *and* a new earth," says II Pet. 3:13. The Christian hope relates not only to my individual fate, but to the entire creation. Through sin the whole creation has become involved in death. This we hear not only in Genesis, but also in Rom. 8:19ff., where Paul writes that the whole creation[22] from

---

21. I use this rather unfortunate term for want of a better. What I mean by it will be clear from the preceding discussion.

22. The allusion in verse 20 to the words "for your sake" of Genesis 3:17 excludes the translation of *ktisis* as "creature" in the sense of man, a translation adovcated by E. Brunner and A. Schlatter. See O. Cullmann, *Christ and Time* (1950), p. 103.

now on waits longingly for deliverance. This deliverance will come when the power of the Holy Spirit transforms all matter, when God in a new act of creation will not *destroy* matter, but set it free from the flesh, from corruptibility. Not eternal ideas, but concrete objects will then rise anew, in the new, incorruptible life-substance of the Holy Spirit; and among these objects belongs our body as well.

Because resurrection of the body is a new act of creation which embraces everything, it is not an event which begins with each individual death, but only at the *end*. It is not a transition from this world to another world, as is the case of the immortal soul freed from the body; rather it is the transition from the present age to the future. It is tied to the whole process of redemption.

Because there is sin, there must be a process of redemption enacted in time. Where sin is regarded as the source of death's lordship over God's creation, there this sin and death must be vanquished together, and there the Holy Spirit, the only power able to conquer death, must win all creatures back to life in a continuous process.

Therefore the Christian belief in the resurrection, as distinct from the Greek belief in immortality, is tied to a *divine total process* implying deliverance. Sin and death must be conquered. We cannot do this. *Another* has done it for us; and he was able to do it only in that he betook himself to the province of death—that is, he himself died and expiated sin, so that death as the wages of sin is overcome. Christian faith proclaims that Jesus has done this and that he arose *with* body and soul after he was fully and really dead. Here God has consummated the miracle of the new creation expected at the end. Once again he has created life as in the beginning. At this one point, in Jesus Christ, this has already happened! Resurrection, not only in the sense of the Holy Spirit's taking possession of the *inner* man, but also resurrection of the *body*. This is a new creation of matter—an incorruptible matter. Nowhere else in the world is there this new spiritual matter. Nowhere else is there a spiritual body—only here in Christ.

The First-Born from the Dead

Between the Resurrection of Christ and the Destruction of Death

We must take into account what it meant for the Christians when they proclaimed: Christ is risen from the dead! Above all we must bear in mind what death meant for them. We are tempted to associate these powerful affirmations with the Greek thought of the immortality of the soul, and in this way to rob them of their content. Christ is risen: that is, we stand in the new era in which death is conquered, in which corruptibility is no more. For if there is really *one* spiritual body (not an immortal soul, but a spiritual body) which has emerged from a fleshly body, then indeed the power of death is broken. Believers, according to the conviction of the first Christians, would no longer die: this was certainly their expectation in the earliest days. It must have been a problem when they discovered that Christians continued to die. But even the fact that men continue to die no longer has the same significance after the resurrection of Christ. The fact of death is robbed of its former significance. Dying is no longer an expression of the absolute lordship of death, but only one of death's last contentions for lordship. Death cannot put an end to the great fact that there is *one* risen body.

We ought to try simply to understand what the first Christians meant when they spoke of Christ as being the "first-born from the dead." However difficult it may be for us to do so, we must exclude the question whether or not we can accept this belief. We must also at the very start leave on one side the question whether Socrates or the New Testament is right. Otherwise we shall find ourselves continually mixing alien thought-processes with those of the New Testament. We should for once simply listen to what the New Testament says. Christ the first-born from the dead! His body the first resurrection body, the first spiritual body. Where this conviction is present, the whole of life and the whole of thought must be influenced by it. The whole thought of the New Testament remains for us a book sealed with seven seals if we do not read behind every sentence there this other sentence: Death has already been overcome (death, be it noted, not the body); there is already a new creation (a new creation, be it noted, not an immortality which the soul has always possessed) the resurrection age is already inaugurated.[23]

Granted that it is only inaugurated, but still it is *decisively* inaugurated. *Only* inaugurated: for death is at work, and Christians still die. The disciples experienced this as the first members of the Christian community died. This necessarily presented them with a difficult problem.[24] In I Cor.

---

23. If, as the Qumran fragment [4 Q Florileqium i.8; see A. Dupont-Sommer, *The Essene Writings from Qumran* (Meridian Books, 1962), p. 312] seems to confirm, the "teacher of righteousness" of this sect really was put to death and his return was awaited, still what most decisively separates this sect from the original Christian community . . . is the absence in it of faith in a resurrection which has *already* occurred.

24. See in this regard Ph. H. Menoud, "La mort d'Ananias et de Saphira," *Aux sources de la tradition chrétienne. Mélanges offerts à Goguel* (1950), particularly pp. 150ff.

11:30 Paul indicates that basically death and sickness should no longer occur. We still die, and still there is sickness and sin. But the Holy Spirit is already effective in our world as the power of new creation; he is already at work visibly in the primitive community in the diverse manifestations of the Spirit. In my book *Christ and Time* I have spoken of a tension between present and future, the tension between "already fulfilled" and "not yet consummated." This tension belongs *essentially* to the New Testament and is not introduced as a secondary solution born of embarrassment,[25] as Albert Schweitzer's disciples and Rudolf Bultmann maintain.[26] This tension is already present in and with Jesus. He proclaims the Kingdom of God for the future; but on the other hand, he proclaims that the Kingdom of God has already broken in, since he himself with the Holy Spirit is indeed already repulsing death by healing the sick and raising the dead (Matt. 12:28, 11:3ff., Luke 10:18) in anticipation of the victory over death which he obtains in his own death. Schweitzer is not right when he sees as the original Christian hope *only* a hope in the future; nor is C. H. Dodd when he speaks *only* of realized eschatology; still less Bultmann when he resolves the original hope of Jesus and the first Christians into existentialism. It belongs to the very stuff of the New Testament that it thinks in temporal categories, and this is because the belief that in Christ the resurrection is achieved is the starting-point of all Christian living and thinking. When one starts from this principle,

---

25. See particularly F. Buri, "Das Problem der ausgebliebenen Parusie," *Schweiz. Theol. Umschau* (1946), pp. 97ff. See in addition O. Cullmann, "Das wahre durch die ausgebliebene Parusie gestillte neutestamentliche Problem," *Theol. Zeitschr.*, 3 (1947), pp. 177ff.; also pp. 428ff.

26. R. Bultmann, "History and Eschatology in the New Testament," *New Test. Stud.*, 1 (1954), pp. 5ff.

then the chronological tension between "already fulfilled" and "not yet consummated" constitutes the *essence* of the Christian faith. Then the metaphor I use in *Christ and Time* characterizes the whole New Testament situation: the decisive battle has been fought in Christ's death and resurrection; only V-day is yet to come.

Basically the whole contemporary theological discussion turns upon this question: Is *Easter* the starting-point of the Christian Church, of its existence, life, and thought? If so, we are living in an interim time.

In that case, the faith in resurrection of the New Testament becomes the cardinal point of all Christian belief. Accordingly, the fact that there is a resurrection body—Christ's body—defines the first Christians' whole interpretation of time. If Christ is the "first-born from the dead," then this means that the end-time is already present. But it also means that a temporal interval separates the first-born from all other men who are not yet "born from the dead." This means then that we live in an interim time, between Jesus' resurrection, which has already taken place, and our own, which will not take place until the end. It also means, moreover, that the quickening power, the Holy Spirit, is already at work among us. Therefore Paul designates the Holy Spirit by the same term—*aparche*, firstfruits (Rom. 8:23)—as he uses for Jesus himself (I Cor. 15:23). There is then already a foretaste of the resurrection. And indeed in a twofold way: our inner man is already being renewed from day to day by the Holy Spirit (II Cor. 4:16; Eph. 3:16); the body also has already been laid hold of by the Spirit, although the flesh still has its citadel within it. Wherever the Holy Spirit appears, the vanquished power of death recoils, even in the body. Hence miracles of healing occur even in our still mortal body. To the despairing cry in Rom. 7:24, "Who shall deliver me from this body of death?" the whole New Testament answers: the Holy Spirit!

The foretaste of the end, realized through the Holy Spirit, becomes most clearly visible in the early Christian celebration of the breaking of bread. Visible miracles of the Spirit occur there. There the Spirit tries to break through the limits of imperfect human language in the speaking with tongues. And there the community passes over into direct connection with the Risen One, not only with his soul, but also with his resurrection body. Therefore we hear in I Cor. 10:16: "The bread we break, is it not communion with the body of Christ?" Here in communion with the brethren we come nearest to the resurrection body of Christ; and so Paul writes in the following chapter (a passage which has received far too little consideration): if this Lord's Supper were partaken of by all members of the community in a completely worthy manner, then the union with Jesus' resurrection body would be so effective in our own bodies that even now there would be no more sickness or death (I Cor. 11:28-30)—a singularly bold assertion.[27] Therefore the community is described as the body of Christ, because here the spiritual body of Christ is present, because here we come closest to it; here in the common meal the first disciples at Easter saw Jesus' resurrection body, his spiritual body.

Yet in spite of the fact that the Holy Spirit is already so powerfully at work, men still die; even after Easter and Pentecost men continue to die as before. Our body remains

---

27. Also to be understood in the light of this is F. J. Leenhardt's study, "This is My Body," in Cullmann-Leenhardt, *Essays on the Lord's Supper* (Ecumenical Studies in Worship 1; 1958).

mortal and subject to sickness. Its transformation into the spiritual body does not take place until the whole creation is formed anew by God. Then only, for the first time, there will be nothing but Spirit, nothing but the power of life, for then death will be destroyed with finality. Then there will be a new substance for all things visible. Instead of the fleshly matter there appears the spiritual. That is, *instead of corruptible matter there appears the incorruptible.* The visible and the invisible will be spirit. But let us make no mistake: this is certainly not the Greek sense of bodiless Ideal! A new heaven *and* a new earth! That is the Christian hope. And then will our bodies also rise from the dead. Yet not as fleshly bodies, but as spiritual bodies.

The expression which stands in the ancient Greek texts of the Apostles' Creed is quite certainly not biblical: "I believe in the resurrection of the flesh!"[28] Paul could not say that. Flesh and blood cannot inherit the Kingdom. Paul believes in the resurrection of the *body*, not of the *flesh.* The flesh is the power of death, which must be destroyed. This error in the Greek creed made its entrance at a time when the biblical terminology had been misconstrued in the sense of Greek anthropology. Our body, moreover (not merely our soul), will be raised at the end, when the quickening power of the Spirit makes all things new, all things without exception.

An incorruptible body! How are we to conceive this? Or rather, how did the first Christians conceive of it? Paul says (Phil. 3:21) that at the end Christ will transform our body into the body of his own glory (*doxa*), just as in II Cor. 3:18:

---

28. W. Bieder, "Auferstehung des Leibes oder des Fleisches?," *Theol. Zeitschr.*, 1 (1945), pp. 105ff., seeks to explicate the expression "resurrection of the flesh," both from the point of view of biblical theology and of the history of dogma.

"We are being transformed into his own likeness from glory to glory (*apo doxes eis doxan*)." This glory (*doxa*) was conceived by the first Christians as a sort of light-substance; but this is only an imperfect comparison. Our language has no word for it. Once again I refer to Grünewald's painting of the resurrection. He may have come closest to what Paul understood as the spiritual body.

Those Who Sleep

The Holy Spirit and the Intermediate State of the Dead

And now we come to the last question. When does this transformation of the body take place? No doubt can remain on this point. The whole New Testament answers, at the *end*, and this is to be understood literally, that is, in the temporal sense. That raises the question of the "interim condition" of the dead. Death is indeed already conquered according to II Tim. 1:10: "Christ has conquered death and has already brought life and incorruptibility to light." The chronological tension, which I constantly stress, concerns precisely this central point: death is conquered, but it will not be abolished until the end. According to I Cor. 15:26, death will be conquered as the *last enemy*. It is significant that in the Greek the same verb *katargeo*[29] is used to describe both the decisive victory already accomplished and the not-yet-consummated victory at the end. John's Apocalypse describes the victory at the end, the annihilation of death: "Death will be cast into a pool of fire" (Rev. 20:14); and a few verses farther on it is said, "Death will be no more."

---

29. Luther translates *katargeo* by "er hat ihm 'die Macht genommen'" in II Tim. 1:10, and by "er wird aufgehoben" in I Cor. 15:26.

That means, however, that the transformation of the body does not occur immediately after each individual death. Here too we must once again guard against any accommodation to Greek philosophy, if we wish to understand the New Testament doctrine. This is the point where I cannot accept Karl Barth's position as a simple restatement of the original Christian view, not even his position in the *Church Dogmatics*[30] where it is subtly shaded and comes much nearer[31] to New Testament eschatology than in his first writings.[32] Karl Barth considers it to be the New Testament interpretation that the transformation of the body occurs for everyone immediately after his individual death— as if the dead were no longer in time. Nevertheless, according to the New Testament, they *are* still in time. Otherwise, the problem in I Thess. 4:13ff. would have no meaning. Here in fact Paul is concerned to show that at the moment of Christ's return "those who are then alive will have no advantage" over those who have died in Christ. Therefore the dead in Christ are still in time; they, too, are *waiting*. "How long, Oh Lord?" cry the martyrs who are sleeping

---

30. K. Barth, *Die kirchliche Dogmatik*, II, 1 (1940), pp. 698ff.; III, 2 (1948), pp. 524ff., 714ff.

31. It is another question, of course, whether Barth does not have the *right* to adduce relationships in this whole matter which yet lie outside the New Testament circle of vision. But if so, then this "going beyond the New Testament" should perhaps be done consciously and should always be identified as such with clarity and emphasis, especially where a constant effort is being made to argue from the point of view of the Bible, as is the case with Barth. If this were done, then the inevitable danger which every dogmatician *must* confront (and here lies the dignity and greatness of his task) would be more clearly recognized: namely, the danger that he may not remain upon an extension of the biblical line, but rather interpret the biblical texts primarily *ex post facto*, from the point of view of his "going beyond the New Testament." Precisely because of this clear recognition of the danger, discussion with the exegete would be more fruitful.

32. Especially *The Resurrection of the Dead* (1926).

under the altar (Rev. 6:10). Neither the saying on the cross, "Today you will be with me in paradise" (Luke 23:43), the parable of the rich man, where Lazarus is carried directly to Abraham's bosom (Luke 16:22), nor Paul's saying, "I desire to die and to be with Christ" (Phil. 1:23), proves as is often maintained that the resurrection of the body takes place immediately after the individual death.[33] In none of these texts is there so much as a word about the resurrection of the body. Instead, these different images picture the condition of those who die in Christ before the end— the interim state in which they, as well as the living, find themselves. All these images express simply a special proximity to Christ, in which those dying in Christ before the end find themselves. They are "with Christ" or "in paradise" or "in Abraham's bosom" or, according to Rev. 6:9, "under

---

33. Also the much-disputed words of Luke 23:43, "Today you will be with me in paradise," belong here. To be sure it is not impossible, though artificial, to understand semeron (today) as modifying lepo soi (I tell you). The statement is to be understood in the light of Luke 16:23 and of the Jewish conception of "paradise" as the place of the blessed (Strack-Billerbeck, ad. loc.; P. Volz, Die Eschatologie der judischen Gemeinde im neutest. Zeitalter [find ed., 1⅝flff], p. 265). It is certain that Luke 16:23 does not refer to resurrection of the body, and the expectation of the Parousia is in no way supplanted. Such an interpretation is also decisively rejected by W. G. Kümmel, Promise and Fulfilment (1957), p. 74. A certain disparity here over against Pauline theology does exist insofar as Christ himself on the day referred to as "today" has not yet risen, and therefore the foundation of the condition wherein the dead are bound up with Christ has not yet been laid. But in the last analysis the emphasis here is on the fact that the thief will be with Christ. Menoud (Le sort des trépassés, p. 45) correctly points out that Jesus' answer must be understood in relation to the thief's entreaty. The thief asks Jesus to remember him when he "comes into his kingdom," which according to the Jewish view of the Messiah can only refer to the time when the Messiah will come and erect his kingdom. Jesus does not grant the request, but instead gives the thief more than he asked for: he will be united with Jesus even before the coming of the kingdom. So understood, according to their intention, these words do not constitute a difficulty for the position maintained above.

the altar." All these are simply various images of special nearness to God. But the most usual image for Paul is: "They are asleep."[34] It would be difficult to dispute that the New Testament reckons with such an interim time for the dead, as well as for the living, although any sort of speculation upon the state of the dead in this interim period is lacking here.

The dead in Christ share in the tension of the interim time.[35] But this means not *only* that they are waiting. It means that for them, too, something decisive happened with Jesus' death and resurrection. For them, too, Easter is the great turning point (Matt. 27:52). This new situation created by Easter leads us to see at least the possibility of a common bond with Socrates, not with his teaching, but with his own behavior in the face of death. Death has lost its horror, its "sting." Though it remains as the last enemy, death has no longer any final significance. If the resurrection of Christ were to designate the great turning-point of the ages only for the living and not for the dead also, then the living would surely have an immense advantage over the dead. For as members of Christ's community the living are indeed even now in possession of the power of the resurrection, the Holy Spirit. It is unthinkable that, according to

---

34. The interpretation which K. Barth (*Die kirchliche Dogmatik*, III, 2, p. 778) gives of the "sleeping," as if this term conveyed only the "impression" of a peaceful going to sleep which those surviving have, finds no support in the New Testament. The expression in the New Testament signifies more, and like the "repose" in Rev. 14:13 refers to the *condition* of the dead before the Parousia.

35. The lack of New Testament speculation on this does not give us the right simply to suppress the "interim condition" as such. I do not understand why Protestant theologians (including Barth) are so afraid of the New Testament position when the New Testament teaches only this much about the "interim condition": (1) that it exists, (2) that it already signifies union with Christ (this because of the Holy Spirit).

the early Christian point of view, nothing should be altered for the dead in the period before the end. It is precisely those images used in the New Testament to describe the condition of the dead in Christ which prove that even now, in this interim state of the dead, the resurrection of Christ— the anticipation of the end—is already effective. They are "with Christ."

Particularly in II Cor. 5:1-10 we hear why it is that the dead, although they do not yet have a body and are only "sleeping," nevertheless are in special proximity to Christ. Paul speaks here of the natural anxiety which even he feels before death, which still maintains its effectiveness. He fears the condition of "nakedness," as he calls it; that is, the condition of the inner man who has no body. This natural dread of death, therefore, has not disappeared. Paul would like, as he says, to receive a spiritual body in addition, directly (ependysasthai) while still living, without undergoing death. That is, he would like to be still alive at the time of Christ's return. Here once again we find confirmation of what we said about Jesus' fear of death. But now we see also something *new*: in this same text alongside this natural anxiety about the soul's nakedness stands the great confidence in Christ's proximity, *even in this interim state.* What is there to be afraid of in the fact that such an interim condition still exists? Confidence in Christ's proximity is grounded in the conviction that our inner man is already grasped by the Holy Spirit. Since the time of Christ, we, the living, do indeed have the Holy Spirit. If he is actually within us, he has already transformed our inner man. But, as we have heard, the Holy Spirit is the power of life. Death can do him no harm. Therefore something is indeed changed for the dead, for those who really die in Christ, i.e., in possession of the Holy Spirit. (The horrible abandonment in death, the separation from God, of which we have spoken, no longer exists, precisely because the Holy Spirit does exist. Therefore the New Testament emphasizes that the dead are indeed *with Christ*, and so not abandoned. Thus we understand how it is that, just in II Cor. 5:1ff., where he mentions the fear of disembodiment in the interim time, Paul describes the Holy Spirit as the "earnest."

According to verse 8 of the same chapter, it even appears that the dead are nearer Christ. The "sleep" seems to draw them even closer: "We are . . . willing rather to be absent from the body, and to be 'at home' with the Lord." For this reason, the apostle can write in Phil. 1:23 that he longs to die and be with Christ. So then, a man who lacks the fleshly body is yet nearer Christ than before, if he has the Holy Spirit. It is the flesh, bound to our earthly body, which is throughout our life the hindrance to the Holy Spirit's full development. Death delivers us from this hindrance even though it is an imperfect state inasmuch as it lacks the resurrection body. Neither in this passage nor elsewhere is found any more detailed information about this intermediate state in which the inner man, stripped indeed of its fleshly body but still deprived of the spiritual body, exists with the Holy Spirit. The apostle limits himself to assuring us that this state, anticipating the destiny which is ours once we have received the Holy Spirit, brings us closer to the final resurrection.

Here we find fear of a bodiless condition associated with firm confidence that even in this intermediate, transient condition no separation from Christ supervenes (among the powers which cannot separate us from the love of God in Christ is death—Rom. 8:38). This fear *and* this confidence are bound together in II Cor. 5, and this confirms the fact that even the dead share in the present tension.

Confidence predominates, however, for the decision has indeed been made. Death is conquered. The inner man, divested of the body, is no longer alone; he does not lead the shadowy existence which the Jews expected and which cannot be described as life. The inner man, divested of the body, has already in his lifetime been transformed by the Holy Spirit, is already grasped by the resurrection (Rom. 6:3ff., John 3:3ff.), if he *has* already as a living person really been renewed by the Holy Spirit. Although he still "sleeps" and still awaits the resurrection of the body, which alone will give him full life, the dead Christian *has* the Holy Spirit. Thus, even in this state, death has lost its terror, although it still exists. And so the dead who die in the Lord can actually be blessed "from now on" (*ap' arti*),[36] as the author of the Johannine Apocalypse says (Rev. 14:13). What is said in I Cor. 15:54b, 55 pertains also to the dead: "Death is swallowed up in victory. O death, where is thy victory? O death, where is thy sting?" So Paul writes: "Whether we live or die, we belong to the Lord." Christ is "Lord of the living and the dead" (Rom. 14:8-9).

One could ask whether in this fashion we have not been led back again, in the last analysis, to the Greek doctrine of immortality, whether the New Testament does not assume, for the time after Easter, a continuity of the "inner man" of

---

36. In view of the places in the New Testament where *ap' arti* can only mean "from now on" (for instance, John 13:19), and in view of the good sense which the sentence makes when *ap'arti* is so translated, I continue to subscribe to the usual translation "from now on" and see it as modifying *apothneskontes*, although many factors support A. Debrunner's view. (Blass-Debrunner-Funk, *A Greek Grammar of the New Testament* [1961] §12), following A. Fridrichsen's suggestion, which understands *aparti* as the colloquial Attic word for "exactly, certainly" and then finds in P⁴⁷'s omission of *nai* a support for reading *ap' arti* as *aparti*, modifying *legei to pneuma*, not *apothneskontes*.

converted people before and after death, so that here, too, death is presented for all practical purposes only as a natural "transition."[37] There is a sense in which a kind of *approximation* to the Greek teaching does actually take place, to the extent that the inner man, who has already been transformed by the Spirit (Rom. 6:3ff.), and consequently made alive, continues to live with Christ in this transformed state, in the condition of sleep. This continuity is emphasized especially strongly in the Gospel of John (3:36, 4:14, 6:54, and frequently). Here we observe at least a certain analogy to the "immortality of the soul," but the distinction remains none the less radical. Further, the condition of the dead in Christ is still imperfect, a state of "nakedness," as Paul says, of "sleep," of waiting for the resurrection of the whole creation, for the resurrection of the body. On the other hand, death in the New Testament continues to be the enemy, albeit a defeated enemy, who must yet be destroyed. The fact that even in this state the dead are already living with Christ does not correspond to the natural essence of the soul. Rather it is the result of a divine intervention from outside, through the Holy Spirit, who must already have quickened the inner man in earthly life by his miraculous power.

Thus it is still true that the resurrection of the body is awaited, even in John's Gospel—though now, of course, with a certainty of victory because the Holy Spirit already dwells in the inner man. Hence no doubt can arise any more: since he already dwells in the inner man, he will certainly transform the body. For the Holy Spirit, this quickening power, penetrates everything and knows no barrier. If he is really

---

37. We have already spoken above of K. Barth's attempt (which indeed goes too far) to place a positive valuation in dialectical fashion alongside the negative valuation of death.

within a man, then he will quicken the whole man. So Paul writes in Rom. 8:11: "If the Spirit dwells in you, then will he who raised Christ Jesus from the dead call to life your mortal bodies also *through the Spirit dwelling in you.*" In Phil. 3:21: "We wait for the Lord Jesus Christ, who will conform our lowly body to the body of his glory." Nothing is said in the New Testament about the details of the interim conditions. We hear only this: we are nearer to God.

We wait, and *the dead* wait. Of course the rhythm of time may be different for them than for the living; and in this way the interim-time may be shortened for them. This does not, indeed, go beyond the New Testament texts and their exegesis,[38] because this expression *to sleep,* which is the customary designation in the New Testament of the "interim condition," draws us to the view that for the dead another time-consciousness exists, that of "those who sleep." But that does not mean that the dead are not still in time. Therefore once again we see that the New Testament resurrection hope is different from the Greek belief in immortality.

Conclusion

On his missionary journeys Paul surely met people who were unable to believe in his preaching of the resurrection *for the very reason* that they believed in the immortality of the soul. Thus in Athens there was no laughter until Paul spoke of the resurrection (Acts 17:32). Both the people of whom Paul says (in I Thess. 4:13) that "they have no hope" and those of whom he writes (in I Cor. 15:12) that they do not believe there is a resurrection from the dead are probably not Epicureans, as we are inclined to believe. Even those

---

38. Here I follow R. Mehl's suggestion, *Der letzte Feind,* p. 56.

who believe in the immortality of the soul do not have *the* hope of which Paul speaks, the hope which expresses the belief of a divine miracle of new creation which will embrace everything, every part of the world created by God. Indeed for the Greeks who believed in the immortality of the soul it may have been harder to accept the Christian preaching of the resurrection than it was for others. About the year 150 Justin writes of people "who say that there is no resurrection from the dead, but that immediately at death their souls would ascend to heaven" (Dialogue, 80). Here the contrast is indeed clearly perceived.

The emperor Marcus Aurelius, the philosopher who belongs with Socrates to the noblest figures of antiquity, also perceived the contrast. As is well known, he had the deepest contempt for Christianity. One might think that the death of the Christian martyrs would have inspired respect in this great Stoic who regarded death with equanimity. But it was just the martyrs' death with which he was least sympathetic. The alacrity with which the Christians met their death displeased him.[39] The Stoic departed this life dispassionately; the Christian martyr on the other hand died with spirited passion for the cause of Christ, because he knew that by doing so he stood within a powerful redemptive process. The first Christian martyr, Stephen, shows us (Acts 7:55) how very differently death is bested by him who dies in Christ than by the ancient philosopher: he sees, it is said, "the heavens open and Christ standing at the right hand of God!" He sees Christ, the conqueror of death. With this faith that the death he must undergo is already conquered by him who has himself endured it, Stephen lets himself be stoned.

---

39. M. Aurelius, *Med.*, XI, 3. To be sure, as time went on he more and more gave up the belief in the soul's immortality.

The answer to the question, "Immortality of the soul or resurrection of the dead in the New Testament," is unequivocal. The *teaching* of the great philosophers Socrates and Plato can in no way be brought into consonance with that of the New Testament. That their *person*, their *life*, and their *bearing in death* can nonetheless be *honored* by Christians, the apologists of the second century have shown. I believe it can also be demonstrated from the New Testament. But this is a question with which we do not have to deal here.

Afterword[40]

A German edition of this Ingersoll Lecture was published in the *Festschrift* to Karl Barth,[41] and a summary has appeared in French periodicals. No other publication of mine has provoked such enthusiasm or such violent hostility. The editors of the periodicals concerned have been good enough to send me some of the letters of protest which they have received from their readers. One of the letter writers was prompted by my article to reflect bitterly that "the French people, dying for lack of the Bread of Life, have been offered instead of bread, stones, if not serpents." Another writer takes me for a kind of monster who delights in causing spiritual distress. "Has Mr. Cullmann," he writes, "a stone instead of a heart?" For a third, my study has been "the

---

40. When Professor Cullmann's Ingersoll Lecture was published in book form (London: The Epworth Press, 1958), it appeared with a 1956 preface, dated at Chamonix on September 15, in which the author took cognizance of the critique aroused by his views on the topic of resurrection and immortality. This preface is here reprinted as an Afterword.

41. "Festgabe für Karl Barth zum 70. Ceburtstag I," *Theol. Zeitschr.*, 12 (1956), pp. 126-56. See also *Verbum Caro* (1956), pp. 58ff.

cause of astonishment, sorrow, and deep distress." Friends who have followed my previous work with interest and approval have indicated to me the pain which this study has caused them. In others I have detected a malaise which they have tried to conceal by an eloquent silence.

My critics belong to the most varied camps. The contrast, which out of concern for the truth I have found it necessary to draw between the courageous and joyful primitive Christian hope of the resurrection of the dead and the serene philosophic expectation of the survival of the immortal soul, has displeased not only many sincere Christians in all communions and of all theological outlooks, but also those whose convictions, while not outwardly alienated from Christianity, are more strongly molded by philosophical considerations. So far, no critic of either kind has attempted to refute me by exegesis, that being the basis of our study.

This remarkable agreement seems to me to show how widespread is the mistake of attributing to primitive Christianity the Greek belief in the immortality of the soul. Further, people with such different attitudes as those I have mentioned are united in a common inability to *listen* with complete objectivity to what the texts teach us about the faith and hope of primitive Christianity, without mixing their own opinions and the views that are so dear to them with their interpretation of the texts. This inability to listen is equally surprising on the part of intelligent people committed to the principles of sound, scientific exegesis and on the part of believers who profess to rely on the revelation in Holy Scripture.

The attacks provoked by my work would impress me more if they were based on exegetical arguments. Instead, I am attacked with very general considerations of a philosophical, psychological, and, above all, sentimental kind.

It has been said against me, "I can accept the immortality of the soul, but not the resurrection of the body," or "I cannot believe that our loved ones merely sleep for an indeterminate period, and that I myself, when I die, shall merely sleep while awaiting the resurrection."

Is it really necessary today to remind intelligent people, whether Christians or not, that there is a difference between recognizing that such a view was held by Socrates and accepting it, between recognizing a hope as primitive Christian and sharing it oneself?

We must first listen to what Plato and Paul said. We can go further. We can respect and indeed admire both views. How can we fail to do so when we see them in relation to the life and death of their authors? But that is not reason for denying a radical difference between the Christian expectation of the resurrection of the dead and the Greek belief in the immortality of the soul. However sincere our admiration for both views, it cannot allow us to pretend, against our profound conviction and against the exegetical evidence, that they are compatible. That it is possible to discover certain points of contact, I have shown in this study; but that does not prevent their fundamental inspiration being totally different.

The fact that later Christianity effected a link between the two beliefs and that today the ordinary Christian simply confuses them has not persuaded me to be silent about what I, in common with most exegetes, regard as true; and all the more so, since the link established between the expectation of the "resurrection of the dead" and the belief in "the immortality of the soul" is not in fact a link at all but renunciation of one in favor of the other. I Cor. 15 has been sacrificed for the Phaedo. No good purpose is served by concealing this fact, as is often done today when things that are really incompatible are combined by the following type of oversimplified reasoning: that whatever in early Christian teaching appears to us irreconcilable with the immortality of the soul, viz., the resurrection of the body, is not an *essential* affirmation for the first Christians but simply an accommodation to the mythological expressions of the thought of their time, and that the heart of the matter is the immortality of the soul. On the contrary we must recognize loyally that precisely those things which distinguish the Christian teaching from the Greek belief are at the heart of primitive Christianity. Even if the interpreter cannot himself accept it as fundamental, he has no right to conclude that it was not fundamental for the authors whom he studies.

•   •   •   •   •

In view of the negative reactions and "distress" provoked by the publication of my thesis in various periodicals, should I not have broken off the debate for the sake of Christian charity, instead of publishing this booklet? My decision has been determined by the conviction that "stumbling blocks" are sometimes salutary, both from the scholarly and the Christian point of view. I simply ask my reader to be good enough to take the trouble of reading on till the end.

The question is here raised in its *exegetical* aspect. If we turn to the Christian aspect, I would venture to remind my critics that when they put in the forefront, as they do, the particular manner in which they *wish* themselves and their loved ones to survive, they are involuntarily giving grounds to the opponents of Christianity who constantly repeat that the faith of Christians is nothing more than the projection of their desires.

In reality, does it not belong to the greatness of our Christian faith, as I have done my best to expound it, that we do not begin from our personal desires but place our resurrection within the framework of a cosmic redemption and of a new creation of the universe?

I do not underestimate in any way the difficulty one may experience in sharing this faith, and I freely admit the difficulty of talking about this subject in a dispassionate manner. An open grave at once reminds us that we are not simply concerned with a matter of academic discussion. But is there not therefore all the more reason for seeking truth and clarity at this point? The best way to do it is not by beginning with what is ambiguous, but by explaining simply and as faithfully as possible, with all the means at our disposal, the hope of the New Testament authors, and thus showing the very essence of this hope and—however hard it may seem to us—what it is that separates it from other beliefs we hold so dear. If in the first place we examine objectively the primitive Christian expectation in those aspects which seem shocking to our commonly accepted views, are we not following the only possible way by which it may perhaps nonetheless be given us, not only to undersand that expectation better, but also to ascertain that it is not so impossible to accept it as we imagine.

I have the impression that some of my readers have not troubled to read my exposition right through. The comparison of the death of Socrates with that of Jesus seems to have scandalized and irritated them so much that they have read no farther, and have not looked at what I have said about the New Testament faith in the victory of Christ over death.

For many of those who have attacked me, the cause of "sorrow and distress" has been not only the distinction we

313

draw between resurrection of the dead and immortality of the soul, but above all the place which I with the whole of primitive Christianity believe should be given to the intermediate state of those who are dead and die in Christ before the final days, the state which the first-century authors described by the word "sleep." The idea of a temporary state of waiting is all the more repugnant to those who would like fuller information about this "sleep" of the dead who, though stripped of their fleshly bodies, are still deprived of their resurrection bodies although in possession of the Holy Spirit. They are not able to observe the discretion of the New Testament authors, including Paul, in this matter; or to be satisfied with the joyful assurance of the Apostle when he says that henceforth death can no longer separate from Christ him who has the Holy Spirit. "Whether we live or die, we belong to Christ."

There are some who find this idea of "sleep" entirely unacceptable. I am tempted to lay aside for a moment the exegetical methods of this study and ask them whether they have never experienced a dream which has made them happier than any other experience, even though they have only been sleeping. Might that not be an illustration, though indeed an imperfect one, of the state of anticipation in which, according to Paul, the dead in Christ find themselves during their "sleeping" as they wait for the resurrection of the body?

However that may be, I do not intend to avoid the "stumbling block" by minimizing what I have said about the provisional and still imperfect character of this state. The fact is that, according to the first Christians the full, genuine life of the resurrection is inconceivable apart from the new body, the "spiritual body," with which the dead will be clothed when heaven and earth are re-created.

314

In this study I have referred more than once to the Isenheim altarpiece by the medieval painter Grünewald. It was the resurrection body that he depicted, not the immortal soul. Similarly, another artist, Johann Sebastian Bach, has made it possible for us to hear, in the Credo of the Mass in B Minor, the musical interpretation of the words of this ancient creed which faithfully reproduces the New Testament faith in Christ's resurrection and our own. The jubilant music of this great composer is intended to express not the immortality of the soul but the event of the resurrection of the body: *Et resurrexit tertia die. . . . Expecto resurrectionem mortuorum et vitam venturi saeculi.* And Handel, in the last part of the *Messiah,* gives us some inkling of what Paul understood by the sleep of those who rest in Christ; and also, in the song of triumph, Paul's expectation of the final resurrection when the "last trumpet shall sound and we shall be changed."

Whether we share this hope or not, let us at least admit that in this case the artists have proved the best expositors of the Bible.

Scripture Index

WHAT THE BIBLE SAYS ABOUT RESURRECTION

Subject Index

329